In a Dream,
In a Vision of the Night

by

Susan Noone Riddle

© 1998, 2002 by Susan Noone Riddle.
All rights reserved.

No part of this book may be reproduced, stored in a retrieval system, or transmitted by any means, electronic, mechanical, photocopying, recording, or otherwise, without written permission from the author.

ISBN: 1-4033-9301-X (e-book)
ISBN: 1-4033-9302-8 (Paperback)

This book is printed on acid free paper.

1stBooks – rev. 07/16/03

CONTENTS

INTRODUCTION ix

Chapter 1: What Does the Bible Say?
    We Know In Part 1
    Dreams Viewed as Gifts of the Spirit 2
    Dreams, Trances and Visions 3
    Dreams and Parables as Dark Sayings............. 6

Chapter 2: Are All Dreams and Visions from
    God? Know His Voice.................................... 11
    Dreams That Come From the Kingdom of
    Darkness 11
    Dreams That Come Out of Our Own
    Hearts.. 14
    Dreams That Come From the Lord................ 15

Chapter 3: To Interpret or Not to Interpret,
    Is that the Question? 17
    Eight Major Ways to Understand
    A Dream... 18
        Attributes of Places
        Attributes of Characters

    Attributes of Objects
    Attributes of Animals
    Actions or Conduct
    Attitudes or Feelings
    Array of Colors
    Analogy of Numbers
The Parable of the Sower 20

Chapter 4: Dreams and Symbolism 26
    The WISE Use of Symbols 26
    Symbolism: Types, Shadows and Parables 28

Chapter 5: Symbols and their Scriptural Meaning 40
    Animals & Reptiles & Insects & Birds 40
    Colors 50
    Metals 52
    Numbers 54
    People: 59
    Places: 71
    Different Rooms and Locations: 76
    Vehicles 83
    Symbolic Actions 90
    Symbolic Body Parts 103
    General Symbols 114
    Dealing with Symbols, Types and
    Shadows 231

Chapter 6: Dreams That Do Not Necessarily
  Use Symbolism 235
  Dream - Signs of Victory 236
  Dream: And the Governor Will Be 239
  Night Communication 240
  Dreams: My Father's Death 241
  One of the Last Dreams 242
  Warnings in the Night 244
  Psalms 46: 4 245
  Dream of Suffering Marriage 246
  The Dream of a Move 247
  This is NOT My Will 248
  The Gospel is Preached on
  an Exploding 747 249

Chapter 7: Dreams that Use Symbolic Language
  Based on Bible Truths 255
  Fed By an Angel 255
  The Mosquito Dream 257
  The Fly Dream 258
  Just Chop It Off!!! 259
  Snakes in the Living Room 260
  Drug Addicts or Sorcerers? 262
  Tornadoes Are Coming! 265
  The Big One 267

v

The Tsunami Tidal Wave 268
Sheol and the Pit 270
Pray In the Spirit 272
Dream: Healing an Offense 274
Our Dreams About Hitler 274
Dream: Falling Hard 277
Missing Money 280

Chapter 8: So What's All the Fuss About? 282
    A Black Wedding Dress 284

Chapter 9: Tying It All Together 287

Chapter 10: Frequently Asked Questions 288

Bibliography 301

How Can I know the Lord Personally? 304

About the Author 309

DEDICATION

I want to dedicate this book to the awesome and deep flow of the Holy Spirit of God who reveals the Lord Jesus Christ to us. Knowing a Holy God who loves to speak to His people fulfills the first commandment of the two commandments that Jesus left us with, "Jesus said to them, 'You shall love the Lord your God with all your heart, with all your soul, and with all your mind.'" *(Matt. 22: 37-40)* He created us to fellowship with Him. He wants us to talk to Him. He also wants to talk to us. In His Word He was faithful to instruct, give revelation and warn His children. He is so personal that he will gently speak anything that is necessary for His children to stay close in their walk with Him.

I also want to dedicate this book to my mother who has always believed in her heart that God is a supernatural God. She always listened to my dreams with special interest. To my husband, Charles, for being such a stabilizing force in my life. Thank you to Joe Ann and Peggy, and the dreamsfromHim e group for all the long hours on the phone and e-mail. We have learned so much from one another.

INTRODUCTION

As a child I can remember having dreams that really influenced my life. Many times they were vivid and so real. As a teenager, I began to have dreams that came true. Some of them were very serious. My mother was always encouraging, viewing this as a gift from God. There was little available at that time that actually taught what the Lord says in the Bible about prophetic dreams and visions. The only thing that was available was "Psychic" and "spirit guide" type of stuff. In my heart, I knew something was off where all of that was concerned.

Entering my teenage years, I attended a revival in a church where the supernatural was frowned upon. Being saved and rooted in this church, I was never taught about how to walk in the Spirit, or resist the devil. Unfortunately, no matter how much I loved the Lord and wanted to serve Him, I backslid. While actively attending this church, I experienced many vivid dreams. I spoke to the Pastor of this church about it, earnestly seeking help. He shared his view that God did not speak to His people prophetically in dreams anymore. He also said that it was the devil who used people in this way for evil. In his experience and belief system, the devil was powerful and supernatural, and the LORD was not! I believe that even though he meant well, this confused me greatly.

Needless to say, I was terrified and closed my heart to the supernatural! Thinking that the devil could use my mind in this way caused me to close my heart to the possibility that God would speak through dreams and visions. It was difficult later in life to believe that God was more powerful than the devil and kingdom of darkness!

It was not until after I was married and came back under the grace of God that dreams began to surface again. Once again He began to pour out His Spirit in a manner that really got my attention. A wondrous journey began as He taught me about His language in the Spirit and from His Word.

It is for this reason that this book concerning dreams and visions has come about. In ministry, I have encountered more than I can count who do not understand what they see and hear in the night season. It is evident that we are in the latter days. Soon our Lord will return! When the Spirit was poured out at Pentecost, Peter quoted *Joel 2: 28-31* when he said in *Acts 2*, *"17* - And it shall come to pass in the last days, says God, That I will pour out my Spirit on all flesh,

Your sons and daughters shall prophesy, Your young men shall see visions, Your old men shall dream dreams, *18* - And on My men servants and My maidservants." Peter was speaking of the days before the return of the Lord. No one knows the day or hour that He will return, but He did tell us to discern the times. The signs we see today of the eminent return of the Lord are very clear. The light of the Lord is getting brighter, while the darkness is getting darker. Though the devil is busy blinding the eyes of the world, the Lord is beginning to pour out His latter rain! The Spirit is beginning to move in the body of Christ like never before.

One of the ways that He is moving in and through His people today is in dreams and visions. This is more and more evident in this 21st century. There is rarely a day that goes by that some sort of communication from someone in the body of Christ about a dream or vision they have received from the Lord comes across my path. The Lord has poured out his anointing on me in order to be able to reach in the Spirit and discern what a dream may mean according to the Scriptures. At times I see the dreams as though I had them myself! Other times, I may receive revelation from the dream after a period of prayer. I believe that the Lord has called me to train and teach other believers truths from His Word so that they can in turn teach and train others how to understand the imagery of the Bible and how it relates to the parables or dreams we receive. For certain, none of the ability to interpret dreams or visions comes from man. If the Lord does not reveal the interpretation by His Spirit, there is no interpretation. Dream interpretation is part of the gifts of the Spirit including prophecy, discerning of spirits, words of knowledge, and words of wisdom, and must come from the Holy Ghost. *(1 Corinthians 12: 11)* As the Lord continues to pour out His Spirit in these last days, more and of God's people are going to see and hear the Lord through dreams and visions. It is so important that we know the Word of God. The Word of God will interpret itself.

In the Old Testament there were different types of Prophets. One type that is described is the "Seer." I believe that many seeing Prophets are rising up to aid the body of Christ in these perilous days.

In A Dream, In A Vision of the Night
Job 33:15-18

Chapter One
What Does the Bible Say?
We Know In Part

At one time in my life I was led to believe that there is nothing in the Bible which tells us as believers that dreams and visions are for us today. It is very important that we search the scriptures out ourselves on any and every matter. The enemy knows the scripture. He twisted the Word of God in the garden with Adam and Eve, as well as in the wilderness with Jesus. When anyone talks to someone else about a dream or vision that they have had, they should not accept one word of counsel as LAW! People are human and make mistakes. The Apostle Paul himself said in *1 Corinthians 13: 12* that we only know in part. He said that we see through a glass darkly. No one person has the whole revelation from the Lord! It is when we come together with our "parts" we have received from His heart that a total picture begins to emerge. The Lord designed us that way so that we would fellowship with and need one another. It is very dangerous to let anyone have the kind of control over anyone else as the all knowing and seeing part of their life. Seek the counsel of others you trust in the Lord, but seek the Lord and His Word by His Spirit through prayer and reading the Word of God.

Dreams Viewed as Gifts of the Spirit

A dream interpretation should be regarded like a prophecy, word of wisdom, word of knowledge, or any word from anyone. There should be confirmation from deep down in your spirit as well as from the Word of God. Remember, it was your dream, not the interpreters' dream. We are still human beings and can miss it! You have the Holy Spirit in you, the teacher! *(1 John 2: 27)* Listen to Him. If you feel a lack of peace about what you are hearing, don't judge the interpreter; judge the interpretation! A constant study in the Word on a daily basis will keep you fresh in the Word as well as fine tuned to the Spirit of God. As is stated in *2 Timothy 2: 15*, "Be diligent to present yourself approved to God, a worker who does not need to be ashamed, rightly dividing the word of truth." *John 7: 38* says that OUT OF OUR HEARTS will flow RIVERS OF LIVING WATER! In *Romans 8: 11*, Paul tells us that the same Spirit that raised Jesus from the dead dwells in us and will quicken our mortal

In A Dream, In A Vision of the Night
Job 33:15-18

bodies! The gifts of the Spirit are not floating around out in the atmosphere somewhere waiting for us to catch them and use them. HE IS WITHIN US. We are the temple of the Holy Spirit. *(1 Cor. 6: 14)* We can all learn to hear His voice and follow His direction if we will learn that the Kingdom is within. I developed a "saying" years ago that I felt was from the Lord. I use this statement many times in my own life, and when I minister to God's children. It says, "Victory comes without a doubt, when we learn to live from the inside out!" Circumstances we "feel" and "see" should not motivate our dreams or actions, but the moving of the Holy Spirit deep on the inside of us. When we learn to walk in the Spirit in our waking hours, we will learn to do the same in our sleep.

Dreams, Trances and Visions

There is certainly a lot in the Word of God about dreams and visions. In the research that I have done personally, dreams are mentioned about 122 times in the entire Bible. The trance is mentioned about 4 times. Visions are mentioned about 101 times.

In the Greek language of the New Testament and the Hebrew language of the Old Testament the word "dream" is translated simply to dream, or a dream. In the Greek language, the word "trance" is translated as a displacement of the mind. In the Hebrew language the word "vision" is translated in several ways. One is a view, an appearance, a shape. Another translation is a dream, revelation oracle, a sight, or a striking appearance. Another translation is to gaze at, mentally perceive, contemplate, behold, prophesy, see. A last translation found for the word vision in the Hebrew language is for one to mentally dream; a seer.

In Webster's Dictionary the definitions for these very same words are as follows:

Dream: A series of thoughts, images, or emotions, occurring during sleep.

Trance: A state of partly suspended animation or inability to function.

Vision: Something seen in a dream, trance, or ecstasy. A supernatural appearance that conveys a revelation. Paula M. Cavu, in his book "Dreams and Visions With a Difference for all Believers," tells us that the period of time that Abraham, Isaac, and Jacob were on the earth the Lord communicated a great deal through dreams and visions. *(Genesis 12 through 49.)* Cavu says, "Because we, the church, live in the time of the fulfillment of the promise of Abraham in Jesus Christ we become interested in the way in which God

In A Dream, In A Vision of the Night
Job 33:15-18

spoke to the people of this era. We would expect God to be speaking to us in similar ways."

Many of the Prophets of old saw visions and had dreams from the Lord. Ezekiel saw the throne of God *(Ezekiel 1)*, Daniel dreamed dreams that deeply disturbed him and were prophetic *(Daniel 8: 27, Daniel 10)*, Isaiah saw the seraphim worshiping God *(Isaiah 6)* In the New Testament, John, in the book of Revelations, saw most of what is in this book as a vision. Peter was resting and saw the vision of the sheet and the animals *(Acts 10: 9-22)*. It even says in verse 17 that Peter was perplexed and wondered what the vision meant. He wondered within himself what the vision was, after thought and prayer it was revealed to him. In *Numbers chapter 12: 6* it says, "If there is a Prophet among you; I the Lord, make Myself known to him in a vision, And I speak to him in a dream. Not so with my servant Moses; He is faithful in all my house. I speak with him face to face; even plainly, and not in dark sayings; And he sees the form of the Lord. Why then were you not afraid to speak against My servant Moses?" The Lord is specifically pointing out that he speaks to us in different ways. Moses had a particular purpose that he was to accomplish. The Lord chose to speak to him face to face on Mount Sinai. Moses was a type of Jesus for us. Father God spoke to Jesus face to face. The Lord points out that he speaks to His prophets in dark sayings, dreams and visions. As we walk with Him and our relationship with Him develops more and more, we begin to find that our dreams are shorter and more to the point.

Dreams and Parables as Dark Sayings

It is interesting to note the relationship between what Paul said in *1 Corinthians 13: 12*, and what the Lord said in *Numbers chapter 12*. That scripture says in the King James Version, "For now we see through a glass darkly; but then face to face: now I know in part: but then shall I know even as also I am know." If the Apostle Paul, with all of the revelation that he had, saw through a glass darkly, how much more do we? I know that we are ever increasing in understanding as we approach the coming of the Lord, but most of us do not have what Paul taught down pat yet! He said we know in part. Dreams are imparted knowledge given in part. A dream must come from the Holy Spirit, through our born again spirit, and then through our soul that is still being renewed day by day. Our souls still remember who we were. Our Lord uses language that our soul man can understand in dreams. They are

In A Dream, In A Vision of the Night
Job 33:15-18

dark because we are in need of being continually ENLIGHTENED. Light dispels darkness! *(Romans 12: 1-2; 2 Corinthians 4: 6)*

In the New Testament, Jesus spoke to the disciples and others in parables. Parables are much like dreams. They needed to be interpreted. In *Matthew 13: verses 10-14*, Jesus speaks about why He spoke in parables. The disciples asked Him, "Why do you speak to them in parables?" Jesus answered them saying, "Because it has been given to you to know the mysteries of the kingdom of heaven, but to them it has not been given." Why had it been given to the disciples and not to the multitude? Because the disciples were, and those of us today that are disciples of Christ are, being enlightened by His Word and Spirit! Jesus is still speaking to us in parables today. In verse 13 Jesus said, "Therefore I speak to them in parables, because seeing they do not see, and hearing they do not hear, nor do they understand." However, those of us that are called to the mysteries of the kingdom can know and interpret the parables we receive from the Lord in the form of a dream, trance or vision. Those that are not believers do not understand because their natural minds cannot understand the language of the Spirit. *(1 Cor. 2: 14) Proverbs 25: verse 2* says, "It is the glory of God to conceal a matter, But the glory of kings to search out a matter." We as kings and priests in Jesus are called to search all the wonderful jewels hidden in the Word of God. Speaking to us in parables, dreams, and visions is one way that the Lord causes us to dig deeper into the Word. Many people find that when they first begin to have dreams from the Lord, the dreams are very long and full of details. As we grow in knowledge of the Word of God, receiving the light of the truth of His Word, renewing our minds on a daily basis, we will find that these dreams become shorter and more to the point. When we are born again, our spirit man is totally brand spanking new in the Lord! However, our soul still remembers the desires and lust and pleasures of sin. It takes time to get a strong supply of the WORD of God built up to begin to replace these memories with truth. This process can be seen in the dreams and visions that we have. There are even some dreams that are all entwined with our own feelings and desires. The longer we truly walk with the Lord and yield to His will we find that less and less of our own will and way is found in the dreams we dream.

I love the scripture in *Mark chapter 4 verses 33 and 34*. Mark says, "And with many such parables He spoke the word to them as they were able to hear it. But without a parable He did not speak to them. And when they were alone, He explained all things to His

In A Dream, In A Vision of the Night
Job 33:15-18

disciples." If we will draw away from the crowd everyday spending quality time with our Lord, He will speak to us also. He will explain all things to us. We are meant to know the mysteries as we walk with Him everyday.

When Job was questioning God's continuing trials, he said this, "When I say that my bed shall comfort me, my couch will ease my complain, Then you scare me with dreams and terrify me with visions, so that my soul chooses strangling and death rather than my body." *(Job 7: 13-15)* What I understand this to mean is that when we are in danger of feeling too comfortable where we are, and where we are is in danger, the Lord loves us so much that he will warn us in a dream even to the point of scaring us. This may be at times what it takes to get our attention. In *Job 33: 14-18*, it says, "For God may speak in one way or in another, yet man does not perceive it. In a dream in a vision of the night, when deep sleep falls upon men, While slumbering on their beds, Then He opens the ears of men, and seals their instruction. In order to turn man from his deeds, and conceal pride from man, He keeps back His soul from the Pit, and his life from perishing by the sword." What I understand this to mean is that if we have a dream, which we cannot understand, we can rest. The Lord will seal the instruction of the dream. In other words, we will understand what we need to understand while the Lord does the rest. Time after time people have expressed confusion over counsel they have received about dreams and visions they did not understand or dreams that made them sick at heart. They had been counseled to forget it, it was not from God unless it was positive in nature. This does not agree with the Bible. John and Daniel died not understanding the visions they had of a fearful time in the future.

Certainly, dreams, trances and visions are not the only way that our Lord speaks to us. There are many other ways in which we can hear the Lord and receive direction, counsel, revelation, etc. The purpose of this writing however is to deal specifically with the voice of the Lord in the form of dreams, trances and visions.

In A Dream, In A Vision of the Night
Job 33:15-18

Chapter Two
Are All Dreams and Visions from God? Know His Voice

The answer to this question is a definite NO! Even though we know that the Lord is the one who created all things, He has instructed us to take care and know his voice. In *John 10: 4* the Lord clearly says that His sheep know His voice. In verse 5 it states that they do not even know the voice of a stranger! The devil, our enemy, does attempt to speak to us in the night season. It is up to us to know the Word of God as well as yield to the Spirit of God in order to discern what is of God and what is not. The kingdom of darkness and even our own flesh will try and tempt us to sin, discourage us, lie to us, scare us, and many other things. We can also dream from the business of our day, or from the desires of our own heart.

Dreams That Come From the Kingdom of Darkness

An example of this in my life was several years ago. I dreamed of a dark angel. This dark angel said that I would never finish the race in the Lord. He proceeded to tell me why this was true. When I woke up I was deeply disturbed. At first, I thought the Lord was telling me my fate. But as I began to meditate on the dream, I realized that this dream was not from the Lord. As I understood that the angel was dark, I knew that the dream revealed the evil plan of Satan, not the victorious plan and perfect will of the Lord!

At another time, several years ago, I kept having a recurring dream that greatly troubled me. I will not reveal the content of the dream to avoid giving glory to the enemy. The dream was causing me to dwell on the temptation to commit a certain sin. At first, I thought that the Lord was trying to show me what was in my heart. Yet, I never even had a thought of this sin until I would have the dream. For days after the dream I would fight for my life not to give into temptation. The thoughts would leave, and I would be fine for weeks. Suddenly, I would have this dream again. I was too embarrassed to talk to anyone but my husband about it. I was so afraid that Christian friends would judge me, and then write me off.

Finally one day I told a sister in the Lord all about it. She shared these words, "The Lord would never give you a dream that would tempt you to sin, in order to show you the evil desires in your heart. The only

In A Dream, In A Vision of the Night
Job 33:15-18

reason He would give you the dream would be to help you overcome, not fall!" I cannot tell you how those simple, true statements SET ME FREE!! I prayed with her and rebuked the enemy in the name of Jesus. As a result, in the name of Jesus, I NEVER HAD THE DREAM AGAIN! God is good!

I have received many demonic dreams from people all over the world. There is a common thread through all of them. I bring this up to say that the enemy is not original or creative. He has been trying to terrorize people for as long as he has been seeking those he wants to sift and devour. It is important to remember that he is crafty and wise and his schemes are real, however, let us remember that the Lord is wiser and has REAL plans for us to deliver us! The enemy wants us to be ashamed and hide the attacks he sends against us to keep us in bondage. The Lord wants us to share with others who can help and pray for us. Sometimes we trust a Psychologist or doctor more than we do a brother or a sister in Christ because we are afraid of being judged and rejected. I encourage everyone to find someone they can trust in the Lord and get help to be the best you can be in Christ. It is true that we don't need to share our deepest fears with just anyone. The Lord has someone you can trust. It is best for women

Susan Noone Riddle

to confide in women, and men in men, unless it is your spouse, to avoid other problems that can arise.

Dreams That Come Out of Our Own Hearts

Another place that dreams can come from is out of our own heart. *(Ecc. 5: 3)* Recently I had a dream about my father waiting in line at a doctor's office. There was a long line. I kept looking at him to be sure he was fine. In 1997, in reality, my father left this life and went on to be with Jesus. Months before he died, we spent many hours at the doctors office waiting. The very day before the dream my mother and I had been to the doctor for a medical problem that she had. The dream about my father was probably from the business of the day before. The fact that he was waiting to see a doctor was probably in the dream because we had waited the day before, and it brought back the memory of what we had been through with my dad.

In A Dream, In A Vision of the Night
Job 33:15-18

Dreams That Come From the Lord

The only three places that I know of dreams come from are the Lord, from the devil, and from within us. The Lord will speak to us in this manner for many different reasons. Some of these reasons may be to tell us something about ourselves that is good, or that needs to be changed. Another reason may be to warn us of things to come. Sometimes the Lord may desire to reveal a spiritual truth. Other times He may reveal something to us about a brother or sister so that we can pray for them (He will only do this if He knows He can trust us, not so that we can gossip with what He has shown us). It is not always God's purpose for us to go to a person with information He has revealed. This must carefully be considered in prayer to know from the Spirit what the Lord's will is concerning information a dream from the Lord has provided. The Lord may want to confirm something to the dreamer. The Lord may want to give direction in a dream. It is best to seek confirmation and not make a decision too soon when it comes to serious changes in life and ministry. One should never make a change based on a dream alone. We should always remember that the Word is true in its entirety. We need to conform our

Susan Noone Riddle

lives and dreams to His Word, not try and conform His Word to our lives and dreams!

A very important thing to remember is that if we listen we will hear the voice of the Lord in many different ways. We must be sure to stay in the Word of God and seek counsel from those in the body whom we know walk close to the Lord. *(Proverbs 11: 14)* Then, we must take it all to the Lord in prayer, as we wait for direction!

In A Dream, In A Vision of the Night
Job 33:15-18

Chapter Three
To Interpret or Not to Interpret, Is that the Question?

Does a dream really need to be interpreted? Why would the Lord speak to us in dark sayings, when we have the fullness of the LIGHT within our very being? If we have to interpret, then why should we not just "KNOW" what the Lord is saying?

Yes, dreams really do need to be interpreted. Sometimes they are what they are. Other times they are what they are, and they are also symbolic. We do have the fullness of LIGHT within us. The Lord DOES speak to us in many other ways other than in dreams. There are some Christians who are deeply spiritual who never remember any dreams that they have. These same people may not understand a dream that someone else may share with them. Yet, they hear the Lord very clearly. For those of us that are visionary Christians, it is very important to learn what the Lord is saying. The question of "just knowing" is easily answered with scriptures. I have addressed this question all throughout this book.

Susan Noone Riddle

Eight Major Ways to Understand A Dream

Our dreams are parables with Biblical imagery that usually involves modern language. When we want to understand a dark saying or parables of the night, there are EIGHT MAJOR things that we must consider:

1. **Attributes of Places:**
   What is the significance of the location of the dream?
   What does this place mean to me?
   What characteristics does this place have in the Bible?
   Is it a positive or a negative force in the dream? (Can be both).

2. **Attributes of Characters:**
   What is the significance of the people in the dream?
   What do they mean to me?
   Are they a positive or a negative force in the dream? (Can be both).
   What characteristics do they have that people in the Bible have?

3. **Attributes of Objects:**

In A Dream, In A Vision of the Night
Job 33:15-18

What are the significances of the objects in the dream?

What do they mean to me?

What characteristics do these objects have that are in the Bible?

Are they a positive or a negative force in the dream? (Can be both).

4. **Attributes of Animals:**

   What is the significance of the animal or animals in the dream?

   What do they mean to me?

   What characteristics do they have to animals in the Bible?

   Are they a positive or a negative force in the dream? (Can be both).

5. **Actions or Conduct:**

   What are my actions or behavior in this dream?

   What are the actions and behavior of others in this dream?

   How do these actions relate to the actions and behavior of the characters of the Bible?

   Are these actions a positive or a negative force in the dream? (Can be both).

6. **Attitudes or Feelings:**

What are my feelings and attitudes in this dream?
What are the feelings and attitudes of others in this dream?
How do these emotions relate to the feelings and attitudes of the characters of the Bible?
Are the feelings a positive or a negative force in the dream? (Can be both).

7. Array of Colors:
What are the significant colors of clothes and objects in this dream?
How do these colors relate to the meaning of colors in the Bible?

8. Analogy of Numbers:
What are the significant numbers of people and objects in this dream?
How do these numbers relate to the meaning of numbers in the Bible?

The Parable of the Sower

In The Parable of the Sower, *(Matt. 13: 1-23; Mark 4: 1-20; Luke 8: 1-15)*, Jesus makes it clear that the parable takes place in a field. How do we know? The parable itself causes images to form in the heart of the

In A Dream, In A Vision of the Night
Job 33:15-18

hearer. There are words mentioned like, "earth," "stony places," "thorns," and "good ground." The hearer does not picture the sower throwing his seed on a couch, or roof, or hardwood floor! If these objects and places were used in the parable, it would take on a whole new meaning. Almost everything we encounter in our lives can serve as a parable or story with symbolic images, and can inform us, warn us, and teach us. This parable can be viewed as a natural event. However, the main message of the parable is not the natural event, but the message in the actions, places and people of the parable.

The symbols in the dream must be looked at collectively. While the symbols are important, we need not get loaded down with extreme detail. When looking at a dream to understand the message, that message can easily be lost in a dream that is given too much attention to long, particular data. I have received dreams from dreamers that were pages and pages long. These dreams are full of details that came out of the soul of the dreamer, which made it difficult and time consuming to find the message within. If we will learn to use the questions above, we will be able to organize our thoughts better when retelling the dream for understanding.

In the parables that Jesus gave us, He gave only the details that communicated the allegory. We need to look at our dreams the same way. If someone were to ask you to give a summary of a story or book you read, you would retell the parts of the story that were significant to you, adding only the details that strongly impressed you. When seeking to interpret someone else's or our own dream by the Spirit, we would do the same thing, view the summary. Look carefully at the overall message first.

In The Parable of the Sower, Jesus did this very same thing. He told the parable to the whole multitude, but in *Matt. 13: 10-23* and in *Luke 8: 9-10*, He told the meaning to the disciples. Why? Because they asked Him why He spoke in parables. He will answer us as well. *Luke 8: 9-10* tells us that the disciples asked Jesus to tell them what the parable means. He calls parables "mysteries," and says it is given to the disciples to understand them! In interpreting the parable, He starts with the main symbol that unlocks the rest of the parable, "seed." In *Luke 8: 10*, Jesus says, "Now the parable is this: The seed is the Word of God." Jesus is telling us that scriptural imagery opens up the entire understanding of the rest. From this we learn that seeds can be the Word of God, and words of man. Whether evil or anointed

In A Dream, In A Vision of the Night
Job 33:15-18

with the Word, they can, if planted in good soil, grow into something strong. If an evil word is planted in soil that is fertile with lust of the flesh, it can grow. If that same word goes forth, but reaches fertile ground with the strength of the Holy Spirit and crucified with Christ, that evil seed will NOT GROW! If the Word of the Lord is sown in a heart that is ready and willing to receive, the Word will take root and will yield a crop of good fruit!

Symbols can sometimes have meaning to us because of our culture or personal feelings, but their basic meaning is rooted and grounded in the Word of God. If someone dreams of eating seeds from a lemon, and they hate lemons because of the sour taste it possesses, that does not change the fact that the seed of that lemon represents the potential for words to be planted and grow. In a dream like this, that word or seed may mean that something bitter and sour has been planted and may take root in the fleshly ground, growing up to defile many. On the other hand, if the dreamer comes from a cultural background where seeds are worshiped somehow, that person may dream of a seed in a safe mounted on a wall while they stand silently looking at it. The basic meaning of the seed is still the Word of God. Why? Because the Word of God says it is! The message in the usage of the seed by the Lord may mean something entirely different from the dream of a lemon's meaning. The Lord may be saying to this dreamer to, "Get the Word off of the page (wall) and out of the box (tradition) and into their mouth!"

In this same parable, Jesus taught us to pay attention to the person or persons involved in the dream. It would do no good to have symbols in "things" (seed) or "places" (soil) without a person to sow the seed in the place (sower) and the hearer or recipient of the seed. The condition of their hearts is what determines their ability to receive. Another character is the devil who steals the Word out of the hearts of the hearers. In this parable, the devil was represented in the symbol, "birds." Birds will usually follow this pattern all throughout the scriptures and in dreams and represent "spirits." The birds may represent the Holy Spirit (dove) or they may be unclean, demonic spirits.

Actions are shown in the response of the hearts of the hearers. This parable reveals four responses or actions that cause the hearer to reject or not be able to completely receive the fullness of the Word or seed, and one reaction that does cause fullness. Numbers are significant in showing the different stages of development in the hearers. One hundred-fold is

In A Dream, In A Vision of the Night
Job 33:15-18

revealing the hearer that receives the fullness of the Word. The 60-fold hearer represents the one who receives more than half, but not the fullness. The one who receives 30-fold received some impartation of revelation from the Word of God, but not much. Then there is the one who received absolutely nothing at all!

Many other parables and dreams will use color also to represent something important. In the parable of the Rich Man and Lazarus in *Matt. 17: 4*, the color purple is used to represent wealth and riches.

Chapter Four
Dreams and Symbolism

We have already established that dreams are dark sayings and parables. Jesus taught us that parables needed to be interpreted. Some of our Old Testament characters taught us that dreams are symbolic and must be interpreted. Joseph had symbolic dreams that were actually prophetic about his own life as well as his family and ultimately all of Israel. He shared these dreams with his jealous brothers. This only brought him a life full of struggle and trouble! We can learn a valuable lesson from Joseph sharing his dreams with his brothers. Jesus said not to cast our pearls before the swine. *(Matt 7: 6)* There are those in the body of Christ that will persecute those who dream because of ignorance (not understanding), jealousy or carnal mindedness. Joseph was very skilled at understanding the dreams that Pharaoh had.

The WISE Use of Symbols

The dreamer as well as those who interpret dreams must exercise caution when using symbols. We cannot

In A Dream, In A Vision of the Night
Job 33:15-18

make hard fast rules. As with everything in the Kingdom, dreams and visions must be viewed through the eyes of the Word of God that is truth, as well as the Spirit of God. The Word without the Spirit is legalistic and dry. The Spirit without the Word can be dangerous, too. There are many voices in the Spirit realm. We need the Word of God to determine that the voices we hear are correct. The Lord Jesus Christ has provided the balance for us. Without it, we can be misled. The Bible is a great literary work full of types and shadows and symbolism. The imagery that the Lord put in His Word is unceasingly inspiring and captivating to the Spirit filled reader. Many times the scriptures will have both a real, natural meaning about something that really happened, as well as a symbolic lesson and teaching within it.

We are richly blessed with the inward witness of the Spirit of God. Many times someone has shared an interpretation with me that did not sit right. When this happens, the next step is to pray, asking the Lord why it is not sitting right. There are two vital questions we can ask ourselves about why it isn't setting right with us:

1. Is my flesh in the way, preventing me from receiving what the Lord may be wanting to say to me? Or,

2. Is the information shared coming from someone else's flesh, making it incorrect?

1 *John 2: 26-27* says, "These things I have written to you concerning those who try to deceive you. But the anointing which you have received from Him abides in you, and you do not need that anyone teach you but as the same anointing teaches you concerning all things and is true, and is not a lie, and just as it has taught you, you will abide in Him." What John is wanting us to understand here is that HE LIVES IN US! HALLELUJAH! We have the King of Kings and the Lord of Lords in us! Listen to His voice on the inside when it comes to dreams or anything at all!!

Symbolism: Types, Shadows and Parables

The Bible itself is full of rich types, shadows, symbols and parables. There are differing opinions within the body of Christ about what a type is as opposed to a shadow. I would like to give an overview

In A Dream, In A Vision of the Night
Job 33:15-18

of all of the views I have seen and heard. While there is only one God and one truth, we become troubled and confused by strong opinions of man. The important thing to remember is that symbols used in the Word of God are the same symbols used in dreams and visions, but are sometimes clouded or darkened by the experience of the soul. This is true of Bible interpretation as well. Oh how glorious it will be to see Him face to face and be like Him! *(1 John 3: 1-3)*

1. **Symbol**: This is the most commonly used term; the vocabulary that a community has in common; an image that represents a position on something that is added to its meaning that is generally considered literal; the general distinctions between the person, place, animal or thing used as a symbol and its definition; something that is what it is, and also means something else.
2. **Type**: A person, place or thing having common characteristics with another. A person, place or thing serving as an illustration of something. Isaac was a type of the Lord Jesus Christ.
3. **Shadow**: A trace or remnant of something more substantial. The lambs that were sacrificed in the Old Testament for the covering of sin, were a

Susan Noone Riddle

SHADOW of the sacrifice that Jesus made on the cross.
4. **Parable**: An allegory, riddle, dream or vision. A descriptive narrative told or written with the purpose of illuminating the hearer or reader of a spiritual principle. A descriptive narrative presenting pictures and symbols, which have meaning.

When reading through the book of Revelations, one might throw their hands in the air and say, "I can't understand a word of this!" I really feel that much of what the Apostle John saw, he did not understand as well. He wrote down what he saw the best way that he could describe it all. In *Revelations 4:3* the rainbow is mentioned. We know from *Gen. 9: 12-17* that the rainbow is symbolic of God's covenant with us concerning the earth. It was a symbol of His promise to us never to destroy the earth by flood again. This is a promise that cannot and will not be broken. The Bible itself can interpret the symbols in the Bible. Dreams can be interpreted by the meaning of the symbols in the Word of God.

Another example is in *Psalm 64*. In *Psalm 64: 3* it says, "Who sharpen their tongues like sword, And bend their bows to shoot their arrows — bitter words."

In A Dream, In A Vision of the Night
Job 33:15-18

Wow! If you dream that someone is shooting arrows at you, or guns (our modern day arrows) it may be that the Lord is wanting you to know that it is possible that someone is speaking bitter words against you. This is important to know because the Lord told us in *Isaiah 54: 17* that "No weapon formed against you shall prosper, and every tongue which rises against you in judgment YOU SHALL CONDEMN. This is the heritage of the servants of the Lord, and their righteousness is from Me, Says the Lord." The Lord may let you know that someone is speaking against you because He has given us the responsibility to condemn the words in His name so that they, as weapons formed against us, cannot prosper against us. Some may say, "Why doesn't the Lord just simply tell us in plain language, or let us over hear someone talking about us?" He does speak to us in plain language, also. He does what He wants the way He wants to do it! It is His choice to speak to us the way He chooses when He wants to. He does not always have to tell us why! That is also His choice. Sometimes the purpose of using parables and dreams is to teach us a deeper meaning of the Word.

Once we begins to understand the language of the Bible and the Spirit, and how to listen to the voice of the Lord, the language of dreams and visions becomes more and more clear. One of the mistakes that many people make in understanding the dreams and visions of the Lord, is that of taking the dreams too literally. For example, I once had a series of dreams in which my sons were the main characters. In one dream my middle son fell off of our porch. In another dream a police officer brushed passed my youngest son and knocked him over, also knocking his shoes off. In another dream, my youngest son was kidnapped and disappeared. My initial reaction was to protect my children. Then I began to realize that the dream was about something very near to my heart. It was a warning that something that I viewed in my heart as a "spiritual child" was about to be under serious attack by the enemy.

Sure enough, it happened. The policeman was someone who was in authority at the time. The shoes represented my walk with the Lord. The whole time was a very difficult time that really could have knocked me off the porch and off my feet, but because I was fully warned in advance, I was able to pray through and overcome! Had I not recognized the voice of the Lord in that these dreams were symbolic, I could have really panicked concerning my children! At the same time, I prayed for my children because dreams can many times be multilevel in meaning. I know now

In A Dream, In A Vision of the Night
Job 33:15-18

that it was important to pray for them at that time because of problems that have come into their lives, as they grew older. Thank God that sometimes we pray mysteries, planting seeds of the Word for future events.

Some dreams, like these spoken of above, have a level of truth in a natural meaning, and a level of truth in the symbolic or spiritual meaning. How do you know the truth about a dream? Study the Word of God and pray, be patient and trust the Lord! As humans we would like hard fast rules that would make it easy for us to figure out. The Lord wants us to meditate and dwell on His Word. Instant answers would not encourage us to linger where He is for answers! There are some symbols that come right out of the Bible like the word, "arrows" from *Ps. 64: 3*, "Who sharpen their tongues like swords, and bend their bows to shoot their arrows — bitter words." If we are shooting arrows or guns in a dream and the Word is going forth bringing healing, then the work of the Lord is being done! If we are shooting arrows or guns in a dream and they are representing the words of accusation, then we need to stop talking about our brethren! Another example of this is wine. The Bible calls it "new wine" speaking of the Spirit. However, if you dream that you are drinking wine and doing something destructive, this would not

Susan Noone Riddle

indicate the work of the Spirit! Most symbols have a good and evil side to them.

Another example of this is the symbol, water. Water is a type of the Holy Spirit in the Bible. In *John 7: 38* Jesus told us that "rivers of living water" would flow out of our hearts. He goes on to explain that this water is the promise of the Holy Spirit. In many scriptures fountain, rivers, brooks and springs are used as symbols to describe how the Holy Spirit might move in individuals. *(Isaiah 58: 11)* Water is used so often in the Bible that there are many references to it such as, the deep ocean, baptisms, rivers, storms, brooks, rain, dew, wells, fountains, being satisfied, thirsting for, having drought without it, and many more. So when a person dreams of water, the dreamer must consider if the water in the dream was a life flow or a destructive flow in order to know its particular meaning in that dream. If you dream of clear, pure flowing water, then you are probably dreaming of the Holy Spirit. If you dream of murky, muddy water, then the Holy Spirit is not what is being represented here. This dirty water is more than likely a wrong or unclean spirit.

As we saw in the Parable of the Sower, numbers are very significant in the Word of God as well as in dreams. If you dream of the number seven in

In A Dream, In A Vision of the Night
Job 33:15-18

connection with your ministry and life, this could really be a good thing! The number seven is symbolic of perfection and completion. Seven is one of God's perfect numbers. It is used about 600 times throughout the Bible. In *Genesis 2: 1; 3* we learn that the work of creation was completed and God rested on the seventh day! In *Revelations 16: 17* the seventh vial was poured out into the air. A great voice came from the throne saying, it is done!! The blood of the sacrifice spoken of in *Lev. 16: 14, 19* gave complete purification of sinfulness. In *Matthew 18: 21-22* Jesus speaks of forgiveness being "seven times seventy." Jesus was using the multiples of seven to speak to us of complete forgiveness which holds no malice.

As we also saw in the parable of The Rich Man and Lazarus, colors are also important to note of in a dream. Many times a color will stand out so vividly in a dream that you just know it is important to its meaning. I would not suggest taking every color from a dream and picking it apart. However, if something stands out as significant, pay close attention to it. An example of this would be a dream that my husband had. In the dream the streets of a downtown portion or the heart of the town we live in was full of water. The water was crystal clear and a beautiful blue color. He and I were diving in the water, swimming and having a wonderful time. Water, representing Spirit, *(Eph. 5: 6)*, crystal clear, representing purity and transparency of heart, *(Revelations 15: 22-3 and Revelations 5: 6)* and blue, representing the Holy Spirit as well as something heavenly. *(Numbers 15: 23 and John 14: 26)*, leaves a clear picture right out of the Word of God as to the meaning of this dream. The dream indicates revival coming forth into our hearts and the hearts of the people of this town. At the end of the dream, others began to jump in and enjoy the sea of glass and the anointing of God! *Ezekiel 47: 1- 12* describes this river that flows from the throne of God. The Lord God caused Ezekiel to swim in this river!! It brought healing and life. GLORY TO GOD!! Verse 9 says, "And it shall be that every living thing that moves, wherever the river goes, will live. There will be a great multitude of fish, because these waters go there; for they will be healed, and everything will be healed wherever the river goes!"

All creatures such as animals, reptiles, insects and the like are usually significant in dreams. Animals in the Bible give rich imagery. Some of the figurative meanings of animals are: Demonic powers *(Rev. 12: 4-9)*, the instinctive characteristics of man *(Jer. 13: 23)*, demonic dominion in the world *(Dan. 7: 2-8)* and the sacrifice that Jesus made on the cross *(1 Peter 1: 18-*

In A Dream, In A Vision of the Night
Job 33:15-18

20). To dream of a pet such as a dog or cat, would have a different meaning than to dream of a vicious growling dog or a snarling cat! I have dreamed of my pet dog being wounded before. I learned that this type of dream can be symbolic of something very near and dear to the heart being wounded. I have also dreamed of a dog that was trying to bite me. This is a warning from the Lord of an attack planned by the evil one. Many times the warning itself is enough to send us to our knees in prayer. Because of this, the event that we were warned about may come and go with little detrimental significance! The Lord, through prayer, gets the victory! Most of the time the nature of the animal speaks for the meaning it represents in the dream. A rat or a reptile is rarely ever anything but a demonic spirit. If a rat is a pet in a dream, this could be an indication of a "pet sin" that the dreamer has allowed to "hang around!"

Another significant type of symbol that we must understand in dreams is that of places, buildings and rooms. When one is deeply involved in a body at a church, many times the Lord will speak to us about that church. However, the dream itself may not always take place in an actual church setting. It may be in a setting where people gather together a lot. I've had dreams pertaining to church or the fellowship of believers that took place in a restaurant, or school, or auditorium. These places represented the church. This was clear also by the content of the dreams.

Another significant room in a dream is the kitchen. Many times the kitchen can represent the heart of the dreamer. The reason for this is that the kitchen is the heart of one's home! I had a dream that I was standing on the table in our kitchen at home. A full group of unseen worshippers were playing live music. I could not see them, but I could hear the music. There were black bands or belts that were attached to the ceiling and to my waist. I was pulling the bands one by one and break them! As they broke I would sing, "I break these chains — that bind me!" Finally, all of the bands were broken. I turned to leave the kitchen. As I did, I looked around and shadows began to try to come back into the kitchen. I turned to face them. As I did, the music started again. The shadows disappeared. When I awoke I realized that the song I was singing was a totally new song. We now sing it frequently in our praise and worship services.

It is very important to remember that a symbol should not always be used in an interpretation simply because it meant something in another dream. Dreams are abstract and cannot be interpreted concretely. Use these symbols only with prayer and by the Spirit. They

In A Dream, In A Vision of the Night
Job 33:15-18

are only meant to be used as a means to learn the language of the Spirit ad truth of the Word. I cannot stress this enough. Deep in our human sin nature, our soul man and our flesh, we want to be in control. If we make hard fast rules with symbols, we run into the danger of forcing our dreams to mean things that they don't. I have seen churches torn apart because an individual or two had dreams that they used to cause discord and strife with. The things of the Spirit should never be used to manipulate ours or another's circumstances to suit what we want.

Here are some symbols that may be found in dreams.

Chapter Five
Symbols and their Scriptural Meaning

ANIMALS & REPTILES & INSECTS & BIRDS

Alligator: <u>See Leviathan, Also Crocodile and Dinosaur.</u>

Ant: Hardworking; ability to prepare; wisdom. *(Prov. 6: 6-8; 30:25)*

Bat: Night dweller; blood suckers; unclean; flying creature often related to witchcraft and vampires. *(Du. 14: 18; Is. 2: 19-21; Lev. 11: 19)*

Bear: Evil men; danger; if one plays dead or if a body is dead, a bear will not pursue them (dead in Christ); Russia; wicked ruler over poor people, vindictiveness that is severe; antichrist of the last days; end time dominion and rule; financial matters as in: bear market. *(2 Sam. 17: 8; Dan. 7: 5; Is. 11: 7; Rev. 13: 2; Amos 5: 19; 2 Kings 2: 23-24; Prov. 17: 12)*

In A Dream, In A Vision of the Night
Job 33:15-18

Bees: Busy bodies; gossip; group of people; can produce sweet honey, or sting and wound; enemies that crowd around us. *(1 Tim. 5: 13; Judges 14: 8; Du. 1: 44; Psalms 118: 12)*

Bird: Holy Spirit; evil spirits; wicked rulers; nations that are hostile; Kingdom of God; a mother's love; God's provision. *(Matt. 6: 29; 13: 32; 23: 37; Is. 46: 11)*

Buzzards: **Also Ravens and Vultures**: Unclean spirits; length with the dead and evil supernatural realm; forsaken by all in death to self. *(2 Sam. 21: 10; Jer. 7: 33)*

Crane: Alone. *(Is. 38: 14; Hos. 7: 11)*

Dove: The Holy Spirit; peace and new life; a sin offering; burnt offering; cleansing; mercy. *(Gen. 8: 8-12; Matt. 3: 16; 10: 16; Lev. 5: 7-14; 14: 21-22; John 1: 32)*

Eagle: Soaring in the Spirit; good or evil leader; strength, power, and swiftness in both judgment and in delivering God's people from trouble; the United States of America; Prophet of God. *(Isaiah 40: 31, 46: 11; Jer. 48: 40, Ez. 17: 3, 7; Ex. 19: 4; Rev. 12: 14)*

- **Feathers**: Protection; shield; provision of ability to fly and sore. *(Ez. 17: 3-7; Ps. 91: 4; Dan. 4: 33)*
- **Fowler**: To mesmerize; to be trapped. *(Ps. 91: 4)*
- **Owl**: **Also Liliths, Screech Owls and Night Hags**: Wisdom through earthly means or from above; evil spirit; unclean spirit; night creature; routinely secluded. *(Is. 13: 21; 34: 13-14; 43: 20; Ps. 102: 6; Job 30: 29)*
- **Raven**: **See buzzard**.
- **Sparrow**: Provision; food; God's care for his creation. *(Matt. 10: 29-30)*
- **Wings**: Refuge; God's presence; safety; ability to fly away and escape danger. *(Ps. 91: 4, 17: 8, 61: 4)*

Camel: A servants heart; to bear the load. *(Gen. 24: 10, 31-32)*

Cat: **Also Tigers, Leopards and Cheetahs**: Unclean spirit; danger lying in wait; crafty; mysterious, strong self will; witchcraft; someone that is unattainable; unless personal pet. In the case of a personal pet, a cat can mean something or someone dear to your heart. A personal pet that is a

In A Dream, In A Vision of the Night
Job 33:15-18

leopard, could be a pet sin! *(Jer. 5:6, 13: 23; Hos. 13: 7)*

Cheetahs: **Also Tigers, Leopards and Cats**: Unclean spirit.

Chicken: **Also Hen, Rooster, and Chick**: A gatherer; to mother; Israel. *(Luke 13: 34; 22: 34; Matt. 23: 27; John 18: 27)*

Cow: **Also Heifer, Bull, Calf and Cattle**: The young: believers who are sanctified; agile; sacrifice; food; playful; worship of golden: immorality; great sin; punishment; an apostasy; blood of is not sufficient; evil men; mighty men; God's sacrifice and strength; ashes of sacrifice kept, mixed with water to purify; slaughtered and burned outside the camp; for sacrifice must be without blemish and never been in bondage to sin (never yoked); fall short of the sacrifice of Christ; expediency that is not proper; festive joy with shame. *(Num. 18: 17; 19: 1-22; Lev. 9: 2-3; Amos 6: 4; Ps. 22: 13; 29: 6; 68: 30; Ex. 32: 4-6, 21-35; 1 Cor. 10: 6-8; Matt. 10: 29-30; Luke 15: 23, 27; Heb. 9: 13; 10: 4; Du. 33: 17; Is. 34: 6-7; Gen. 15: 9; Judges 14: 18; Jer. 50: 11)*

Crocodile: **See Leviathan, Also Dinosaur and Alligator.**

Deer: **Also Hind:** Seeking water; ability to leap; quickness in stride; comeliness; our soul longing for the Lord. *(Is. 35: 6; Ps. 18: 32; 42: 1-2; Song 2: 17; 2 Sam. 22: 34)*

Dinosaur: **See Leviathan, Also Crocodile and Alligator.**

Dog: Note type of dog and relationship to dog: biting dog is dissension; hypocrite; attack against God's work; accusation; if a personal pet: something or someone dear to your heart; personal pet that is a wolf: pet sin, or warning you of an attack on the sheep; Judizers; watchman as in Elder or prophet as watchdog; returning to sin; false teachers. *(Prov. 26: 11-17; Phil. 3:2; Ez. 3: 17; Gal. 5 15; Ps. 22: 16; Rev. 22: 15; 2 Peter 2: 22; Matt. 7: 6)*

Donkey: **Also Mule:** Hard headed; endurance; self willed, single-minded, determined, and unyielding; riding: victory over self-will and humility. *(Ex. 4: 20; Mark 11: 2; Prov. 26: 3; Num. 22: 25; 2 Peter 2: 16; Hosea 8: 9)*

In A Dream, In A Vision of the Night
Job 33:15-18

Dragon: A high level of demonic attack; spiritual wickedness in high places; antichrist; Satan. *(Rev. 12:3-9; 13: 2-4; 16: 1; 20: 2)*

Fish: The newly saved; men's souls; clean and unclean men or spirits; miraculous provision of food in mass. *(Ez. 4: 19; Lev. 11: 9-12; Matt 4: 19; 17: 24)*

Flea: Not substantial; annoyance; subtle; inconvenience. *(1 Sam. 24: 14)*

Fly: Beelzebub; demons; corruption of the house or possession by demonic spirits of the person. *(Ecc. 10: 1; Matt. 12: 24)*

Fox: **Also Jackal**: Secret sins; crafty man; enemies of the cross; skill for evil; desolation and crying in the night; divining prophets; suck the life flow from lambs (blood). *(Jer. 9: 11; Rev. 13: 11; Is. 35: 6-7; Ez. 13: 4-6; Song 2: 15; Luke 13: 32)*

Frog: Demon spirits; lying nature; sorcery; speaking curses. *(Rev. 16: 13; Ex. 8: 1-15; Ps. 78: 45)*

Goat: Carnal, fleshly Christians; unbelief; Christian or group of Christians walking in sin; the cursed, "scapegoat" or "goat of removal" showing that our sins have been removed as far as the east is from the west;

opposite of lambs; carriers of sin; our need to obtain forgiveness of sin; mixed with sheep, but not called the shepherds "own." *(Ex. 25: 4; Matt. 25: 31-46; Lev. 16: 8, 15, 20-22; Ps. 103: 12; Heb. 13: 12)*

Grasshopper: **Also Locust**: Trouble and devastation to crops; instrument of God's judgment upon nations that are rebellious; destroyer; subordinate position; numbers of a mighty army; encumberment; trivial; good for eating. *(Ex. 10: 1-20; Rev. 9: 7-11; Is. 40: 22; Num. 13: 33; Joel 2: 1-11, 25; Lev. 11: 20-23; Mark 1: 6; Ecc. 12: 5)*

Hare: **See Rabbit**.

Horse: Instruments of battle; power and strength of the flesh; time period of work; a powerful work of God on the earth, in the Spirit; tenaciousness, single-mindedness and aggressiveness; in transportation: battle; not to trust in over the name of the Lord. (This would carry over into our modern day weapons and modes of transport). *(Job 39: 19; Ps. 32: 9; 33: 17; 66: 12; Prov. 26: 3; Jer. 5: 8; 8: 6; Rev. 6: 1-8; 19: 11, 14, 19, 21; Zech. 1: 8; 10: 3; 2 Kings 2: 11; Hos. 14: 3; James 3: 3; Amos 8: 11; John 16: 2)*

In A Dream, In A Vision of the Night
Job 33:15-18

Different color horses are important:
- **Black**: Famine; evil.
- **Bay (flame-colored)**: Anointing, power, fire.
- **Pale**: Death.
- **Red**: Persecution, bloodshed; enemy warring against God's people.
- **White**: War of conquest; God's mighty army)

Lamb: **Also Sheep**: Jesus as our sacrifice; true believers; gentleness; blamelessness and purity led to the slaughter; saints; the church; Israel. *(Is. 53: 7; 2 Sam. 2: 17; Luke 10: 3; Matt. 10: 6; 25: 33; John 1: 29, 36; 1 Peter 1: 19)*

Leopards: **See Tigers, Cheetahs and Cats**.

Leviathan: **Also Crocodile and Dinosaur**: Creature that cannot be tamed with the natural strength of man; demon; evil spirit; ancient demonic control; only the Lord has power over. *(Job 41: 1-10; Ps. 74: 14; 104: 26)*

Lice: Accusation; shame; plague. *(Ex. 8: 16-18)*

Lion: Jesus; conqueror; overcoming bold saints; Satan the devourer; warrior; transformation; victory; persecution; dominions of the world; antichrist. *(Ez. 1: 10; Prov. 28: 1;*

Susan Noone Riddle

>*30: 30; Is. 11: 6-8; John 18: 37; Rev. 5: 5; 13: 2; 17: 14; 19: 16; 1 Peter 5: 8; Ps. 22: 13; 91: 13; Dan. 7: 1-4)*

Locusts: **See Grasshopper**.

Pig: **Also Sow and Swine**: An unclean (fleshly) people; legalistic Christians; dull minded to spiritual things; phony and hypocritical; a foolish woman; false teachers; detestable things. *(Matt. 7: 6; Prov. 11: 22; Is. 65: 4; 66: 3; 2 Peter 2: 22; Ps. 80: 13)*

Rabbit: **Also Hare**: Satan; evil spirits; pagan celebration of Easter; rapid multiplication. *(Du. 14: 7; Lev. 11: 6; Josh. 19: 20)*

Scorpion: Evil spirits; sin nature; burdens that are heavy; lust of the flesh; deception; a stringing deadly pain; satanic; spirit of the antichrist; poisonous. *(Luke 10: 19; Rev. 9: 3, 5, 10; 1 Cor. 15: 56; Rom. 7: 23; 1 Kings 12: 11; Du. 8: 15; 2 Chron. 10: 11)*

Serpent: **Also Snake**: Satan; earthly, sensual wisdom; crafty and cunning; Christ made sin for us; cursed; criticism and gossip, persecution if viper; divination if python or constrictor; beguiling; drunkenness; malice; evil that is sudden; enemies; vileness of hate of the sinner. *(Gen. 3: 1; 49: 17; Rev.*

In A Dream, In A Vision of the Night
Job 33:15-18

12: 9; 20: 2; 20: 2; Mark 3: 7; Acts 16: 16; Matt. 10: 16; John 3: 14; Prov. 23: 31-32; Ps. 58: 3-4; Ecc. 10: 8; Is. 14: 29)

Sheep: **See Lamb**.

Snake: **See Serpent**.

Spider: False doctrine; unstable; without any deity; enticing demonic presence. *(Is. 59: 5; Ecc. 7: 26; Job 8: 14; Prov. 8: 14; 27: 18; 30: 24)*

Tigers: **Also Cheetah, Leopards and Cats**.

Wolf: Plan to destroy God's flock; deviant; wolf in sheep's clothing; brazen; false prophet; opportunistic; prowl round at night. *(Matt. 7: 15; 10: 16; John 10: 12; Is. 11: 6; Jer. 5: 6)*

Worm: **Also Maggot**: Detested; disease; humility; no dignity; filthiness of the flesh; destruction; eat off of flesh; destructive to vines and tree; likened to the misery and suffering of the lost soul in hell; crucified Messiah. *(Ex. 16: 20; Du 28: 39; Is 14: 11, 66: 24, 51: 8; Job 25: 6; Ps. 22: 6; Mark 9: 48)*

COLORS

Black: Opposite of white and purity; judgment of God; death; famine; sin; ignorance; darkness; demonic army; Jesus' depth on the cross. *(Rev. 6: 2-12; Lam. 4: 8; Jer. 8: 21; Matt 27: 45; Ps. 18: 9, 11; 97:2; 104: 2; Ex. 20: 21; Zeph. 1: 15; Joel 2: 2)*

Blue: The Holy Spirit; heaven; heavenly visitation. *(Numbers 15: 38; Ex. 28; Num. 4)*

Brown (or Tan): Green life turns this color (withers) when dead; born again; without spirit; repentance or turning from dead works. *(1 Peter 1: 24; Ps. 37: 2)*

Gold: is in METALS.

Gray: **See also Silver in METALS**: Mixture of black and white; deception; compromise; truth mixed with tradition. See also Silver in METALS section. *(Hosea 7: 9)*

Green: Life; can be good or evil life; life of the flesh;. provision; rest and peace. *(1 Peter 1: 24; Gen. 1: 30; 9: 3; Ps. 23: 2)*

Orange: **Also Peach and Tan**: If Halloween orange or warning street sign, orange can mean:

In A Dream, In A Vision of the Night
Job 33:15-18

        Great danger; forceful power; warning; caution. Strong anointing as in fire of God; Holy Spirit in fire; God's protection;. purification; persecution; love; God's vengeance; angels. *(Prov. 6: 27; Acts 2: 3; Zech. 5: 2; Is. 6: 5-7; Luke 12: 49-53; Song 8: 6; Heb. 12: 29; Heb. 1:7)*

Pink: **See Red, Tan and Orange (Peach.)** It can mean flesh, as it is the color of flesh; can be watered down blood, or a watered down gospel, or lack of passion for gospel. *(Rev. 6: 7, 17: 3-6; Ex. 26: 14)*

Purple: Kingly; wealth; prince; authority; political power and wealth in the sense of dishonesty and wickedness (Babylon); royalty; majesty power in wealth and royalty; expensive to buy. *(Dan. 7: 5, 16, 29; Judges 8: 26; John 19: 2, 5; Rev. 17: 4; 18: 16; Acts 16: 14; Prov. 6: 27; Acts 2: 3; Zech. 5: 2; Is. 6: 5-7; Luke 12: 49-53; Song 8: 6; Heb. 12: 29; Heb. 1:7)*

Red: **Also Scarlet and Crimson**: The blood of Jesus; warfare; sacrifice; passion; strong emotion; forgiveness; cleansing; zealousness; deep sins; conquest; wine; complexion. *(Lev. 4: 7; Prov. 23: 31; Rev.*

6: 4-7, 12: 3; 17: 3-6; Ex. 26: 14; 2 Kings 3: 22; Lev. 14: 4, 6, 49-52; Heb. 9: 11; Is. 1: 18; Na. 2: 3; Josh 2: 18, 21)

Silver: **See MEDALS**.

White: Purity that dispels the darkness; righteousness; God's majesty; blameless; washed white by the blood; redeemed; God's glory; white is associated with light and the new heavens and earth; victory; completion; can also be purely evil. *(Rev. 1: 14; 2: 17, 3: 4; 6: 2, 11; 20: 11; Is. 1: 18; Dan. 7: 9; John 4: 35; Mark 16: 4)*

Yellow: **See also Gold in MEDALS**: Something good; honor; infirmity; sin. *(Ps. 68: 13)*

METALS

Brass: Judgment of sin; hardness of heart; Word of God; strength; Christ's glory; willful disobedience; judged; man's word; replacement. *(Ex. 26: 19; Num. 21: 9; Rev. 1: 15; Is. 48: 4; Heb. 13: 10-13; Ex. 27: 13; 1 Corinthians; 13: 1; 2 Chron. 12: 10)*

Gold: The riches of the glory of God; enduring capacity of the believer as overcomer;

unchanging holiness; wisdom; glory; righteousness; glorifying self when used as adornment or as idol worship. *(Lam. 4: 2; Ps. 19: 10, 119: 72; Rev. 3: 18, 21: 18. 21; 1 Cor. 3: 12; Ex. 20: 23; Is. 40: 19; Job 22: 25)*

Iron: **Also Steel**: Power; strongholds; stubborn; strength; blight; strict rules; crushing power; judgment. *(Rev. 2: 27; Du. 28: 23; 48; Dan. 2: 40)*

Lead: Heaviness; burden; sinfulness. *(Zech. 5: 8; Ex. 15: 10)*

Silver: Understanding; knowledge; purity; cleanliness; redemption; idolatry; Words of God; promises of God; worldly knowledge; cleansed and ready for use; very precious to God; used as betrayal; furnace of adversity. *(Proverbs 2: 3-4; Ex. 26: 19; Gen. 37: 28; Judges 17: 4; 1 Kings 7: 51; Ez. 7: 19-20; Matt. 26: 15; Is. 1: 22; Acts 19: 24; 1 Cor. 3: 12; Job 28: 1; Ps. 12: 6)*

Tin: Cheap; flimsy; imitation; dross. *(Is. 1: 25; 51: 17-22; Ez. 22: 18-19; Ps. 75: 8; 119: 119)*

Susan Noone Riddle

NUMBERS

One: **Also First**: New; beginning; unity; timing; position or order primacy; deity; sufficiency. *(Du. 6:4; John 17: 21; Matt. 6: 33; Ex. 20: 3; Rev. 1: 11, 17; 2: 8; Is. 44: 6; 45: 5-6)*

Two: Witnessing; separation; discernment; wholeness in marriage; division; enmity; opposition; dividing light and darkness; relationship between God and man is closely tied to our relationship with man. *(Gen. 1: 6-8, 27; 2: 24; 16: 21; Ex. 31: 18; Ecc. 4: 9-10; Matt. 19: 5-6; 22: 37-40; 1 Tim. 5: 19; John 8: 17; Rev. 11: 2-4)*

Three and Third: Complete; perfection; witness; divine fullness; solid attributes; Godhead; conform; resurrection power over sin; divine fullness. *(Romans 3: 9; 6: 9; 1 Sam. 3: 8; Jonah 1: 16-17; 20: 1-9; 1 John 5: 6-7; Col. 2: 9; Eph. 3: 19; 4: 13; John 1: 16)*

Four: World; earth; creation; creative work; four winds; four seasons; four corners of the earth; rule and reign over the earth; global implications such as east, west, north,

In A Dream, In A Vision of the Night
Job 33:15-18

south; territorial specific realm implications. *(Gen. 2: 10; 41: 34; Rev. 5: 9; 7: 1, 9; 13: 7; Is. 58: 6-10; Ez. 42: 20; 46: 21; Lev. 11: 20-27; 27: 31; John 8: 34; 1 Cor. 15: 39)*

Five: Grace; atonement; fivefold ministry; service (five fingers on the hand); bondage; complete wellness. *(Is. 1: 12-14; Matt. 25: 2; Eph. 4: 11; Mark 6: 38-40; Luke 9: 13-16; Gen. 1: 20-23)*

Six: Man; beast; Satan; flesh; carnal; toil and strain of the flesh or natural realm; work; sorrow; secular completeness. *(Rev. 13: 18; 1 Sam. 17: 4-7; Gen. 1: 26-31; 4: 17-18; 2 Peter 3: 8; 2 Sam. 21: 20; Num. 35: 15)*

Seven: Completion; finished work; perfection; rest; perfection in the Spirit. *(Gen. 2: 1-3; Lev. 14: 7; 16: 14, 19; Matt. 18: 21-22; Jude 14; Rev. 2: 1; 8: 2; 12: 3)*

Eight: Circumcision of the flesh; liberty; salvation; new beginning; resurrection life; die to self. *(Gen. 17: 12; 1 Peter 3: 20-21; 2 Chron. 29: 17; 2 Peter 1: 14)*

Nine: Fruit of the Spirit; gifts of the Spirit; finality; harvest; fullness of development.

Susan Noone Riddle

>*(Matt. 27: 45; Judges 4: 1-3; Gal. 5: 22-23; 1 Cor. 12: 4-11)*

Ten: Government; law (commandments); order; tithe; measure; trial; testing. *(Lev. 27: 32; Ex. 34: 28; Rev. 2: 10; 12: 3; Matt. 25:1-13)*

Eleven: End; finish; final; incomplete; disorder; lawlessness. *(Gen. 27: 9; 32: 33; Du. 11: 8; Ex. 26: 7; Matt. 20: 9-12)*

Twelve: Divine government and election; apostolic fullness; discipleship; The Church; people of God; united; oversight. *(Gen. 49: 28; Numbers 13: 1-16; Matt. 3: 14; Luke 9: 1-2; 22: 30; Rev. 12: 1; 21: 12; Rev. 22: 2; Ex. 15: 27; 29: 15; 1 Cor. 1: 10)*

Thirteen: Rebellion; rejection; backsliding. *(Gen. 14: 4; Esther 9: 11; 1 King 7: 1)*

Fourteen: Passover; recreate, reproduce; servant. *(Ex. 12: 6; 1 Kings 8: 65; Num. 9: 5; Gen. 31: 41)*

Fifteen: Deliverance; grace; freedom; rest. *(Lev. 23: 6-7; Hos. 3: 2; Gen. 7: 20; 2 Kings 20: 6)*

Sixteen: Not under the law because of love; free; salvation. *(Acts 27: 34; 37-38)*

In A Dream, In A Vision of the Night
Job 33:15-18

Seventeen: Spiritual order; incomplete; immature. *(Gen. 37: 2; 1 Chron. 25: 5; Jer. 32: 9)*

Eighteen: Bondage; judgment; destruction; captivity. *(Judges 10: 7-8; Luke 13: 11-16)*

Nineteen: Faith; void of self-righteousness; ashamed; barren of flesh or of Spirit; repentance. *(2 Samuel 2: 30; Rom. 6: 21)*

Twenty: Holy; redemption. *(Ex. 30: 12-14; Rev. 4: 4)*

Twenty-four: Perfection in government; priesthood; consecration; maturity. *(Rev. 4: 4-10; Josh. 4: 2-9; 1 Chron. 24: 3-5; 25: 1-12; 1 Kings 19: 19)*

Thirty: Beginning of ministry; maturity for ministry; blood of Christ. *(Luke 3: 23; Gen. 41: 16; Num. 4: 3)*

Forty: Trials; testing. *(Matt. 4: 2; Num. 13: 25; 14: 33-34; Ex. 34:27-28; Matt. 26: 15; Acts 1: 6; 7: 30)*

Fifty: Pentecost; Holy Spirit; jubilee; liberty; freedom. *(Lev. 23: 16; 25: 10-11; Ex. 26: 5-6; 2 Kings 2: 7; Num. 8: 21)*

Seventy: Transference of God's Spirit; multitude; increase; restoration. *(Num. 11: 16-29; Gen. 4: 24; 11: 26; 46: 27; Ex. 1: 5-6; 15: 27; 24: 1-9; Luke 10: 1)*

Seventy-five: Cleansing and purifying; separating. *(Gen. 12: 4; Dan. 12: 5-13)*

One hundred:Fullness; people of promise. *(Mark 5: 20; 10: 30; Gen. 26: 12)*

One hundred and Twenty: Start of life in the Spirit; end of flesh life. *(Acts 1: 5; 2 Chron. 3: 4; 5: 12; Gen. 6: 3; Du. 34: 7)*

One hundred and forty-four: God's fullness in all He has creation. *(Rev. 7: 1-6; 14: 1-3; 21: 17; 1 Chron. 25: 7)*

One hundred and Fifty: End of the judgment by water. *(Gen. 8: 3)*

One hundred and Fifty-three: Bringing in the harvest; revival. *(John 21: 6-4)*

Two Hundred: Inadequacy of needs being met in the natural and/or in the Spirit. *(2 Sam. 14: 26; Josh. 7: 21; John 6: 7; Gen. 11: 19)*

Three hundred: God's chosen; God's remnant. *(Judges 7 & 8; 15: 4; Gen. 5: 22; 6: 15)*

Three hundred ninety: God's chosen; God's remnant as in the nation of Israel. *(Is. 7: 8; Ez. 4: 5)*

Six-Six-Six: Antichrist; Satan; number of man; mark of the beast. *(Rev. 13: 18; Dan. 3: 17)*

In A Dream, In A Vision of the Night
Job 33:15-18

Thousands: Coming to maturity. *(Joshua 3: 3-4; 1 Sam. 17: 5, 33; Eph. 4: 13; Rev. 12: 18; 14: 9-11)*

Two Thousand: Church age ending in resurrection. *(Joshua 3: 4)*

Ten Thousand: God's army taught and led by God. *(Du. 33: 2-3, Jude 14)*

Twelve Thousand: The Lords mighty army. *(Rev. 7: 5-8)*

One hundred and forty-four thousand: The salvation of the world. *(Rev. 7: 4)*

PEOPLE:

Callings, Characteristics, Relationships, Relatives, Personalities, Professions and More

Baby: New birth; barren women pitied; reproductive; ministry in its infancy stage; helpless; new Christian; baby Christian; new move of God; spiritual immaturity; reward; fruitfulness; new covenant; miracle. *(1 Corinthians 3: 1; Gen. 21: 6; 1 Sam. 2: 1-10; 2 Kings 4: 11-17; Gen. 16: 1-6; Ps.*

127: 3; Ex. 1: 15-22; 2: 1-10; 1 Peter 2: 2; Heb. 5: 13)

Bride: **See also Wife, Marriage and Groom**: Covenant relationship; the church or the remnant; unfaithfulness or faithfulness in the natural things or the spiritual things; miraculous transformation. *(Ephesians 5: 31-32; Hos. 1: 2; 2 Corinthians 6: 14; 11: 2; Rev. 19: 7-9; 20-22; John 21-10; Is. 62: 5)*

Brother: **See also Sister and Friend**: The Holy Spirit; a spiritual brother in the church; yourself; someone who has similar qualities to you; the brother himself; can be disorderly, or in need of admonishment, or weak, or evil, in need, or can be falsely judged. *(Hebrews 13: 3; 1 Cor. 1: 1; Amos 1; 9; 1 Cor. 8: 11-13; 2 Thess. 3: 6; James: 1: 9; Romans 14: 10-21; 2 Thess. 3: 15; 1 Timothy 5: 1)*

Brother-in-law: **See also Sister-in-law**: Same as a brother, yet under the law; minister involved in another church; yourself; the brother-in-law himself; adversity; someone who has similar qualities to him. *(Esther 7:*

In A Dream, In A Vision of the Night
Job 33:15-18

6; *Exodus 18: 17; Gal. 3: 5, 42-26; 4: 21; Romans 4: 13-15; 1 Timothy 5: 1)*

Carpenter: Jesus; a preacher ofd the gospel. *(2 Kings 22: 6; Is. 41: 7; Mark 6: 3)*

Clown: The carnal nature; playing with God; childishness; work of the flesh. *(Ecc. 7: 4)*

Daughter: Child of God; ministry that is your child in the Spirit; look at similar character traits in yourself; the child herself; prophesy; complacent; dutiful; beautiful; given to lust; ideal. *(Ez 16: 44; Joel 2: 28; Proverbs 31: 29; Gen. 19: 30-38; Judges 11: 36-39; Is. 32: 9-11; Ps. 45: 9-13)*

Doctor: **See also Hospital**: Healer; authority; wisdom of the world; minister; Jesus. *(2 Chronicles 16: 12; Mark 2: 17; 5: 26)*

Driver: The one in control of ministry or marriage, or life, etc. What is the of the driver, and who is he or she driving? *(2 Kings 9: 20)*

Drunkard:**Also Drug Addict**: Under the influence of a spirit that is either righteous or wrong; controlled; rebellion; completely overcome in an addicted manner to something other than the Lord (like having another god before them); self indulging; destruction; turbulent seas; lightheadedness; error;

spiritual blindness; global commotion; persecution; debased mind; poverty; justice that is corrupted; mind turmoil; unbridled lust; disorderly behavior; slumber. *(Acts 2: 13-18; Eph. 5: 18; Luke 21: 34; Rev. 17: 4; Is. 49: 26; 19: 14; 28: 7; 29: 9-11; 5: 22, 23; ; Jer. 25: 15-29; Prov. 20: 1; 23: 21; Ps. 107: 25-27; 1 Thess. 5: 6, 7; Rom. 13: 13)*

Employee: **Also Servants**: Showing who is in submission in a certain situation; actual person; servant. *(Col. 3: 22)*

Employer: **Also Master**: Showing who is in charge in a certain situation; Good or evil authority depending on the character and actions of the person in dream; Pastor; satan. *(Col. 4: 1)*

Family: **See also Father, Mother, Daughter and Son**: Church family; or natural family; assembly or team or group that is in covenant together; harmony and oneness; eternal bond; order or disorder; fellowship; relationships. *(Eph. 1: 5; 3: 14-15; 5: 23; Gen. 13: 16; Col. 3: 18-21; Matt. 10: 13; Heb. 9: 15; Col. 1: 12; Rev. 22: 3-5; 1 Cor. 11: 3; Rom. 8: 17)*

Farmer: **See Barn and Field**: Minister in any capacity; Pastor; Preacher; sowing and reaping; diligence; rewards; harvest. *(Mark 4: 14; Prov. 24: 30-34; Luke 12: 16-21; 2 Cor. 9: 6-11; Gen. 8: 22; Matt. 13: 30)*

Father: **See also Family, Mother, Daughter and Son**: Father God; the Holy Spirit; authority that is natural and/or spiritual; birthright; tradition; satan; natural father; supplier of needs; trainer; the one who nourishes; head of household; Father's house can be the Temple or heaven. *(John 8: 44, 54; Hos. 11: 1-3; Matt. 7: 8-11; Is. 1: 2; Ex. 6: 14; John 2: 14-16; 14: 2)*

Father-in-law: **See also Mother-in-Law**: Same as above but a father under the law; the actual father-in-law himself; advisor. *(Exodus 18: 17; Gal. 3: 5, 42-26; 4: 21; Romans 4: 13-15)*

Foreigner: **Also Sojourner, Stranger, Unknown Man and Alien**: Not of the fold; someone to view with care; not a citizen of heaven (because of not accepting Jesus Christ as Lord); wanderer; cursed; no longer a part of the world (as living in but not being of). *(Gen. 11: 1-9; Lam. 5: 2; Ruth 5: 10; Matt.*

Susan Noone Riddle

          8: 20; Eph. 2: 19; 3: 1-6; 1 Cor. 4: 11; 1 Peter 2: 11)

Friend: **See also Brother and Sister**: Jesus; faithfulness; can tempt others to sin; sacrifice; similar to the dreamer in position in society, personality traits both in strengths and weaknesses and things that appeal to them. *(1 Sam. 15: 8; 18: 1; 20: 11-16; Prov. 17: 17; 18: 24; Ps. 41: 9; Prov. 27: 7; John 15: 13; Du. 13: 6-8)*

Giant: Angel; demon; challenge; mountain that needs overcoming. *(Numbers 13: 32-33; 2 Sam. 21: 16-22; Gen. 6: 4; Du. 2: 10-11, 21; 9: 2; 1 Chron. 20: 4-8)*

Governor: **Also Kings, Judges, Caesars, Emperors, Princes, Pharaohs and Rulers**: Person in charge in the church and/or natural; government, authority; the Lord; rule and reign. *(Mal. 1:8; Acts 23: 24, 26; Ps. 84: 3; 100: 4; 2 Chron. 18: 33; 1 Kings 16: 16; Prov. 21: 1)*

Grandchild: Inherited blessing or iniquity; one's spiritual heritage; actual grandchild; ministry that came from someone who came out of your ministry; heir; virtue in the family. *(Ex. 34: 7; 2 Kings 17: 41; 1 Tim. 5: 4)*

Grandmother: **Also Grandfather**: Righteous or unrighteous spiritual inheritance; past; wisdom. *(Proverbs 13: 22; 2 Tim. 1: 5)*

Groom: **See also Marriage and Bride**: Christ the Bridegroom; marriage; headship; God. *(John 3: 29; Ez. 16: 8-14)*

Guard: **See also Police**: Protection and defense; vigilance and sober mindedness; keep prisoners in prison; power; training of soul and flesh; God's ability to keep us. *(2 Tim. 1: 12; Eph. 6: 10-18; 1 Peter 5: 8; 2 Kings 10: 25; Acts 16: 27; Prov. 4: 13; 13: 6; 21: 23)*

Guest: Angel; messenger; celebration; witnesses of God's sovereignty and justice; the Lord Jesus in our hearts; evil presence. *(1 Sam. 16: 5; Zeph. 1: 7; Rev. 19: 9; 22: 17; John 14: 6; Gen. 12: 16; 19: 3, 24)*

Harlot: **Also Prostitute**: Adultery; temptation; snare; covetousness; worldly church; enticement; unfaithful Israel or church; loves God much when forgiven. *(Rev. 17: 5; Jer. 2: 20-24; 3: 3; Is. 1: 2; Prov. 2: 16;-19 5: 3-5; 6: 26; 7: 6-27;-23 9: 13-18;*

Susan Noone Riddle

> *Hos. 2: 7; 4: 12; Luke 7: 36-50; Matt. 21: 31; 1 Cor. 6: 9-11)*

Husband: **Also see Marriage and Groom**: The Lord Jesus; satan; actual person; to be honored; ex-husband could be bondage to the world. *(Is. 54: 5; Prov. 5: 18, 19; 1 Cor. 14: 34, 35; 1 Peter 3: 7; Gen. 3: 16; Jer. 3: 20)*

Judge: **Also Kings, Governors, Caesar's, Emperors, Princes, Pharaohs and Rulers**: Father God; conscienceless toward sin or guilt; authority; satan; one anointed to make decisions; accuser; unjust; Jesus. *(1 Cor. 11: 31; Psalm 75: 7; 94: 20; Acts 23: 3; 17: 31; James 5: 9; Mic. 7: 3)*

Lawyer: **Also Attorney**: Counselor; prosecutor or accuser; defender; Christ; legalism; just advocate; mediator. *(Rev. 12: 10; Luke 11: 46; 22: 66-71; Titus 3: 13; 1 John 2: 1; 14: 16, 26)*

Man (unknown person): **Also see Old Man and Foreigner**: God's messenger; demonic messenger; evil motive; if a kind stranger: Jesus; Son of Man; humanity of Jesus. *(Heb. 13: 2; 2: 14-16; John 3: 16; Luke 19: 10; Gen. 11: 1-9; Lam. 5: 2; Ruth 5: 10;*

Matt. 8: 20; Eph. 2: 19; 3: 1-6; 1 Cor. 4: 11; 1 Peter 2: 11)

Mother: Church; Jerusalem; charity and love; comfort; Holy Spirit; meddler; mother herself; spiritual mother; teacher; tremendously evil end time apostate church. *(Gal. 4: 26; Gen. 3: 20; Ps. 87: 5-6; Rev. 17: 5; Hos. 2: 2, 5; Prov. 31; Rom. 16: 13; Ez. 23: 2; Jer. 50: 12)*

Mother-in-law: **Also see Father-in-law**: Church; Jerusalem above; meddler; mother-in-law herself; false teachers; tremendously evil end time apostate church. *(Gal. 4: 26; Gen. 3: 20; Ps. 87: 5-6; Rev. 17: 5; Hos. 2: 2, 5; Prov. 31; Rom. 16: 13; Ez. 23: 2; Jer. 50: 12)*

Old Man: Carnality; wisdom. *(Rom. 6: 6, 5: 17; Heb. 13: 2; 2: 14-16; John 3: 16; Luke 19: 10; Gen. 11: 1-9; Lam. 5: 2; Ruth 5: 10; Matt. 8: 20; Eph. 2:1, 19; 3: 1-6; 1 Cor. 2: 14; 4: 11; 1 Peter 2: 11)*

Police: **See also Guard, Lawyer and Judge**: Spiritual authority of the church; Pastor or Elders; protection; natural authority; angels or demons; enforcer of the curse of the law. *(Hebrews 1: 7, 14; Luke 12: 11; 22: 25; Ps.*

Susan Noone Riddle

94: 20; 2 Cor. 10: 8; Titus 2: 15; 2 Tim. 1: 12; Eph. 6: 10-18; 1 Peter 5: 8; 2 Kings 10: 25; Acts 16: 27; Prov. 4: 13; 13: 6; 21: 23)

Preacher and/or Pastor: Also Priest and Prophet: Representing God; wife of a preacher could be the church; spiritual authority. *(Jer. 3: 15; 23: 1; Jude 24-25; Rom. 10: 14; 12: 1-2; 2 Cor. 11: 13; Heb. 4: 14-16; Gal. 3: 27)*

Sister: **See Brother**: Sister in Jesus; similar qualities you see in yourself or someone else; herself; the Church. *(Matt. 12: 50; Rom. 14: 10-21; 16: 1; 2 John 13; Hebrews 13: 3; Amos 1; 9; 1 Cor. 1: 1; 8: 11-13; Luke 10: 38-42; 2 Thess. 3: 6, 15; James: 1: 9; 2: 15; 1 Timothy 5: 2)*

Sister-in-law: **See also Brother-in-Law**: Same as sister only under the law; Minister involved in another church; yourself; the sister-in-law herself; someone who has similar qualities to her. *(Esther 7: 6; 1 Timothy 5: 2; Exodus 18: 17; Gal. 3: 5, 42-26; 4: 21; Romans 4: 13-15)*

Soldier: **See also Guard and Police**: Spiritual warfare; God's ability to keep us; angel; warring in the Spirit; demon with the purpose of warring; persecution; working

In A Dream, In A Vision of the Night
Job 33:15-18

for the Lord. *(Rev. 12: 7, 10; 2 Tim. 1: 12; 2: 4; Phil. 2: 25; Eph. 6: 10-18; 1 Peter 5: 8; 2 Kings 10: 25; Acts 16: 27; Prov. 4: 13; 13: 6; 21: 23)*

Son: **See also daughter**: Child of God; ministry that is your child in the Spirit; look at similar character traits in yourself; the child himself; prophesy; complacent; dutiful; characteristics of lust; ideal. *(Ez 16: 44; Joel 2: 28; Proverbs 31: 29; Gen. 19: 30-38; Judges 11: 36-39; Is. 32: 9-11; Ps. 45: 9-13)*

Teacher: **See also Classroom and School**: Jesus Christ; Holy Spirit; the revelation of God; important instruction; gift from God to the body; can be evil; five fold ministry; authority. *(John 3: 2; Eph. 4: 11; Ps. 18: 34;71: 17; 144: 1; Heb. 8: 11; 1 Tim. 4: 1-3; Job 21: 22; 2 Sam. 22: 35; Prov. 3: 5; Mark 11: 13-17; 2 Kings 2: 15; 5: 22; Phil. 2: 5-11; 1 Cor. 11: 1)*

Thief: Satan; deceiver; loss; works of the flesh; condemned if not repented of; cannot be named among the brethren; Jesus coming like a thief. *(1 Cor. 6: 10; Prov. 6: 30; 1 Thess. 5: 2; Rev. 3: 3; 16: 15; Is. 1: 23;*

Susan Noone Riddle

John 12: 6; Job 24: 14; John 10: 1-10; Eph. 4: 28)

Wife: **See also Bride and Marriage**: Israel; the wife herself; joined together; submission; Bride of Christ; Holy Spirit; covenant relationship; the church or the remnant; unfaithfulness or faithfulness in the natural things or the spiritual things; miraculous transformation. *(Ephesians 5: 23-32; Hos. 1: 2; 2 Corinthians 6: 14; 11: 2; Rev. 19: 7-9, 20-22; 21: 8; John 21-10; Is. 62: 5; Ez. 16: 8-14; 1 Corinthians 7:33; Gal. 4: 24)*

Witch: Rebellion; slander; non-submissive wife, lust for power and authority; church member, or employee; controlling spirit type of Jezebel, both in a male or a female; seduction; worldly church; forbidden. *(1 Samuel 15: 23; 2 Kings 9: 22; 2 Chron. 33: 6; Gal. 3: 1; 5: 20; Du. 18: 9-14; Ex. 22: 18)*

Woman (Unknown): **See Man and Harlot**: Angel; demon; witchcraft; seducing spirit; temptation; yourself. *(Proverbs 2: 16; 23: 27; Heb. 13: 2; 2: 14-16; John 3: 16; Luke 13: 21; 9: 10; Gen. 11: 1-9; Lam. 5: 2;*

In A Dream, In A Vision of the Night
Job 33:15-18

Ruth 5: 10; Matt. 8: 20; Eph. 2: 19; 3: 1-6; 1 Cor. 4: 11; 1 Peter 2: 11)

PLACES:

Work Places, Home Places, Worship Places, Marketplaces and More

Airport: The church; family; preparation; preparing to fly in the Spirit; delay; tarry; change; power over demonic forces; provision of nourishment, both natural or spiritual; image of approaching terror. *(1 Kings 9: 26-28; Ez. 30: 9; Acts 27: 1-2; Ps. 48: 7; Matt. 8: 23-27; 24: 38; 1 Peter 3: 20; Luke 5: 4; Psalms 74: 13-14; Prov. 31: 14; Jer. 23: 22)*

Bank: Reward reserved in heaven; the church; storage; safe; safeguarded; security; protected; money changers in temple driven out. *(John 2: 15; Matt. 6: 20; 25: 27; 21: 12; Luke 19: 23)*

Banquet: **See also Food, Cafeteria and Restaurant**: Having plenty and being well satisfied with needs; affluence and luxury; abundance; joy

Susan Noone Riddle

and blessings; not regarding the Lord by partying; church; service; systematic serving of the Word of God; choosing what you want as opposed to receiving what you need; honoring guest; worship; celebrating victory. *(Matt 25: 35; 32: 4; Psalm 19: 9-10; John 6: 27, 48-63; 4: 32, 34; 1 Cor. 3: 1-2; Heb. 5: 14; Ester 1: 3-12; 1 Sam. 25: 11, 36; Jer. 51: 34-44; Prov. 9: 13-18; Is. 5: 11-12)*

Barbershop: **See also Hair**: Changing customs, habits and traditions, covenant of sins, religiousness; turning from wrong beliefs and strong opinions; the church as either a place of vanity, or repentance. *(1 Cor. 11: 14; Lev. 19: 27; 2 Sam. 14; 25, 26; Judges 16: 17, 22; Is. 3: 17, 24; Song 5: 2, 11)*

Barn: Church; provision; place to stored up wealth; deliverance; workplace; security; plenty. *(Du. 28: 8; Luke 12: 18, 24; Prov. 3: 10; Matt. 3: 12; 13: 30)*

Beauty Shop: **See Hair, Barber Shop and Women**: Preparation; vanity; holiness. *(Pro. 31: 30; Hos. 10:5; Ps. 29: 2; 1 Cor. 11:15)*

In A Dream, In A Vision of the Night
Job 33:15-18

Cafeteria: **See also Food, Banquet and Restaurant**: Church; service; systematic serving of the Word of God; choosing what you want as opposed to receiving what you need; honoring guest; worship; celebrating victory. *(Matt 25: 35; 32: 4; Psalm 19: 9-10; John 6: 27, 48-63; 4: 32, 34; 1 Cor. 3: 1-2; Heb. 5: 14; Ester 1: 3-12; 1 Sam. 25: 11; Jer. 51: 34-44)*

Building: **Also Church Building**: The church itself; congregation; an actual service; life choices; edification; new body after resurrection. *(Matt. 16: 18; 7: 24-27; Luke 12: 13-21; 1 Cor.: 3: 9; 16, 17; 6: 19; Col. 2: 7; 1 Tim. 3: 15; Eph. 2: 20; 4: 12; Romans 15: 2; 2 Cor. 5: 1; Hebrews 3: 4)*

City: Characteristics of what the city in the dream is known for; the church; the nature and virtue or lack of in a person; New Jerusalem the City of our God; apostate church. *(Jude 1: 7; Acts 20: 23; Prov. 25: 28; Ez. 16: 49-50; Rev. 18: 10; 21: 18)*

Classroom: **See Teacher and School**: Small group ministry within the church; God's call of one chosen for learning and teaching; training; center of learning; five fold ministry. *(Job 21: 22; Luke 8: 35; Psalm 143: 10; 18 :34; Acts 19: 9; Is. 28: 10; Matt. 21: 23; Mark 1: 21; Eph. 4: 11)*

Countryside: **See Nation**: A quiet time; space to think; peace and tranquility. *(Mark 6: 31; 1 Kings 9: 7; 17: 1-7; 19: 9-13; 1 Sam. 22: 5; Ps. 104: 10-18; Gen. 24: 63)*

Courthouse: **See also Judge**: Time of trial; balance of mercy and judgment; persecution; judgment. *(1 Cor. 6: 1; Is. 43: 12; Ps. 94: 20; Du. 17: 6-13)*

Factory: Smooth service to God and organized or the opposite, the church working properly; unorganized; fervor in service. *(Luke 2: 49; Rom. 12: 11; Prov. 31: 13; 1 Thess. 2: 9; Acts 20: 35)*

Garden: **See also Yard**: Increase; work; ministry; church; pleasant; fruitfulness; prospering; pastime; field of labor. *(Gen. 2: 8-10; 4: 2-3; Is. 51: 3; 58: 11; Jer. 2: 21; 1 Tim. 4: 14-15)*

Hospital: **Also Healing**: Ministry of healing; place to caring; love; wounded church in need of healing; place of healing because of hearing the Gospel; or learning of Christ God's Son; extended to the broken hearted;

In A Dream, In A Vision of the Night
Job 33:15-18

healing as a result of repentance; turning from backsliding; because of faithfulness; healing from spiritual sickness or there because of it; healing from being obedient and following God's will. *(Ez. 47: 8-11; Is. 53: 5; 19: 22-25; 6: 10; Jer. 17: 11; 3: 22; P. 137: 3; 41: 4; 2 Chron. 7: 14; Mal. 4: 2; Pro. 4: 20-22; John 9: 1-3; 2: 16)*

Hotel: Temporary; migratory; socially accepted place to gather; changing church. *(Luke 10: 3-31, 33-34)*

House: **See also Sanctuary, Temple, Tent or Tabernacle**: **Also Home**: The church; or one's own home; person or family; dwelling place; Tabernacle or Temple of God; the true church; heaven; security or insecurity depending on dream; center of the family or family of God; people in the church are the household of God; our present life and its condition; place to relax and be entertained with ungodly things; people in the church are the members of His household; resting place; place to return to; eternal home or heaven; reference to ones character or reputation; place where evil demonic spirits dwell; the human body or body as an earthly tent; our body as a place for God and His Spirit to live. *(Luke 11: 24; 15: 6; 2 Sam. 14: 13-24; Ruth 1: 21; 4: 3; Acts 16: 31, 34; Heb. 3: 6; 3: 10-21; 1 Chron. 17: 5; Judges 11: 34; 19: 9; Acts 16: 34; Gen. 14: 14; 8: 9; 2 Cor. 5: 6; Eph. 2: 19; 3: 17; Ecc. 12: 5; Matt. 12: 44; Luke 11: 25; 2: 4; 2 Corinthians 5: 1-10; Mark 13: 34-35; 2: 1, 4-5; 3: 24; John 14: 1-4, 23; 1: 11; Job 30: 23; 2 Cor. 5; 1; Heb. 10: 21; Ps. 119: 54; 122: 1; Ex. 34: 26;13: 3; Prov. 2: 18; Luke 15: 6; 11: 25; 1 Tim. 5: 4; Is. 65: 10)*

DIFFERENT ROOMS AND LOCATIONS:

Attic: **See also Upstairs, Roof and Two Story**: Of the spirit; the mind; thought; right and/or wrong attitudes; stored, memories; learning; Spirit realm; upper room. *(Acts 1: 12; 2: 1-4)*

Basement: Storage place; flooding; hidden; forgotten; carnal nature; soul; lust; depression; secret sin. *(Jer. 38: 6)*

In A Dream, In A Vision of the Night
Job 33:15-18

Bathroom: Repentance; confession; desire; cleansing; removing; expelling. *(Lev. 8: 5-6; 14: 8-9; Ps. 51: 1-2; 7-10; Rev. 21: 26-27)*

Bedroom: Rest; privacy; peace; good covenants and wrong covenants; intimacy; slumbering; laziness. *(Ps. 4: 4; 139: 8; Is. 28: 18-20; Heb. 18: 4)*

Childhood home: Something from the past that is influencing you today for good or evil; same for a church; family; etc. *(1 Timothy 5: 4)*

Den: Relaxed fellowship; too relaxed; notice where the focus is. *(Mark 2: 4-5)*

Dining Room:See also Eating: The table of the Lord; communion with the Lord or with the brethren; feeding on the Word. *(Ho. 7: 6; Heb. 4: 12; 1 Corinthians 11: 24)*

Dirty and neglected: Church or home in need of attention. *(Matt. 25: 25-28; Heb. 10: 22; 2 Cor. 7: 1)*

Garage: Protection; storage; ministry potential for outreach. *(Du. 28: 8; Luke 12: 18; Matt. 13: 30)*

Kitchen: **See also Cafeteria and Restaurant**: Preparation for teaching or preaching; heart of the matter; hunger for the Word;

Susan Noone Riddle

>motives; revealing. *(Ho. 7: 6; Heb. 4: 12; 1 Corinthians 11: 24)*

Living Room: **See also Den**: Formal fellowship of church or family or friends. *(Mark 2: 4-5)*

New: New birth; change for the better or worse according to the condition of the home; fresh move of the Spirit; revival. *(2 Corinthians 5: 17; 2 Cor. 5: 1)*

Old: Old man or ways; past; spiritual inheritance; religious traditions; natural inheritance. *(Gen. 12: 1; Jer. 6: 16; Heb. 2: 3)*

Porch: **See also Yard**: Outreach and evangelism to the church; public place, exhibited; displayed; exposed. *(Mark 14: 68; Acts 5: 12; Joel 2: 17)*

Roof: **See also Upstairs and Attic**: The mind; meditation; logic or natural; shield or covering of protection; heavenly revelation; prayer; declaration; complete overview; ability to see all, both good and evil. *(Acts 10: 9; Matt. 10: 27; Luke 12: 3; 2 Sam. 11: 2; Is. 30: 1)*

Twostory: **See also Upstairs, Two Story and Attic**: Multilevel situation; Spirit and flesh of a

In A Dream, In A Vision of the Night
Job 33:15-18

person or a church or ministry. *(Acts 1: 13-14; 20: 7-8)*

Upstairs: Roof, Two Story and Attic: Going higher in the Spirit; something that is of the Spirit; Upper room; Pentecost; thought, good or bad; prayer; Spiritual service. *(Acts 1: 13-14; 20: 7-8)*

Work Area: Service under development in the Spirit; or of God; work of the flesh. *(Gen. 2: 15; Ps. 104: 23; Gal. 2: 16; Eph. 5: 11; John 6: 29; Phil. 3: 2; 1 Cor. 3: 9)*

Yard: **See also Garden and Porch**: Public part of personal life; in back could be event that is behind or over or hidden. *(2 Sam. 17: 18; Esther 1: 5; 1 Kings 6: 36; Ex. 27: 9)*

Library: Exploration into knowledge; knowledge stored up; schooling; abundance of the Word; earthly, sensual wisdom. *(2 Tim. 2: 15; James 3: 13-18; 1 Cor. 8: 1; Rom. 2: 20; Col. 1: 9)*

Nation: **See also Country**: Nation may represent actual nation; known characteristics of the nation. *(Mark 6: 31; 1 Kings 9: 7; 17: 1-7; 19: 9-13; 1 Sam. 22: 5; Ps. 104: 10-18; Gen. 24: 63)*

Park: **See also Garden and Yard**: Worship; enjoying God; playful; garden experience (Adam fell, Jesus faced the cross); rest; tranquility; transient's home. *Gen. 2: 8-10; 4: 2-3; Is. 51: 3; 58: 11; Jer. 2: 21; 1 Tim. 4:14-15)*

Pit: Hell; sepulcher; tomb; entrapment; enticement; self ruination. *(Jer. 18: 20; Is. 14: 15; 24: 22; 38: 17-18; Rev. 9: 1-2; 20: 1-3)*

Prison: Lost souls; Christian held captive by the enemy; rebellion; lawlessness; bondage; persecuted saints; slavery; Sheol or Hades; imprisoned unjustly; release from prison is God's blessing; confinement of personal circumstances; a spiritual condition that is fallen; death; in need of recognition to God. *(Gen. 39: 20; Jer. 37: 18; Ps. 68: 6; 142: 7; Gal. 3 22; Rev. 1: 18, 24; Matt. 5: 25-26; 2 Peter 2: 4)*

Restaurant: **See also Cafeteria and Kitchen**: Place of ministry; atmosphere is important; church with good or bad teaching and serving ministry of the Word; gluttony. *(Psalm 19: 9-10; John 6: 27; 48-63; 4: 32,*

In A Dream, In A Vision of the Night
Job 33:15-18

34; Matt 25: 35; 32: 4; 1 Cor. 3: 1-2; Heb. 5: 14)

School: **See Classroom**: Church; place of teaching and discipleship; people or work; training; teaching ministry. *(Job 21: 22; Luke 8: 35; Psalm 143: 10; 18 :34; Acts 19: 9; Is. 28: 10; Matt. 21: 23; Mark 1: 21; Eph. 4: 11)*

Elementary: Beginning level of walk with God; milk. *(1 Cor. 3: 1-3)*

Middle or Junior High: Level of maturity of person or teaching being given or received; or of one's walk. *(1 Cor. 14: 20)*

High School: Promotion in level of dreamer to a higher level or could be of teaching being received or given. *(1 Cor. 2: 6)*

College: Highest level of learning; promotion in the Spirit; strong meat. *(Rom. 15: 21)*

Shopping Center: **Also Marketplace**: Too much to choose from; churches within the church; view of spiritual, soulish and political atmosphere that is in a church or a community or nation or even in your heart; not to be in temple of God or present during worship; leaders there to show off how grand they are; can be dishonest gain; wisdom calls out to the people there. *(Prov.*

7: 12; 2 Kings 7: 1, 8; Ps. 55: 11; Gen. 34: 10, 21; Amos 8: 5; Neh. 10: 31; John 2: 16; Mark 6: 56)*

Skyscraper: **Also see Tower, Ascend, Up, Mountain, Hills and Elevator**: Prophetic church of great revelation; high places; above earthly experience; higher spiritual things; Mt. Zion; sacrifice of worship; Mt. Sinai and the Ark of the Covenant in the Temple; Songs of ascent unto Him; Tower of Babel; Mt. Carmel; dominance; control; obstacle; Jesus returning from the heavens to earth; symbolic of victory; Jesus being lifted up on the cross; wisdom that comes from above; Beatitudes in the Sermon on the Mount. *(Acts 1: 13-14; 20: 7-8; Ps. 103: 11; 1 Sam. 9: 12-14; Matt 5; 1 Kings 18; John 3: 7; James 3: 15, 17; Heb. 1: 3; 1 Thess. 4: 13-18; 1 Kings 12: 31)*

Trailer: Transitory and indefinite circumstances. *(James 4: 14)*

Vineyard: Jewish Nation; God's Kingdom; growing in grace; peace; fruitful wife or church; worthlessness. *(Matt. 20: 1-6; Hos. 14: 7; John 15: 1-2, 6; Is. 5: 1-7; Ps. 128: 3; 1 Kings 4: 25)*

In A Dream, In A Vision of the Night
Job 33:15-18

VEHICLES

Airplane: They are air "ships;" ministry flowing in spiritual or heavenly places; ministry on the move; high powered; church. *(1 Kings 9: 26-28; Ez. 30: 9; Acts 27: 1-2; Matt. 8: 23-27; 24: 38; Luke 5: 4; Prov. 31: 14; Ps. 18: 10; 48: 7; 74: 13-14)*

    Crashing: Total devastation and swift destruction.
    High: In the heavenlies.
    Large: Large ministry or entire body of Christ.
    Low: Not totally ministering in the Spirit.
    Small: Personal ministry or church.
    Soaring: Deep in the Spirit.
    War Plane: Warfare in the Spirit.

Automobile: Similar to horses, camels, boats, and chariots as well as any and all modes of transporting a person on the ground from place to place, only they are modern day modes; Church or personal ministry; warfare and battles; personal life. *(1 Kings*

12: 18; 2 Kings 2: 11-12; 10:16; Ps. 104: 3; Acts 8: 28-38; 1 Thess. 2: 18)

Brakes: Wait; hindrance; stop something; something or yourself stopping you.

Convertible: Revelation ministry; uncovered and lack of submission.

Four Wheel Drive: Ground breaking powerful ministry. Full gospel base (four gospels).

Junk Yard: Ministries destroyed that were meant to be; need repair and healing to start again.

Large: Large ministry or entire body of Christ; clunky and burdensome; prideful.

New: New ministry; new church.

Old: Old church; old ministry; Church and religious tradition.

Rearview Mirror: Looking back; warning that you should be watching your back.

Seat belt: Safety; prepare for a problem; unfastened, lack of prayer; careless; lack of commitment.

In A Dream, In A Vision of the Night
Job 33:15-18

Small: Personal ministry or church; light and easy yoke; cramped and in need of expanding ministry.

Tires: Notice if flat, driving without air or Spirit; if big and powerful, ministry the same; if too small for vehicle, need more prayer and Spirit; indicates Spiritual condition.

Topless: Lack of covering; free of burdens.

Trunk: Secret place; locked and hidden; secret sin or joy; safe place.

Van: Group ministry; family ministry.

Wreck: Warning of clash or confrontation in ministries; people in strife; real crash.

Bicycle: Ministry in the flesh; struggling in ministry; trying to go with only manpower; light and easy burden *(Gal. 5: 4)*

Blimp: Heavy and awkward ministry; ineffective; bloated with hot air; pride; sluggish and lazy. *(1 Kings 9: 26-28; Ez. 30: 9; Acts 27: 1-2; Ps. 48: 7; Matt. 8: 23-27; 24: 38; Luke*

5: 4; Psalms 74: 13-14; Prov. 31: 14; Ps. 18: 10)*

Boat: **See also Sailboat, Rowboat and Ship**: Local church ministry; personal ministry. *(1 Kings 9: 26-28; Ez. 30: 9; Acts 27: 1-2; Ps. 48: 7; Matt. 8: 23-27; 24: 38; Luke 5: 4; Psalms 74: 13-14; Prov. 31: 14; Ps. 18: 10; 48: 7)*

Bus: Large group ministry. *(1 Kings 12: 18; 2 Kings 2: 11-12; 10:16; Ps. 104: 3; Acts 8: 28-38; 1 Thess. 2: 18)*

    Church Bus: Ministry in the church on the move.

    City Bus: Transport of groups of ministry for the church or the City of God.

    School Bus: Youth ministry; teaching ministry.

    Tour Bus: Christian sightseers out for the fun; watches not doers.

Helicopter: Ministry that is suspended in air; in a fixed position; great warfare ministry. *(1 Kings 9: 26-28; Ez. 30: 9; Acts 27: 1-2; Matt. 8: 23-27; 24: 38; Luke 5: 4; Psalms 74: 13-14; Prov. 31: 14; Ps. 18: 10; 48: 7)*

In A Dream, In A Vision of the Night
Job 33:15-18

Motor: **Also Engine and Battery**: Anointing; incentive; the stimulus of the Spirit; energy force or power in the Spirit; strong fleshly power. *(Acts 1: 8; 10: 38; Eph. 3: 7; Jude 11; Zech. 4: 6)*

Motorcycle: Loner; personal; ministry; rebellion; pride. *(1 Kings 12: 18; 2 Kings 2: 11-12; 10:16; Ps. 104: 3; Acts 8: 28-38; 1 Thess. 2: 18)*

Moving Van: Spiritual or natural move; changing churches; relocation; change needed. *(1 Kings 12: 18; 2 Kings 2: 11-12; 10:16; Ps. 104: 3; Acts 8: 28-38; 1 Thess. 2: 18)*

Raft: Adrift; without any direction; aimless; no power. *(1 Kings 9: 26-28; Ez. 30: 9; Acts 27: 1-2; Matt. 8: 23-27; 24: 38; Luke 5: 4; Psalms 74: 13-14; Prov. 31: 14; Ps. 18: 10; 48: 7)*

Rocket: Powerful ministry; deep into the heavens and Spirit; great speed. *(Ps. 64: 7; Prov. 6: 15; 29: 1)*

Roller coaster: Ministry that survives on signs and wonders; excitement oriented rather than faith based. *(1 Kings 12: 18; 2 Kings 2: 11-*

Susan Noone Riddle

> *12; 10:16; Ps. 104: 3; Acts 8: 28-38; 1 Thess. 2: 18)*

Rowboat: Ministry doing the works of men; earnest prayer ministry. *(1 Kings 9: 26-28; Ez. 30: 9; Acts 27: 1-2; Ps. 48: 7; Matt. 8: 23-27; 24: 38; Luke 5: 4; Psalms 74: 13-14; Prov. 31: 14; Ps. 18: 10)*

Sailboat: Ministry totally dependent on the wind of the Spirit. *(1 Kings 9: 26-28; Ez. 30: 9; Acts 27: 1-2; Ps. 48: 7; Matt. 8: 23-27; 24: 38; Luke 5: 4; Psalms 74: 13-14; Prov. 31: 14; Ps. 18: 10)*

Ship: Large, complicated, flowing ministry or church. *(1 Kings 9: 26-28; Ez. 30: 9; Acts 27: 1-2; Ps. 48: 7; Matt. 8: 23-27; 24: 38; Luke 5: 4; Psalms 74: 13-14; Prov. 31: 14; Ps. 18: 10)*

- **Battleship**: Warfare in the Spirit.
- **Crashing**: Total devastation and swift destruction.
- **Fast**: In power.
- **Large**: Large ministry or entire body of Christ.
- **Sinking**: Not totally ministering in the Spirit.
- **Small**: Personal ministry or church.

In A Dream, In A Vision of the Night
Job 33:15-18

Soaring: In the Spirit.

On Dry Ground: Fleshly ministry.

Tractor: Spiritual farmer; seed sower; ground plower in the Spirit. Coming at you, an attack in the realm of the Spirit. *(1 Kings 12: 18; 2 Kings 2: 11-12; 10:16; Ps. 104: 3; Acts 1: 8; 4: 33; 8: 28-38; 1 Thess. 2: 18)*

Train: A great work and move of the Holy Spirit; unceasing work; consistent. *(1 Kings 12: 18; 2 Kings 2: 11-12; 10:16; Ps. 104: 3; Acts 8: 28-38; 1 Thess. 2: 18)*

Truck: **Also see categories under Automobile**: Certain type of personal ministry. *(1 Kings 12: 18; 2 Kings 2: 11-12; 10:16; Ps. 104: 3; Acts 8: 28-38; 1 Thess. 2: 18)*

Van: **Also see categories under Automobile**: Family or small church ministry. *(1 Kings 12: 18; 2 Kings 2: 11-12; 10:16; Ps. 104: 3; Acts 8: 28-38; 1 Thess. 2: 18)*

Susan Noone Riddle

SYMBOLIC ACTIONS

Adultery: Spiritual adultery; actual adultery; sexual sin; idolatry; pornography. *(Gal 5: 19-21; James 4: 4; Ez. 23: 45)*

Anoint: Set apart divine appointment in service; prayer for the sick; sanctification. *(James 5: 14; 2 Chron. 22: 7; 1 John 2: 20, 27; 2 Cor. 1: 21; Ex. 28: 41)*

Awakening: Discernment; attentive to wiles of the devil; watchman; sober; stimulated to act. *(Eph. 5: 14; Rom. 13: 11-14; Is. 52: 1; 1 Thess. 4: 6; 5: 6-7; 1 Cor. 15: 34)*

Baking: Hospitality; God's provision; worship. *(Gen. 25: 34; Lev. 26: 26; 23: 17)*

Baptizing: Burial of the old lifestyle; total submersion in something; repentance; preparation for the coming Kingdom; death; burial; resurrection; inner conversion; overwhelmed by water or the Holy Spirit. *(Matt. 3: 9; Mark 10: 38; Rom. 6: 9; 1 Peter 3; Acts 2: 17-18)*

Barrenness: Unable to be productive for life of the Spirit; rejection; cursed; judgment; unfruitful; death of the Spirit; death of a

In A Dream, In A Vision of the Night
Job 33:15-18

ministry. *(1 Sam. 1; Gen. 11: 30; Du. 28: 1-4, 15-18; Is. 5: 1-10)*

Bathing: Cleansing; repentance; totally clean; temptation; purification; ceremonial cleansing; Jewish ritual, before performing duties of the priesthood. *(Ez. 37: 9; Ex. 30: 19-31; Lev. 14: 8; 16: 4, 24; Gen. 2: ; 24: 32; John 13: 10; 20: 22; Mark 7: 2; 2 Sam. 11: 2, 3)*

Choking: Too much too fast; hatred; obstacle that hinders; opposite of breathing in the Holy Spirit. *(Mark 4: 19)*

Crawling: Unclean; humility; to have been cursed; disgraced; snake; idol worship. *(Gen. 3: 14; 1 Sam. 14: 11; Lev. 22: 5; Ez. 8: 10)*

Crying: Grief; sorrow; anguish; repentance; prayer; judgment; humility; sadness; sometimes tears of joy. It is important to note what the dreamer is feeling while shedding the tears). *(Mark 9: 24; Ps. 34: 6)*

Dancing: Worship; spiritual sacrifice; joy; rejoice; idolatry; seduction; whirling; evil and sensual; victory; return of a son. *(Ps. 30: 11; 149: 3; 1 Sam. 18: 6, 7; Ex. 32: 19; 2 Sam. 6: 14, 16; Luke 15: 21-25; Matt. 11: 16-17; 14: 6; Judges 11: 34; Lam. 5: 15)*

Drawing: **See also Painting**: Covering; regenerate; remodel; renovate; love. *(1 Peter 4: 8; Matt. 23: 27; Titus 3: 5; Acts 18: 24)*

Artist's paint: Words; illustrative message; eloquent; humorous; articulate.

House painter's brush: Ministry or minister.

Paint: Doctrine, truth or deception.

Dreaming: To dream that you are dreaming, a message within a message, instruction from God; revelation of God's will or the future; keep dreamer from some evil; a vision; a deep Spiritual truth. *(Gen. 40: 8; 20: 3; 28: 11-22; 37: 5-10; Matt. 1: 20; 27: 13; 19; Judges 7: 13-15)*

Drinking: Consuming upon own lust; fellowship; as in wine and communion; whether good or evil; drinking in the Holy Spirit; under the power of sorrow; affliction; overcome; idolatry; under a strong delusion; from the blood of the saints (persecution); cup of the crucified life. *(Acts 2: 13; Jer. 2: 18; 51: 7; Is. 29: 9-11; 63: 6; Ez. 23: 33; Rev. 14: 8-10; 17: 2, 6; Du. 32: 4; 7; Zech. 9: 15-17)*

In A Dream, In A Vision of the Night
Job 33:15-18

Drowning: **See also Flood**: Overcome; self-pity; depression; grief; being in debt; suffering; temptation; to backslid. *(1 Tim. 6: 9; Rev. 12: 15-16; Is. 61: 3)*

Eating: **See also Dining Room under House**: Experience; covenant; agreement; partake; friendship; fellowship; devour; consume; consuming wisdom; meditation; digesting the Word of God; forbidden fruit; no blood; no unclean foods; gluttony; adoption; must work to eat; respect a brother when choosing food. *(Gen. 2: 16-17; Ex. 24: 11; Jer. 15: 16; 52: 33-34; Rev. 10: 9-10; Luke 13: 26; 22: 15-20; Du. 14: 1-29; 20: 14; Matt. 11: 18; Ez. 3: 1-3; John 4: 34; 13: 18; Acts 14: 22; 15: 19-20; Phil. 2: 12; 3: 19; Josh. 9: 14-15; Prov. 30: 20; Rom. 14: 1-23; 2 Thess. 3: 7-10)*

Falling: Watch for a fall into sin; unsupported; loss of support; trial; succumb; separation from God; backsliding; born in sin; power of God to change; to be depraved; evil heart; corrupted, bondage to satan or/and sin; spiritually blind; Falling and getting up: A righteous man seven times. *(John 3: 6; 3: 16; Titus 1: 15; Eph. 4: 18; Heb. 2: 14, 15;*

Matt. 15: 19; Rom. 3: 12-16; 6: 19; Col. 2: 13; James 1: 2; Prov. 16: 18; 22: 14; 11: 28; 24: 16; Micah 7: 8)*

Feeding: **Also being Fed**: To be supplied in a spiritual or supernatural way; narcissism; works that are righteous; basic teaching; change in basic traits of one's nature; to become impure in character. *(Rev. 12: 6; 1 Cor. 3: 2; Hos. 12: 1; Matt. 25: 37; Is. 11: 7; Ps. 49: 14)*

Flying: Spirit; minister; prophet; Holy Spirit; defense and shelter. *(Mal. 4: 2; Is. 40: 31; Ex. 19: 4; Ps. 91: 4)*

Gardening: Increase; work; ministry; church; pleasant; fruitfulness; prospering; pastime; field of labor. *(Gen. 2: 8-10; 4: 2-3; Is. 51: 3; 58: 11; Jer. 2: 21; 1 Tim. 4:14-15)*

Ironing: Correction; change; sanctification; exhortation; instruction in righteousness; God's discipline; repentance; working out problem relationships; reconciliation; pressure from trials. *(Eph. 5: 2)*

Kiss: Agreement; covenant; enticement; betrayal; covenant breaker; deception; seduction; friend. *(Ps. 2: 12; Prov. 7: 10, 22-23, 27; 27: 6; Luke 22: 48; 2 Sam. 20: 9-10)*

In A Dream, In A Vision of the Night
Job 33:15-18

Kneeling: Submission; worship; prayer; total surrender. *(Dan. 6: 10; Ps. 95: 6; Mark 10: 17; Acts 20: 36)*

Laughing: Rejoicing; joy of worship and walk with God; sarcasm. *(Ps. 59: 8; Job 5: 20; Gen. 18: 11-15; 2 Chron. 30: 10; Prov. 1: 26; 2: 4; 22: 7; 37: 13; 80: 6; 126: 2, 3)*

Lifting Hands: Worship and adoration; praise; total surrender. *(Ps. 141: 2; Rev. 10: 5; 1 Tim. 2: 8; Neh. 8: 6)*

Limping or Unable to Walk: Shortcomings; weakness; inconsistency; not fit for priesthood. *(Prov. 26: 7; 2 Sam. 5: 8; Lev. 21: 17-23; Job 29: 15; Is. 35: 6)*

Moving: Change in ministry; change in the natural; dissatisfaction with where you are. *(Ez. 12: 3; Gen. 11: 31; 12: 1-3; Acts 7: 2-4)*

Painting: **Also Drawing**: Covering; regenerate; remodel; renovate; love. *(1 Peter 4: 8; Matt. 23: 27; Titus 3: 5; Acts 18: 24)*

Artist's paint: Words; illustrative message; eloquent; humorous; articulate.

House painter's brush: Ministry or minister.

Paint: Doctrine, truth or deception.

Playing: Worship; idolatry; covetousness; true worship; spiritual warfare; striving; competition. *(1 Cor. 9: 24; 10: 7; Col. 3: 5)*

Playing an Instrument: Prophesying; worship and praising Him; warring in the Spirit; soothing the soul; worship of self; idolatry; activity or action that proceed from the heart; joy; praise; ministry of the gifts of the Spirit; temptation to sin; mesmerized; seduced; words are important to know what the message is; entertainment; teaching; admonishing; edifying. *(Ez. 33: 32; Dan. 3: 5; Is. 5: 1; Jer. 7: 34; 1 Cor. 9: 24; 10: 7; Gen. 31: 27; Matt. 9: 18, 23; Ex. 15: 20-21; 2 Chron. 5: 11-13; Eph. 5: 19; Col. 3: 16; 3: 5)*

Raining: God's blessings; God's Word and Spirit outpoured; life; revival; Holy Spirit; trial; disappointment. *(Zech 10: 1; Is. 55: 10-11; Matt. 7: 27; Jer. 3: 3)*

  Drought: Blessings withheld because of sin; without God's presence.

Reaping: Fruitfulness for acts; perverse or uprightness deeds being rewarded. *(1 Cor. 9: 11; Prov. 22: 8; Hos. 8: 7; Gal. 6: 8-9; Lev. 26: 5)*

In A Dream, In A Vision of the Night
Job 33:15-18

Rending: (as in Garment or Hands): Anger; deep grief; discord and disunity. *(Matt. 7: 6; 9: 16; 26: 65; Luke 5: 36; 1 Sam. 28: 17)*

Resting: Refreshing; ceasing from activity; relaxation; too relaxed; not paying attention; insolent. *(Ps. 132: 8, 14; Is. 11: 10; 14: 63: 14; Matt. 11: 28-30)*

Rocking: Old; past memories; meditation; rest; retirement; prayer. *(Jer. 6: 16)*

Rowing: Work; working out life's problems; earnest prayer; spiritual labor. *(Mark 6: 48; Phil. 2: 30)*

Running: Swiftness; striving; working out one's salvation; faith; haste; trial. *(1 Cor. 9: 24; Jer. 12: 5; Prov. 1: 6; Rev. 9: 9; 1 Cor. 9: 24; Is. 40: 31)*

Singing: **See also Song and Music**: Rejoicing; thanksgiving; prayer; praise; worship of God or of idols. *(Ps. 7: 17; 9: 2; 13: 6; 18: 49; 21: 13; 27: 6; James 5: 13; Ex. 15: 1; Is. 12: 5; 23: 16-19)*

Sitting: **See also Chair and Throne**: Power; throne of authority; rulership; rest; position; concentration; receiving; place of authority; inner court of the temple; throne of God; satanic powers; mercy seat; Kingship of the

Susan Noone Riddle

Lord. *(Rev. 13: 2; Ps. 1: 1; 7: 7; Job 23: 3; 2 Chron. 9: 18; 19: 8; Matt. 17: 19; Heb. 9: 5-12; Ex. 25: 22; 29: 42-43; 1 John 2: 2; Num. 7: 89; Rom. 3: 24-25; 2 Cor. 5: 20; 1 Tim. 2: 5)*

Skiing: Faith; support by God's power through faith; fast progress. *(John 6: 19-21; Matt. 14: 29-31)*

Sleeping: Indifference; death; rest; unconscience; unaware (hidden or covered); ignorant; danger; laziness; refreshing; spiritual stupor; indifference. *(Is. 29: 10; Rom. 13: 11; Ps. 127: 2; Prov. 20: 13)*

Overslept: Danger of missing a divine appointment.

Smiling: Friendly; kindness; benevolent; good will; without offense; seduction. *(Prov. 18: 24)*

Sowing: Dispersing seed; seed can be righteous or evil. *(Gal. 6: 7-8; 2 Cor. 9: 6; Job 4: 8; Ps. 126: 5; Matt. 13: 3-9; 11-33; 37-53; Mark 4: 1-20; Luke 13: 18-19)*

Speaking: **See Tongue, Voice and Arrows**: Thunder; compelling; words of Christ; indication to open the door of our hearts to receive Jesus; sound of many waters; but sheep know HIS voice; sign of a covenant; requires obedience; important to test the spirit by the Word; language; speech; can be used for good or evil; blessings; cursing; something only God can tame; life and death in it's power; can start a fire for good or evil. *(Zech. 9:7-8; Is. 7: 16; Rom. 5: 3-4; Col. 2: 8; 1 Tim. 6: 20; Prov. 25: 18-19; Ez. 18: 2; Ps. 11: 2; 45: 5; 64: 3; 76: 3; 91: 5; 119: 9; 127: 4; Jer. 9: 8; Job 6: 4; Du. 32: 23, 42; John 4: 1; 10: 4; Heb. 5: 8; 12: 26; Rev. 1: 15; 3: 20; Is. 66: 6; Matt. 3: 3; Josh 24: 24-25; Gen. 3: 1-19; 22: 6-18; 1)*

Sprinkling: Washing for cleansing; consecrating. *(1 Peter 1: 2; Lev. 1: 5-11; 14: 7; Heb. 9: 13)*

Standing: Incomplete task; virtue; standing on or committed to a point of view or belief. *(Acts 7: 55-56; Heb. 10: 11; Eph. 6: 13)*

Straight: Sitting, Standing or Walking: Going in the right direction; not crooked spiritually; unyielding. *(Heb. 12: 13; Matt. 3: 3; Ps. 5: 8; Luke 3: 4-5)*

Stumbling: Barrier in the way preventing the truth; sin; backslide; mistake; become deceived; to be overcome; ignorance. *(Jer. 50: 32;*

Susan Noone Riddle

> *Rom. 11: 9; Is. 5: 24; Ex. 15: 7; 1 Cor. 1: 23; 8: 9; 1 Peter 2: 8; Prov. 3: 23)*

Suicide: Self destructive; self hatred; grief; remorse; foolish action. *(Ecc. 7: 16; Matt. 27: 5)*

Sweating: The effort of man; fleshly works; striving in the flesh. *(Gen. 3: 19; Luke 22: 44)*

Sweeping: Cleaning house (own tent, tabernacle that the Holy Spirit lives in); repentance; change; actively taking barriers down; admonishment of sinners. *(Is. 28: 17; Eph. 4: 31; 2 Cor. 7: 1; 2 Cor. 7: 11; 1 Tim. 5: 20)*

Swimming: Conducting spiritual activity; worship; gifts of the Spirit being applied; service to God; prophecy in operation. *(Ez. 47: 5; Eph. 3: 8)*

Swimming Pool: Spiritual place or condition; church; home; family; God's blessings.

> **Dirty or Dry**: Corrupt or destitute spiritual condition; backslide.

Swinging: Peaceful; rest; quietness; romance; fellowship. *(Is. 30: 15)*

Swinging High: Danger; thrill seeking; immorality; infidelity.

In A Dream, In A Vision of the Night
Job 33:15-18

Tasting: Experience; discern; try; test; judge. *(Ps. 34: 8; 119: 103; Heb. 2: 9; 6: 4; Ex. 16: 31; John 2: 9; Matt. 27: 34)*

Upward Motion: **Also see Tower, Mountain, Hill, Skyscraper, and Elevator**: Prophetic church of great revelation; high places; above earthly experience; higher spiritual things; spiritual ascension; pride; self exaltation; strength; protection; safety; Tower of Babel; dominance; control; obstacle; Jesus returning from the heavens to earth; symbolic of victory; Jesus being lifted up on the cross; wisdom that comes from above; Mt. Zion; sacrifice of worship; Mt. Sinai and the Ark of the Covenant in the Temple; Songs of ascent unto Him; Mt. Carmel; Beatitudes in the Sermon on the Mount. *(Acts 1: 13-14; 20: 7-8; Ps. 61: 3; 103: 11; 144: 2; 1 Sam. 9: 12-14; Matt 5; 1 Kings 18; John 3: 7; James 3: 15, 17; Heb. 1: 3; 1 Thess. 4: 13-18; 1 Kings 12: 31; Prov. 18: 19; Is. 30: 25)*

Urinating: If full, pressure; compelling urge; temptation, repentance; if infection or cancer: offense or enmity. *(Prov. 17: 14; 1 Sam. 25: 22)*

Susan Noone Riddle

Walking: Progress; living in the Spirit; living in sin; the conduct of the dreamer or their lifestyle and actions. *(Gal. 5: 16-25; Eph. 4: 17; 1 John 1: 6-7; 2 Cor. 5: 7)*
Difficult walking:Trials; opposition.

Warring: Total destruction; death; great ruin; prayer and worship; final war in heaven and in earth. *(Rev. 12: 7-17; 17: 14; 19: 11-19; 1 Peter 2: 11; 1 Tim. 1: 18; James 4: 1-2; 2 Cor. 10: 3; Eph. 6: 10-18; 2 Chron. 20)*

Washing: Cleansing from sin and the filth of this world. *(John 9: 7; 13: 5-14; Lev. 1: 13-19)*

Wind Blowing: **See also Clouds, Thunder, Tornado, Storm and Whirlwind**: Powers of God or satan; breathe of life; spirit or doctrine; Holy Spirit; demonic or strong opposition; empty words such as boasting; vanity; calamity; God's adjudication and correction and quota or portion; demise and failure of man; false teaching. *(Eph. 4: 14; John 3: 8; Acts 2: 2-4; Job 1: 12, 19; 8: 2; Prov. 25: 14; Ez. : 10; Eph. 4: 14; Is. 32: 2; Hos. 8: 7; 13: 15)*

Wrestling:Striving; deliverance; resistance; persistence; trial; tribulation; controlling spirit (in a person); attempting to gain

In A Dream, In A Vision of the Night
Job 33:15-18

control. *(Gen. 32: 24-28; Eph. 6: 12; 2 Tim. 2: 24)*

SYMBOLIC BODY PARTS

Ankles: Faith; weak faith; God will heal. *(Ez. 47: 3; Acts 3: 7)*

Arm: Power and strength; help; Savior; deliverer; striker; God's stretched out hand to take one nation from another; His everlasting power; strong and mighty; holy; glorious; redeeming; God's destroying power; protecting power; strengthening; ruling; victorious; the arm of the evil will be broken. *(Ex. 6: 6; Duet. 4: 34; 33: 27; 7: 19; Ps. 89: 1, 10, 13, 21; 98: 1; 44: 3; 10: 15; Is. 30: 30; 40: 10; 63: 12)*

Backside: Past; something that is behind you; something that is over with; going backwards. backsliding; to put or keep out of site; concealed from view: unleavened cakes; or out of balance; God's backside; cast behind someone's presence; casting sin behind you. *(1 Kings 14: 9; Ex. 33: 23;*

Gen. 22: 13; Josh. 8: 4; Mark 8: 32-33; Phil. 3: 13-14)

Cheek: Trial; beauty; personal attack; victory; patience. *(Mic. 5: 1; Matt. 5: 39; Song 5: 13; Ps. 3: 7)*

Eyes: Longing for God; unnatural desire for someone else's possession; intense desire; lust of the eye; the window to the soul; depth and maturity of spiritual things; foresight; knowledge and understanding revealed; evil desires; spiritual dullness; being of the world; illumination and future glory; unworthiness for service; the state of one's moral behavior; spiritual incapability and dullness; contact with eyes reveal unspoken agreement; grief; resentful or painfully bitter desire to have what someone else has (envy); one's moral state revealed; revealed desire for retribution; revealed evil desires of the heart; not fit for service; promise of tears being wiped away and seeing Jesus; inability and dullness of seeing clearly in the Spirit; God leading us and His protection; omnipotent power; holiness. *(Num. 24: 3; Rev. 1: 7; Judges 17: 6; 7: 17; Is. 29: 18; 33: 17; 42: 6-7;*

In A Dream, In A Vision of the Night
Job 33:15-18

52: 8; 2 Chron. 16: 9; Ps. 19: 8; 32: 8; 33: 18; Hab. 1: 13; 1 Sam. 18: 9; 2 Peter 2: 14; 1 John 2: 16; Eph. 1: 18; 6: 6; 1 Cor. 2: 9; Is. 52: 8; Jer. 9: 1; Matt. 5: 38; 6: 22, 23; 7: 3-5; 13: 15; Mark 8: 17-18)

Winking: Flirting with sin; deceitfulness; cunning; hiding true desire.

Closed: Slumbering; refusing to see; unbelief; willful ignorance.

Face: Character; expression; image; heart; notice expression and mood; nature; to hide: disapproval: to fall on: worship; to cover: mourning; to turn from: rejection; setting toward something: determination. *(Gen. 1: 26-29; 3: 19; 17: 3; Prov. 21: 29; Rev. 4: 7; 10: 1; 22: 4; 2 Chron. 30: 9; 2 Kings 12: 17; 2 Sam. 19: 4; Du. 31: 17-18)*

Feet: **See also Shoes or Sandals**: Walk in Spirit; ways; the way you walk, is the way you think; behavior; formal possession; offense; one's heart attitude; stubborn when still; messenger of God; humble walk; lowly stance. *(Ex. 3: 5; 24: 10; Gal. 2: 14; Rev. 1: 15; Ps. 35: 15; 40: 2; 1 Sam. 2: 9 Eph. 6: 15; Rom. 10: 15; 16: 20; Heb. 12: 13,*

Susan Noone Riddle

15; Prov. 25: 19; Acts 9: 5; 2 Chron. 16: 10, 12; 1 Tim. 5: 10; Luke 7: 44)

Barefoot: Not prepared; without salvation and protection; easily offended; tender; good if one is standing in His presence (Moses and the Priest took their shoes off in His presence).

Diseased: Offense.

Kicking: Rebellion against authority.

Lame: Skepticism and doubt.

Washing: A saints duty to brothers and sisters.

Finger: Feelings; pointed finger could be finger of God or accusation; direction; perversity; instruction; discernment; conviction; works, encouragement; work of God; authority of God. *(Luke 11: 20; Dan. 5: 5; Ex. 8: 19; 29: 12; 31: 18; Prov. 6: 13; Is. 2: 8; 58: 9; Du. 9: 10)*

Forehead: Perception and thought processes; inspiration; shamelessness; stronger power; devotion to the Lord; true servants of the Lord; reason; revelation in dreams and vision; mind; the ability to retain and recall events of the past. *(Rev. 7: 3; 13: 16; 14:*

In A Dream, In A Vision of the Night
Job 33:15-18

9; 17: 5; 22: 4; Ex. 28: 38; Ez. 3: 8-9; 9: 4; 28: 48; 1 Sam. 17: 49; 2 Chron. 26: 19)

Front side: Armor worn on front side. *(Eph. 6: 10-17; Gen. 6: 11; Rev. 1: 19)*

Hair: Covering; covenant; too much attention paid to detail; absolute safety; respect; grief; attractiveness; affliction; destruction; fall; great numbers; humanity; numbered on our head showing His love for us; the old sin nature; doctrine; tradition; on body standing up means fear. *(Pro. 16: 31; 31: 30; Hos. 7: 9; Ps. 40: 12; 1 Cor. 11:14-15; Lev. 19: 27; 1 Sam. 14: 45; 2 Sam. 14; 25, 26; Judges 16: 17, 22; 20: 16; Is. 3: 17, 24; Song 5: 2, 11; Job 4: 14-15; Ezra 9: 3; Jer. 7: 29; John 11: 2; Luke 7: 38)*

Haircut: Removing or breaking covenants or religious tradition.

Long: Man: Provocative and defiant behavior; rebellion.

On a Woman: Glorified person in the Lord; or church in the Lord; submissive wife or church.

Short on a Woman: short like a man: manliness; rebellion; homosexuality; unsubmissive, desire to be in control.

Shaving: Putting away the filthiness and nature of the flesh.

Hands: Deeds; strength; power; action; work both natural or spiritual; possession; labor; service; idolatry; spiritual warfare; God's hand: Pleading; defense; judgment; chastening; miracles; punishment; provision; destiny. *(1 Tim. 2: 8; Ps. 16: 8; 17: 7; 28: 4; 31: 15; 45: 9; 75: 8; 90: 17; 109: 31; 110: 1, 5; 139: 10; 145: 16; Job 9: 30; 19: 21; Is. 1: 15; 62: 8; 65: 2; Zech. 3: 1; Ex. 3: 20; 9: 3; 15: 26; 115: 4; Prov. 14: 1; 17: 16-18; 22: 26; Jer. 2: 37; Mark 14: 62; Song 2: 6; Matt. 5: 30; 25: 33; Gal. 2: 9; John 10: 29; 2 Kings 10: 15; 11: 12; Num. 24: 10; Gen. 47: 29, 31)*

Clapping: Joy and worship.

Fist: Anger; fighting.

Hands covering the face: Despair; grief; guilt; shame; joy; laughter.

Holding hands: Agreement.

Left hand: Judgment; spirit.

Raised: Worship; surrender.

Right hand: Oath of allegiance, power, devotion and love, honor; self denial; fellowship; opposition.

In A Dream, In A Vision of the Night
Job 33:15-18

Shaking hands: Covenant relationship; agreement.

Stretched out hands: Helpless; surrender.

Striking: In security or anger.

Trembling: To fear terribly; a strong weakness; awe at God's presence.

Under Thighs: In oaths.

Washing: Innocence.

Head: Thoughts; authority; mind; intelligence; God; Christ; rulership; pastor; employee; power; lordship; husband; protection; prosperity and joy; exaltation; judgment; pride; trust. *(Matt. 6: 17; 22: 37; 27: 39; Is. 15: 2; Ex. 29: 10; Lev. 1: 4; 3: 2; 13: 45; 1 Cor. 11: 3-7; Eph. 1: 22; 5: 23-24; 2 Sam. 13: 19; 15: 30; Jos. 7: 6; Ps. 23: 5; 27: 6; 83:2; 140: 7; Luke 21: 28)*

Anointed: For dedication.

Covered: Grief; subjection.

Covered with dust: dismay.

Covered with the hand: Sorrow.

Uncovered: Leprosy; sin nature.

Swaying: Scorn.

Heel: Power to crush; crucified with Christ; the woman's seed; where the wicked is snared; friend of David; obtaining victory. *(Gen. 3:*

Susan Noone Riddle

15; 49: 17; Ro. 16: 20; Ps. 41: 9; Job 18: 5-9)

Hips: **Also Loins**: Loins; mind; truth; joint; offense between brothers; reproduction. *(1 Peter 1: 13; Eph. 6: 14; Ez. 47: 4; Heb. 7: 10)*

Knees: Obedience; worship of idols; worship of God; submit; service; unyielding; honor; bruised shows the person has been wounded and may over submit to cruelty; reverence. *(Gen. 41: 3; Ro. 11: 4; 14: 11; Is. 45: 23; Matt. 27: 29; Phil. 2: 19; Eph. 3: 14; Ez. 47: 4)*

Legs: **See also Lame, Limping and Thigh**: Man's walk showing weakness of flesh or God's strength; support of the body (can be body of Christ); Spirit; the appearance of the Lord. *(Song 5: 15; Ps. 147: 10; Prov. 18: 14; 26: 7; Dan. 2: 33, 40)*

Female legs: Could represent the strength of lust to entice.

Lips: Utterance; allurement; testimony. *(Prov. 7: 21; 10: 19-21; 18: 6; Heb. 13: 15; Ps. 12: 2-3; 34: 13; 51: 15; 63: 5; 66: 14; 71: 23; 119: 13; 140: 3-9; Josh. 2: 10)*

In A Dream, In A Vision of the Night
Job 33:15-18

Mouth: Witness or testament either good (God's Word) or evil (accusation). *(Prov. 2: 6; 8: 7; Col. 3: 28; Ps. 62: 4; 63: 5-11; Eph. 6: 9; Rev. 19: 15-21)*

Neck: Self-determination; stubborn; unbelief; strength; authority; command; will; beauty; hardness of Spirit. *(Jer. 17: 23; Gen. 41: 42; Prov. 29: 1; Hos. 10: 11; Gen. 27: 40; Ex. 13: 13; Du. 28: 48; 31: 27; Song 7: 4)*

> **Stiff-necked**: Obstinate; rebellion against authority; unyielding; domineering; control.

Nose: Discern; interfering through meddling; strife; busybody; smell. *(1 Peter 4: 15; Prov 30: 30-33; Ps. 11: 6; 18: 8; 75: 5; Job 4: 9; 39: 20; 2 Kings 19: 28; Ex. 15: 8; 2 Sam. 22: 9, 16)*

Nosebleed: Strife; trouble.

Shoulder: Strength; government; assist; bearer; authority; dependable; stubborn (also relates to the shoulder on a road). *(Ps. 81: 6; Is. 9: 6; Zech. 7: 11; Is. 9: 4; 22: 22; Luke 15: 5; Ez. 2: 4; 2 Chron. 36: 13; Du. 31: 27)*

> **Broad Shoulders**: Strength to carry; solace.

Susan Noone Riddle

> **Drooped shoulders**: Tired; overburdened; discouraged; hopelessness.
>
> **Bare female shoulders**: Witchcraft; enticement; temptation.

Teeth: **See also Arrows, Spears, Lips and Mouth**: Wisdom; experience; to work something out; remorsefulness; intense hate. *(Zech. 9: 7-8; Is. 7: 16; Rev. 9: 8; Rom. 5: 3-4; Col. 2: 8; 1 Tim. 6: 20; Prov. 25: 18-19; Heb. 5: 8, 12-14; Ez. 18: 2; Ps. 1: 2; 3: 6; 35: 16; 45: 5; 57: 4; 64: 3; 76: 3; 91: 5; 119: 9; 127: 4; Jer. 9: 8; Job 4: 10; 6: 4; Du. 32: 23, 42)*

Animal teeth: Sharpness; devouring; serious endangerment.

Baby teeth: Childish; without wisdom or knowledge; inexperienced; unblemished.

Broken teeth: A difficult issue; broken relationships; learning obedience through suffering; approaching agony.

Brushing teeth: Making words or thoughts pure.

False teeth: To replace spiritual understanding with reasoning; substitute; wisdom; religious tradition; error.

In A Dream, In A Vision of the Night
Job 33:15-18

Toothache: Tribulation coming; heartache.

Thigh: Strength; the natural, fleshly man; works of the flesh; lust; seduction. *(Gen. 32: 25-32; Num. 5: 21; Ps. 45: 3; Is. 47: 2)*

GENERAL SYMBOLS

A

Acid: Ridicule and mockery; resentfulness that causes one to hold on to offense; keeping a resentment; hatred. *(Job 6: 4; Heb. 12: 15; Mark 16: 18; Acts 8: 23)*

Adultery: Spiritual adultery; actual adultery; sexual sin; having devotion, love and adoration for anything other than God; pornography. *(Gal 5: 19-21; James 4: 4; Ecc. 7: 26; Ex. 20: 14; Ez. 23: 45)*

Airplane: **See Vehicles: also for Crashing, High, Large, Low, Small, Soaring and War Plane.**

Airport: **See Vehicles**.

Alligator: **See Animals, Reptiles, Insects and Birds**

Altar: **See also Mountain, Table and Skyscrapers**: Prayer; were made with hands in Old Testament; place where the bloodshed is purposefully conducted as a religious ritual; offering as a living sacrifice; Lamb of God, Jesus; table of the Lord. *(Ex. 27: 1; 2 Chron. 4: 1; 2 Sam. 24:*

In A Dream, In A Vision of the Night
Job 33:15-18

18-25; Gen. 8: 20; Heb. 13: 10; Ez. 41: 22)

Anchor: Assurance of hope. *(Heb. 6: 19)*

Ankles: Belief that is not strong; God will heal; the believers faith. *(Ez. 47: 3; Acts 3: 7)*

Anoint: **See also Balm**: Set apart divine appointment in service; prayer for the sick; to be made sacred because of the sacrifice of the Christ. *(James 5: 14; 2 Chron. 22: 7; 1 John 2: 20, 27; 2 Cor. 1: 21; Ex. 28: 41)*

Ant: **See Animals**: **also for Reptiles, Insects and Birds**

Antiques: Good or evil inherited from our ancestries; reflecting and recalling the past. *(Jer. 6: 16)*

Apples: Spiritual fruit; aroma; sweet allure; to be tempted to eat of the fruit of sin; a word fitly spoken; As the Apple of His Eye: God's care; security of the believer; the law. *(Zech 2; 8; Deut. 32: 10; Prov. 7: 2; 25: 11; Ps. 17: 8; Gal. 5: 22-23)*

Ark: Christ our security, strength, and deliverance; the Lord as totally man yet totally God; the Lord's seat of authority; man as God's dwelling place; intermediary or middleman; square container; baptism

Susan Noone Riddle

(Noah); heaven; atonement; holiness; God's law; understanding God's will; remembering His provision; covenant; testimony; authority. *(2 Chron. 6: 41; Ex 25: 16, 21; 16: 33, 34; 25: 22; 30: 6; 1 Sam. 6: 19; Lev. 16: 2, 14-17; 1 Peter 3: 20, 21; Heb. 9: 4; Num. 10: 33; 17: 10)*

Arm: Might; help; the Savior of the World; to be rescued; striker; God's stretched out hand to take one nation from another; God as ever present; strong; holy; glorious; redeeming; God's protector; ruling; victorious; the arm of the evil will be broken. *(Ex. 6: 6; Duet. 4: 34; 33: 27; 7: 19; Ps. 89: 1, 10, 13, 21; 98: 1; 44: 3; 10: 15; Is. 30: 30; 40: 10; 63: 12)*

Armies: Godly or demonic might; armies could be led by God, Judges, Kings, and Commanders; Christian armies and soldiers that war against: vain words; the world; satan; flesh; evil men; spiritual wickedness; Soldiers must: obey, be faithful; have self control; be courageous; be pure and alert; stand firm; fight hard; please Jesus, the Captain: in perfection; in power; and in purity. *(Heb. 2: 10; 7: 26; Eph. 6: 12-13;*

In A Dream, In A Vision of the Night
Job 33:15-18

Jude 3, 4; James 4: 4; 1 John 2: 15-17; 1 Peter 5: 8, 9; 1 Tim. 6: 12; 2 Tim. 3: 8; 4: 7-18; Gal. 5: 17-21; 1 Cor. 9: 25-27; 2 Cor. 10: 5, 6; 1 Peter 5: 8; 2 Sam. 2: 8; 12: 28, 29; Judges 11: 1, 5, 6, 32; Josh. 5: 13-15)

Armor: **See also Breastplate and Breast**: Sacred gear for war; light; righteousness; the Bible and sword; shouldn't be of flesh. *(Rom. 13: 12; Eph. 6: 11-17; 2 Cor. 6: 7; 10: 4, 5)*

Arrows: **See also Bow**: The Word of the Lord's deliverance; lies and deceit; bitter words; God's Word unto affliction; quick and quiet judgments; gossip or deceitful speaking; fierce anguish; the commission of the Lord; the power of God; daily demonic attacks; intentions that are evil towards someone. *(Zech. 9:7-8; Is. 7: 16; Rom. 5: 3-4; Col. 2: 8; 1 Tim. 6: 20; Prov. 25: 18-19; Heb. 5: 8, 12-14; Ez. 18: 2; Ps. 11: 2; 45: 5; 64: 3; 76: 3; 91: 5; 119: 9; 127: 4; Jer. 9: 8; Job 6: 4; Du. 32: 23, 42)*

Ashes: Turning from sins; devastation; total death of the old life; consumed; mourning; sorrow; dejection; victory over hardship; to be worthless; showing total metamorphosis;

deceit; afflictions; devastation; to recall something from the past better left alone; used for miracles and purification. *(Gen; 18; 27; Ex. 9: 8; Is. 44; 20; 61: 3; Ps. 102: 9; Jer. 6: 26)*

Atom Bomb: Last days sign; coming of the Lord in power as on the same scale in the imagery of the Word of God as earthquakes, tornadoes, etc.; sudden terror. *(1 Thess. 5: 3; Acts 2: 17, 19)*

Automobile: **See Vehicles: also for Brake, Convertible, Four Wheel Drive, Junk Yard, Large, New, Old, Rearview Mirror, Seat belt, Small, Tires, Topless, Trunk, Van and Wreck.**

Autumn: To turn from sin; transformation; concluding or termination of something. *(Jer. 8: 20; Is. 64: 6)*

Ax: Gospel; to motivate or give an admonishment to others by cutting away a non-truth; to preach. *(Prov. 27: 17; Matt. 3: 10)*

In A Dream, In A Vision of the Night
Job 33:15-18

B

Baby: **See People**.

Back: (as in direction): Returning to the past; behind you; over with; going backward; backsliding; hidden; unleavened cakes; or out of balance; cast behind someone's presence; casting sin behind. *(1 Kings 14: 9; Ex. 33: 23; Mark 8: 32-33; Phil. 3: 13-14)*

Backside: Past; something that is behind you; something that is over with; going backward; backsliding; to put or keep out of site; concealed from view: unleavened cakes; or out of balance; God's backside; cast behind someone's presence; casting sin behind you. *(1 Kings 14: 9; Ex. 33: 23; Gen. 22: 13; Josh. 8: 4; Mark 8: 32-33; Phil. 3: 13-14)*

Baking: Hospitality; God's provision; worship. *(Gen. 25: 34; Lev. 26: 26; 23: 17)*

Balances: Integrity; judgment that is balanced with mercy or God's justice; man's tribulation; the smallness of man; something being shown as in balance; sickness. *(Job 31: 6;*

Susan Noone Riddle

Ps. 62:9; Rev. 6:5; Dan. 5: 27; Is. 40: 12, 15)

Balm: **See also Anoint**: A special anointing to heal. *(James 5: 14; 2 Chron. 22: 7; 1 John 2: 20, 27; 2 Cor. 1: 21; Ex. 28: 41)*

Bank: **See Places**.

Banner: **Also Flag**: Something lifted up as a measurement that is better and higher than something else; against an enemy; warfare; love; triumph; victory; proclamation. *(Ps. 20: 5; Ex. 17: 15; Song 2: 4; Jer. 50: 2)*

Baptism: Death and burial of the old man (nature) and his ways; total submersion in something; repentance; preparation for the coming Kingdom; death; burial; resurrection; inner conversion; overwhelmed by water or the Holy Spirit. *(Matt. 3: 9; Mark 10: 38; Rom. 6: 3-11; 1 Peter 3; Acts 2: 17-18; Acts 22: 16; Titus 3: 5; John 3: 3-6; 1 Cor. 12: 13; Gal. 3: 27-28)*

Banquet: **See Places**: **also for Food, Cafeteria and Restaurant**.

Barbershop: **See also Hair**.

Barn: **See Places**.

In A Dream, In A Vision of the Night
Job 33:15-18

Barrenness: Unable to be effective in life of the Spirit; rejection; cursed; judgment; unfruitful; death of the Spirit; death of a ministry. *(1 Sam. 1; Gen. 11: 30; Du. 28: 1-4, 15-18; Is. 5: 1-10)*

Basket: One basket equals one day; hiding good works; God provides; Judah and Israel's judgment. *(Matt. 5: 15; Amos 8: 1-3; Gen. 40: 16-19; Jer. 24: 1-10)*

Bat: **See Animals**: **also for Reptiles, Insects and Birds**

Bathing: Repenting from sin; totally clean; to be seduced to sin; to make pure by washing; ceremonial washing; Jewish ritual, before performing duties of the priesthood. *(Ex. 30: 19-31; Lev. 14: 8; 16: 4, 24; Gen. 24: 32; John 13: 10; Mark 7: 2; 2 Sam. 11: 2, 3)*

Beam: God's might and power; supporting item or crutch; cry of vengeance. *(Hab. 2: 11; Ps. 104: 3)*

Bear: **See Animals**: **also for Reptiles, Insects and Birds**.

Beard: To esteem someone highly; years that show wisdom; to be covered in authority; neatly trimmed: sane, together; or messy: crazy;

121

plucked or clipped: mourning; holding on to shows respect; if only half shaven: an indignity; not to be marred; lepers must shave beard off. *(Ps. 133: 2; Ezra 9: 3; Jer. 48: 37, 38; 2 Sam. 10: 4; 20: 9; 1 Sam. 21: 12, 13; Lev. 19: 27)*

Beauty Shop: **See places**: **also for Hair, Barber Shop and Women**.

Bed: **See also Bedroom**: Rest; privacy; peace; to commit in the form of a covenant; intimacy; slumbering; laziness. *(Ps. 4: 4; 139: 8; Is. 28: 18-20; Heb. 18: 4)*

Bees: **See Animals, Reptiles, Insects and Birds**

Bells: The act of showing or displaying, in a tangible way, of the Spirit of God; sound that soothes; consecration. *(Ex. 28: 33, 34: 39: 25; 26; Zech. 14: 20; Is. 3: 16, 18)*

Belly: Sentiment, emotional extremes or feelings; the human spirit; desire; the spirit of man; self centeredness; inner most being; inner turmoil. *(Phil. 3: 19-21; Rom. 16: 18; John 7: 38; Prov. 18: 8; Micah 6: 7)*

Bicycle: **See Vehicles**.

Binoculars: **See also glasses or contacts**: Prophetic vision; inability to focus: without ability to concentrate; a situation or person out of the

In A Dream, In A Vision of the Night
Job 33:15-18

proper focus. *(John 16: 13; 2 Corinthians 3: 13)*

Black: **See Colors**.

Blemish: Apostates; should have none if you are in Christ; man's essence and character having flaws, defects and shortcomings. *(Eph. 5: 27; Lev. 21: 17-24; Heb. 9: 4; 2 Peter 2: 13)*

Blimp: **See Vehicles**.

Blind: Lost; no proper understanding; in need of learning; legalist view of people and things; illiteracy in the things of the Spirit; lack of perceptiveness; no power to discern the true nature of people and situations; weakness and helplessness; unbeliever blinded by satan; could not be a priest in the Old Testament if blind; inability to recognize the truth; perverted judgment; don't want to see; idolaters with wrong worship toward God. *(Matt. 15: 14; 23: 26; Rev. 3: 17; Lev. 19: 14; 2 Sam. 5: 6; John 9: 1; Ex. 23: 8; 2 Peter 1: 9; 2 Cor. 4: 4; 1 John 2: 11; Rom. 2: 19; Is. 43: 8; James 1: 23-24)*

Bird: **See Animals, Reptiles, Insects and Birds** for Buzzards, Cranes, Dove, Eagle, Feathers, Fowler, Owls (Liliths, Screech

Susan Noone Riddle

            Owls and Night Hag), Raven, Sparrow, and Wings.

Blood: Spirit of murder; sin; victory; judgment; vengeance; unclean and corrupted; testify or speak of; covenant; guilt and inherited guilt; life of the flesh; cruelty; abomination; slaughter; In the blood of Christ: innocent; conquering; sufficient; precious; necessary; final; cleansing; His blood brings: reconciliation; sanctification; eternal life; communion; justification; redemption; new life; Wine as: blood and grapes; wine or fruit of the grapes represents blood of Christ communion. *(Matt. 26: 26-29; 27: 4, 25; Hab. 2: 12; Is. 34: 6-8; 49: 25, 26; 59: 3; 66: 3; Ps. 58: 10; Rev. 16: 6; 12: 11; Ez. 35: 6; John 6: 53-56; 1 Peter 1: 19; Hebrews 9:13, 14, 22-28; 10: 29; Eph. 2: 13-16; Ro. 3: 24, 25; 5: 9; 1 John 1: 7; Luke 22: 19; Heb. 10: 10)*

Bleeding: Spiritually dying; traumatize; to be in a state of disagreement with someone; someone speaking against someone else.

Blood transfusion: Saving grace; drastic change; rescued from sure death; conversion.

Blue: **See Colors**.

In A Dream, In A Vision of the Night
Job 33:15-18

Boat: **See Vehicles**: **also for Sailboat, Rowboat and Ship**.

Body Odor: To be unexpected; unclean spirit; corruption of the flesh. *(James 4: 8; 2 Cor. 7: 1; Ecc. 10: 1)*

Bones: The heart's spiritual state or status; someone who has passed away; everlasting things; breath of God; If broken: Broken body of Christ; unbroken bones of Christ; great strength, broken spirit; condition of bones can reflect spiritual, mental and/or physical health; man's need for woman; related by blood; remains of the once living body of God's people. *(Job 20: 11; Ez. 37; Gen. 2: 23; Judges 9: 2; Amos 6: 10; Ps. 22: 15; Matt. 25: 8; John 19: 33-36; Numbers 19: 16)*

Book: The scriptures; learning or gaining understanding; revelation that can only come from God or man's wisdom; acquired information; instruction; important register; book of law; Book of Life; book of God's judgment; scroll: can be prophecy; eating is receiving the Word or whatever is written on what you are eating; genealogies; recorded miracles. *(Dan. 7: 10; Rev. 3: 5;*

Susan Noone Riddle

> 1: 11; 18: 8; 17: 8; 0: 12; Ez. 2: 9- 3: 3; Heb. 12: 23; Josh. 1: 8; 18: 9; Mal. 3: 16-18; 2 Kings 22: 8; Ez. 3: 1-3; Num. 21: 14; Gen. 23: 40-43; 5: 1)

Bottle: Supply of livelihood and life. *(Matt. 9: 17; Judges 4: 19; Luke 5: 37-38; 2 Sam. 16: 1; Gen. 21: 14-19; Mark 2: 22; Ps. 56: 8)*

Bow: **See Arrow or Gun**: The might of a nation; verbal attack; to be the victim of ill words or to bring a charge against someone; to pray with power; to be rescued from certain death; indicating that God is to judge a situation; the tongue; defeat; peace; strength. *(Hos. 1: 5; 2: 18: 19; Ps. 7: 12; 11: 2; 64: 3; 2 Kings 13: 14-19; Job 29: 20)*

Bowl: Of full measure; worship in sanctuary; hide light under; note what it contains; completeness. *(Matt. 26: 23; Rev. 16: 1; Ex. 24: 6; Zech. 9: 14-17)*

Bracelet: **See also Jewelry**: Spirit of the world; commitment; confinement of the wrist which affects service. *(Gen. 24: 22; Ez. 16: 11; Is. 3: 19)*

Branches: Great triumph and conquest; churches; God's people; Israel; Christians, adversity;

In A Dream, In A Vision of the Night
Job 33:15-18

trees; vines; God's people filled with joy; abundance; budding branch can be new birth; salvation; blessing; ceremonial. *(Is. 11: 1; Rom. 11: 16, 21; Job 14: 7-9; 15: 32; John 15: 1- 6; Rev. 7: 9; Luke 22: 39- 44; John 12: 13; Gen. 40: 10; Lev. 23: 40; Ez. : 10)*

Brass: **See Metals**.

Bread: God's Word; Christ our food that came down from heaven; God providing for His own; taught belief system; covenant; meat or essence; requirement for life; Last Supper; divine gift of God; life in Christ. *(John 6; 13: 18; Judges 7: 13-14; Mal. 1: 7; Matt. 4: 4; 15: 2-3, 6; 1 Cor. 5: 8; 11: 24; 2 Thess. 3: 8; Luke 1: 53; 12: 1; 14: 15; Ex. 5: 16; 16: 15)*

Fresh: Revelation of the moment; prophetic; coming directly from the throne of God!

Moldy: Old sermons; no direct revelation; religious ritual; out-of-date; unclean; carnal interpretation of the Word; no Spirit.

Unleavened: Without sin.

Breast: **See also Mother and Breastplate**: Endearment; armor; life sustaining substance; loyalty and devotion between the Comforter and His children. *(John 13: 25; Eph. 6: 14; Is. 59: 17; Ps. 22: 9)*

Breastplate: **See also Mother and Breast**: God as a shield of protection; righteousness. *(Eph. 6: 14; Is. 59: 17; 2 Chron. 18: 33)*

Brick: Stone that is man made; bondage; deeds of man; disobedience in setting up one's own plan. *(Is. 9: 8-21; 65: 3; Gen. 11: 3)*

Bride: **See People**: **also for Wife, Marriage and Groom**.

Bridge: The cross; strong belief or faith; to bear with someone or something as to hold them up; to be connected. *(1 Cor. 10: 13; Gen. 32: 22; Is. 43: 2)*

Bridle: Self-constraint; not to be used on strong demonic forces (Leviathan) for they cannot be restrained in our own power; God's authority over flesh and tongue. *(Job 42: 13; James 1: 26; 3: 2, 3; Ps. 32: 9; Is. 30: 28; Titus 1: 11)*

Briers: To be disciplined; teaching that is false; sinful nature; a request turned down or suffering rejection; thorns; change in

In A Dream, In A Vision of the Night
Job 33:15-18

nature. *(Is. 5: 6; 32: 13; 55: 13; Mic. 7: 4; Heb. 6: 8)*

Brook: **See also Waters, Sea and River**: To make new or as if new again by refreshing; wisdom; prosperity; deception; protection. *(Job 6: 15; 20: 17; Prov. 18: 4; Ps. 110: 7; Is. 19: 6)*

Broom: Cleanings of sin; spells of satan worshipers. *(John 2: 15; Gal. 5: 19-20; Ex. 22: 18)*

Brother: **See People: also for Sister and Friend**.

Brother-in-law: **See People: also for Sister-in-law**.

Brown: **See Colors: also for Tan**.

Bruise: Hurt feelings or spirit; discipline; defeat for the devil; people in need of healing and restoration; injury. *(Lev. 22: 24; Prov. 20: 30; Matt. 12: 20; Is. 53: 10; Rom. 16: 20)*

Building: **See Places: also for Church Building**.

Bus: **See Vehicles: also for Church Bus, City Bus, School Bus and Tour Bus**.

Butter: Smooth words; warring heart; forcing of anger on someone. *(Prov. 30: 33; Ps. 55: 21)*

C

Cafeteria: **See Places: also for Food, Banquet and Restaurant**.

Cake: **See also Bread**: Symbol; heavenly nourishment; leavened cakes; offering permeated by sinfulness of man; offering without sin if unleavened (a pure life given to God); points of grace. *(Judges 7: 13; Hos. 7: 8; Ex. 12: 39)*

Camel: **See Animals: also for Reptiles, Insects and Birds**

Candle: **Also See Lamp and Electricity**: God's justice; both man's spirit and God's Spirit; God's Word; not lit could mean the removal God's presence; Jesus; the Lamb is the light; conscience; prosperity; death; churches. *(Job 18: 6; 29: 3; Rev. 1: 20; 21: 23; 1 Sam. 3: 3; Ps. 119: 102; Matt. 25: 1-13; Zeph. 1: 12; Prov. 20: 27; Job 18: 6; 29: 3)*

Candlestick: Those who carry the light of God; Jesus in the Church; the body of Christ universal and individually. *(Ex. 25: 31-35; Rev. 1: 12, 20; Zech. 4: 1, 2, 11)*

Carpenter: **See People**.

In A Dream, In A Vision of the Night
Job 33:15-18

Cat: **See Animals, Reptiles, Insects and Birds for Tigers, Leopards and Cheetahs**.

Cave: Hiding places of asylum and deliverance; wanderers; place where someone is buried; place of solitude where God speaks. *(1 Sam. 22: 1-2, 24; Heb. 11: 38; 1 Kings 18: 4, 13; 19: 5 Josh. 10: 16, 27)*

Chain: Captivity; to be spiritually oppressed; sin's bondage; disciple; satan's defeat. *(Rev. 20: 2; 2 Peter 2: 4; Jude 6; Lam. 3: 7; Rev. 20: 1; Jer. 40: 3, 4)*

Chair: **See also Mercy Seat and Throne**: To be in a fixed location; concentration; receiving position; place of dominion; inner court of the temple; throne of God; satanic powers; mercy seat; Kingship of the Lord. *(Rev. 13: 2; Ps. 1: 1; 7: 7; Job 23: 3; 2 Chron. 9: 18; 19: 8; Matt. 17: 19; Heb. 9: 5-12; Ex. 25: 22; 29: 42-43; 1 John 2: 2; Num. 7: 89; Rom. 3: 24-25; 2 Cor. 5: 20; 1 Tim. 2: 5)*

Check: **See also Bank and Money**: Money, treasure; the act of depending upon someone; belief in God or man's ways. *(Mark 4: 40; Heb. 11: 1; Luke 17: 5)*

Susan Noone Riddle

Cheek: Trial; beauty; personal attack; victory; patience. *(Mic. 5: 1; Matt. 5: 39; Song 5: 13; Ps. 3: 7)*

Chicken: **See Animals, Reptiles, Insects and Birds: also for Also Hen, Rooster, and Chick**.

Choking: Too much too fast; hatred; obstacle that obstructs the breath of God. *(Mark 4: 19)*

Christmas: New birth; pagan tradition; to merchandise God's gifts; spiritual gifts; performing humanitarian acts; to be full of joy. *(1 Cor. 14: 1; Luke 11: 13)*

Circle: **See also Ring and Round**: Immortality; perfection; never ending; heavenly bodies or planets. *(Is. 40: 22; Esther 1: 6; 8: 8; James 2: 2; Luke 15: 22; Ex. 25: 12-27)*

Circumcision: Connection between people with a bond of agreement; cutting off carnal nature; free in the Spirit; regeneration; of Jewish bloodline; the born again Christian; cutting away of the law. *(Rom. 2: 29; Phil. 3: 3; Col. 2: 11; Jer. 4: 4; Du. 10: 16; 30: 6)*

City: **See Places**.

Clapping: Praising; warfare; worship expression of thanksgiving and great joy. *(Ps. 47: 1; 98: 8; Ez. 25: 6; Is. 55: 12)*

Classroom: **See Places**: also for Teacher and School.

In A Dream, In A Vision of the Night
Job 33:15-18

Clay: Feebleness of carnal nature; kingdom that is not secure; distress through trial; fragile nature of the natural man; miracle; sealing. *(2 Sam. 12: 31; Is. 41: 25; 64: 8; Dan. 2: 33-35, 42; Ps. 40: 2; Job 38: 14; John 9: 6, 15)*

Clock: **See also Watch**: Time to make a change; time running out; not on time for something; an obstacle that causes one to not be on time; time is significant in the Bible for: the last days; coming of the Lord; day of salvation; time of bondage; captivity; wandering in the wilderness. *(Ecc. 3: 1-8, 17; Acts 14: 15-17; Ps. 89: 47; Eph. 5: 16; 2 Peter 3: 9, 15; 2 Cor. 6: 2; 2 Tim. 3: 1; 2 Peter 3: 3; Ex. 33: 5; 2 Kings 20: 9-11; 1 Kings 6: 1; Acts 7: 6; Du. 1: 3)*

Closet: Hidden or secret sin; confidential; prayer that is very personal; alone and obscure; good deeds and prayer done in secret (rewarded openly). *(Matt. 6: 6; Joel 2: 16)*

Clothing: **Also Garments**: Wedding garments denote purity and virginity toward God; clean covering of right standing in Christ; linen garments denote consecration to God;

Susan Noone Riddle

> Tearing clothes: Expression of grief and sorrow; essential for survival; manner of deceit; white and dressing signify celebration; garment signifies varies things the Lord is clothed in and thus provides for us; filthy garments: unsaved; walking in sin; trying to obtain right standing in on one's own works. *(1 Samuel 2: 19; Ps. 45: 13-14; Lev. 16: 23; 2 Sam. 14: 2; Ps. 69: 11; 102: 26; 104: 1-2; 1 Sam. 28: 8; Dan. 7: 9; Acts 10: 30; Gen. 2: 25; 3: 7; 37: 23; Rev. 21: 2; Mark 15: 17-20; Is. 5: 1; Matt. 6: 25-34)*

Clouds: **See also Thunder, Tornado, Storm, Whirlwind and Wind**: Coming storm; manifested presence and glory of God; Shekinah glory; armies of the enemy; transfiguration; armies of the Lord; group of people; spiritual guidance; coming of the Lord; God's hiddenness (by shielding man from seeing Him as no man can see God and live); teachers that are deceptive; trouble approaching; fear of trouble; covering; filling of the temple of God (born again, Spirit-filled men and women). *(Is. 19: 1; 44: 22; Ex. 13: 21-22; 14: 19-20;*

In A Dream, In A Vision of the Night
Job 33:15-18

16: 10; 19: 16; 40: 35; Rev. 14: 14; Ps. 18: 9; 104: 3; 97: 2; Num. 9: 15-22; Heb. 12: 1-2; Jude 12; 2 Chron. 5: 13; Luke 9: 34-35; Matt. 24: 30; Prov. 25: 14; 2 Peter 2: 17; 1 Cor. 10: 1-2; Lam. 2: 2; Dan. 7: 13)

Dark clouds: Judgment or attack from the enemy and can be the appearance of the Lord.

White clouds: Glory of God.

Clown: **See People.**

Coat: **Also Cloak and Clothing**: Protective covering for shelter from the elements; a mantle of overseeing others or anointing; to cover someone's sin or to hide one's own sin. *(Matt. 5: 60; 1 Thess. 2: 5; 1 Peter 2: 16; Psalm 109: 17-29; 2 Kings 2: 14-15)*

Clean: To be covered in righteousness.

If dirty: To be clothed in unrighteousness or self righteousness.

Cord: **See also Rope or Chain**: To be tied to something that holds; sin; love; salvation. *(Ps. 2: 3; 118: 27; 129: 4; Jer. 38: 11; Ez. 27: 24; Job; 36: 8; Prov. 5: 22)*

Couch: **See also Bed**: Too relaxed; laziness; loss of concern; resting; privacy; peace; covenant

Susan Noone Riddle

(good or bad); intimacy; slumbering. *(Ps. 4: 4; 139: 8; Is. 28: 18-20; Heb. 18: 4)*

Countryside: **See Nation**.

Court: Eliminated from His presence or entering into His presence; period of suffering; trial; judgment coming, conviction on a matter; acquittal on a matter; just or unjust system or judge; the accused having a voice; decisions are final; corruption unacceptable; contempt of not allowed. *(1 Cor: 6: 1; Is. 43: 12; Ps. 65: 4; 94: 20; 100: 4; Esther 4: 11; 5: 1, 2; Du. 17: 6-13; Rev. 11: 1-3; Ex. chapters 12-19; 27: 9)*

Courthouse: **See also Judge**.

Cow: **See Animals**: **also for Reptiles, Insects and Birds**: **also for Heifer, Bull, Calf and Cattle**.

Crocodile: **See Animals, Reptiles, Insects and Birds**: **also for Leviathan, Also Dinosaur and Alligator**.

Crooked: Warped view or action; distorted spiritual picture; serpent; not on a straight path; a generation gone astray. *(Is. 42: 16; Phil. 2: 15; Du. 32: 5; Ecc. 1: 15; Job 26: 13; Ps. 25: 8; 125: 5; Prov. 2: 15)*

In A Dream, In A Vision of the Night
Job 33:15-18

Crossroads: Christ crucified; options; job change; to have resolve. *(Luke 18: 22-23)*

Crown: To rule and reign; to be given advancement; honor and glory; might; prizes; eternal life; kingship; joy; righteousness; unable to perish; retribution; thorns on Christ; Christ at His return; the church; Christian's reward; minister's reward; soul winner. *(Prov. 12: 4; 16: 31; 17: 6; 27: 24; 132: 18; Lev. 8: 9; Ps. 65: 11; 132: 18; 2 Sam. 12: 30; Esther 2: 17; 8: 15; Rev. 19: 12; Heb. 2: 7-9; Is. 62: 3; 2 Tim. 2: 5; 4: 8; Phil. 4: 1; 1 Thess. 2: 19; 1 Cor. 9: 25; Ps. 7: 16; Matt. 27: 29; James 1: 12; 1 Peter 5: 4)*

Cup: Drink the cup of the Lord; or of devils; abominations; portion in life; to drink of what shall be suffered; blessing; cup of the new covenant in Christ; to be sanctimonious or hypocritical; we are what we eat or/and drink. *(Matt. 23: 25, 26; 20: 23; Luke 11: 39; Ps. 11: 6; 23: 5; 1 Cor. 10: 16)*

Cymbals: Tremble and quake; praise; worship; to display insincere behavior or to make a lot of noise about love while exhibiting no action. *(1 Cor. 13: 1; 1 Chron. 13: 8; 15: 28, Ps. 150)*

D

Dam: Restriction to the power and flow of God, or of the opposition of the enemy; barrier; source of might. *(Josh. 3: 16)*

Dancing: **See also Worship**: Spiritual sacrifice; joy; rejoice; idolatry; to prophesy; liberty; temptation; praise; to whirl or move in a swift, circular (eternal joy) motion; evil and sensual; victory; return of a son. *(Ps. 30: 11; 149: 3; 1 Sam. 18: 6, 7; Ex. 32: 19; 2 Sam. 6: 14, 16; Luke 15: 21-25; Matt. 11: 16-17; 14: 6; Judges 11: 34; Lam. 5: 15)*

Darkness: **See also Night**: Unfamiliarity; the darkness or shadows seen by a blind person; deep grief; turmoil; spiritual or supernatural darkness; eternal darkness; hell; death; immorality; to be innocently ignorant of truth; afflictions; to be in sin's way. *(Matt. 8: 12; 22: 13; 27: 45; Acts 13: 8-11; Ps. 112: 4; Eph. 5: 11; Rom. 13: 12; 1 John 2: 8-11; Job 10: 21, 22)*

Daughter: **See People**.

In A Dream, In A Vision of the Night
Job 33:15-18

Daytime: **See also Light**: Truth; evil exposed; time of good deeds; present age; eternity; a time for the prophetic; the return of the Lord; believer's; the present time; space; light; length of productive time; understanding being illuminated. *(Dan. 7: 9, 13; 12: 11; Ps. 90: 4; Rev. 2: 10; Heb. 1: 2; Is. 22: 5; Gen. 2: 4; John 9: 4; 2 Peter 3: 8; 1 Thess. 5: 2-8; 1 Cor. 3: 13; Eph. 5: 13)*

Deaf: Not paying attention because of turning a "deaf" ear; spiritually, mentally or physically enabled; long-suffering. *(Matt. 11: 5; Is. 29: 18; Ps. 38: 13; 58: 4; 42: 18, 19)*

Death: Final; the end; completion and conclusion of something; actual death; a church without life; a covenant relationship coming to a permanent end; total separation from sin; result of sin; for the believer: peace; receiving reward of living upright; no eternal death; freedom from the power of sin. *(1 Cor. 15: 31; Heb. 2: 14; 9: 14; Is. 26: 14; Rom. 5: 12; 6: 2-11; 7: 4; Gen. 3: 17-19; Eph. 2: 1; James 2: 17-19; Rev. 3: 1)*

Susan Noone Riddle

Deer: **See Animals, Reptiles, Insects and Birds: also for Hind**.

Desert: Forsaken; seclusion; destitute; ineffective and unable to produce fruit; hopeless; wilderness; temptation; supernatural provision. *(Jer. 17: 6; 50: 12, 39; Is. 21: 1; 27: 10; 33: 9; 40: 3; Ps. 107: 4-5)*

Diamond: Something valuable and precious; gift of the Spirit; stubbornness; cruel; inability to change; everlasting; radiant; majesty. *(Zec. 7: 12; Ez. 3: 8-9; 28: 13; Prov. 17: 8; Zech. 7: 12; Jer. 17: 1)*

Dinosaur: **See Animals: also for Reptiles, Insects and Birds, Leviathan, Crocodile and Alligator**.

Disease: Catastrophe; judgment; attack from satan; trial as part of life. *(2 Cor. 112: 7-10; John 9: 1-3; Luke 13: 16; Job 2: 7; 2 Chron. 21: 12-19; 2 Kings 5: 25-27)*

Ditch: Tradition or ritual that leads to a trap; sin; following the blind; fleshly desires. *(Prov. 23: 27; Matt. 15: 14; Luke 6: 39; 2 Kings 3: 16-20; Ps. 7: 15)*

Doctor: **See People: also for Hospital**.

Dog: **See Animals, Reptiles, Insects and Birds**.

In A Dream, In A Vision of the Night
Job 33:15-18

Donkey: **See Animals, Reptiles, Insects and Birds: also for Mule**.

Door: Jesus; opening; to be given admittance; possibility of danger or good; opening of the mouth to speak edification or idle words. *(Hos. 2: 15; 1 Cor. 16: 9; 2 Cor. 2: 12; Col. 4: 3; John 10: 7, 9; Rev. 3: 8, 20; 4: 1; Ps. 141: 3)*

Down: Spiritual decline; backslide; falling away; humility; prostration. *(Du. 22: 8; 2 Cor. 12: 18; Ps. 37: 31)*

Dragon: **See Animals, Reptiles, Insects and Birds**.

Dreaming: Instruction from God; revelation of God's will or the future; keep dreamer from some evil; a vision; a deep Spiritual truth when given a dream within a dream. *(Gen. 40: 8; 20: 3; 28: 11-22; 37: 5-10; Matt. 1: 20; 27: 13; 19; Judges 7: 13-15)*

Drink: **See also Cup**: Consume; fellowship; famine; pleasures of marriage; to have an alliance that is ungodly; receiving God's blessings; communion; under the influence of an evil spirit or unruly flesh; taking in the Holy Spirit or an evil spirit; unhappiness. *(1 Cor. 10: 4, 21; 12: 13; John 4: 13-14; Prov. 5: 15-19; Rev. 14: 8-*

10; Mark 16: 18; 2 Kings 18: 27; Rom. 12: 20; Eph. 5: 18; Matt. 26: 42; Zech. 9: 15-17; Is. 51: 22-23)

Driver: **See People**.

Drowning: Overwhelmed by events or strong personalities; self centered compassion and sympathy; shame; being in debt; suffering; temptation; dejection and mournfulness; to backslid. *(1 Tim. 6: 9; Is. 61: 3; Rev. 12: 15-16; Matt. 18: 6)*

Drugs: **See also Drunk and Drinking**: Additive personality; gossip; contention; witchcraft as a work of the flesh; controlling; imposing the will of one over another; actual drug problem. *(1 Sam. 15: 23; Prov. 17: 22; Gal. 3: 1)*

Drunk: Intoxicated in the natural, or with wrong beliefs, or in the Spirit; affliction; under the influence of an evil spirit or unruly flesh; overcome; under the power of sorrow; under a strong delusion; from the blood of the saints (persecution); idolatry. *(Acts 2: 13; Jer. 51: 7; 2 Kings 18: 27; Is. 51: 22-23; 63: 6; Prov. 5: 15-19; Ez. 23: 33; Rev. 17: 2; Du. 32: 42)*

Drunkard: **See People**: **also for Drug Addict**.

In A Dream, In A Vision of the Night
Job 33:15-18

Dust: Shame; mockery; descendants; to be cursed or under a curse; death; shortcomings of man; flesh of man. *(Matt. 10: 4; Acts 13: 51; 22: 33; 1 Sam. 2: 8; 2 Sam. 16: 3; Is. 47: 1)*

Dynamite: Imperilment; strong attack from the enemy; potential for God and great spiritual power that is used for good or evil; destruction. *(Matt. 9: 8; Luke 10: 19; 22: 53)*

E

Ear: **See also Deaf**: Hearing spiritual things that either build up or tear down; lack of hearing not good. *(Prov. 2: 2; 4: 20; 17: 4; 28: 9; Is. 1: 10; 1 Cor. 2: 9; Job 13: 1)*

Earthquake: Judgment; shaking of God; to under go a great shaking; a huge sweep causing change; change by crisis; repentance; trial; disaster; something that jars the mind or emotions; shock; God showing forth His power, anger, presence and pulling down Kingdoms. *(Is. 24: 20; 29: 6; Jer. 4: 24; Acts 16: 26; Rev. 6: 12-13; 8: 5; 16: 18-19; Heb. 12: 25-29; Ps. 18: 7; 68: 7-8)*

Susan Noone Riddle

East: Light; God's glory; arising; birth; first; anticipate; false religion; Cherubim; the sun rising; East Gate: in the temple area; East Wind: brings judgment; causes springs and fountains to dry up; causes ships and vegetation to dry up; beginning. *(Ps. 103: 12; Rev. 7: 21; 16: 12; Ge. 3: 24; 11: 12; 41: 6, 23, 27; Ez. 10: 19; 11: 1; 17: 10; 27: 25-27; 43: 1, 2; Is. 27: 8; Ho. 13: 15)*

Eating: **See also Dining Room and Chewing**: Becoming a part of; a binding covenant agreement; partake; relationship between friends; fellowship between brothers/sisters in Christ; to ingest a teaching; to consume the Word; to meditate on God's Word; digesting the Word of God; forbidden fruit; no blood; no unclean foods; gluttony; adoption; must work to eat; respect a brother when choosing food. *(Gen. 2: 16-17; Ex. 24: 11; Jer. 15: 16; 52: 33-34; Rev. 10: 9-10; Luke 13: 26; 22: 15-20; Du. 14: 1-29; 20: 14; Matt. 11: 18; Ez. 3: 1-3; John 4: 34; 13: 18; Acts 14: 22; 15: 19-20; Phil. 2: 12; 3: 19; Josh. 9: 14-15; Prov. 30: 20; Rom. 14: 1-23; 2 Thess. 3: 7-10)*

In A Dream, In A Vision of the Night
Job 33:15-18

Echo: Accusation spoken over and over; many opinions vocalized; to imitate in order to make fun of; meaningless prayer. *(Luke 23: 21; Matt. 6: 7)*

Egg: **See also Seed**: Vulnerable; seed; promise that Abraham received of being many nations; promise of an Isaac or a work of the Spirit of God; the possibility for growth and development in any manner; revelation. *(Luke 11: 12; 1 Tim. 4: 15)*

Egypt: The world and being of the world; blackness; persecution; come out of; superstitious; ambitious; unprofitable; lowly kingdom; will be destroyed. *(Is. 19: 3, 19-25; 30: 1-7; 36: 6; Jer. 46: 8-9; Gen. 15: 13; Ez. 29: 14-15; 30: 24-25; Matt. 2: 15)*

Eight: **See Numbers**.

Eighteen: **See Numbers**.

Electricity: Spiritual power of God or demonic; potential for God, or for evil; destruction; flow. *(Matt. 9: 8; Luke 10: 19; 22: 53)*

> **Fire damaged outlet**: Extreme resentment and bitterness; anger; burned out believer.

Outlet for Electricity: Possibility of plugging into the flow of the Holy Spirit.

Unplugged cord: Not plugged in to the power of the Spirit.

Elevator: **Also see Tower, Mountain, Hill, Up and Stairs**: Jesus returning from the heavens to earth; symbolic of victory; Jesus being lifted up on the cross; wisdom that comes from above; Beatitudes in the Sermon on the Mount. If going up: moving up into the realm where God dwells; Prophetic church of great revelation moving upward; high places of the Lord or of the flesh; moving above earthly experience; higher spiritual things; Mt. Zion; sacrifice of worship; Mt. Sinai and the Ark of the Covenant in the Temple; Songs of ascent unto Him; If going down: spiritual demotion; trial; backsliding. Tower of Babel; Mt. Carmel; dominance; control; obstacle; spiritual decline; backslide; falling away; humility; prostration; position change. *(Du. 22: 8; 2 Cor. 12: 18; Ps. 37: 31; Acts 1: 13-14; 20: 7-8; Ps. 103: 11; 1 Sam. 9: 12-14; Matt 5;*

In A Dream, In A Vision of the Night
Job 33:15-18

1 Kings 12: 31; 18; John 3: 7; James 3: 15, 17; Heb. 1: 3; 1 Thess. 4: 13-18)

Eleven: **See Numbers**.

Employer:**See People**: **also for Master**.

Explosion: Violent pressure being quickly released in a destructive way from emotional unrest; expansion or increase; quick work; devastating change. *(Ps. 11: 6; Du. 32: 22; Is. 48: 3)*

Eyes: Longing for God; unnatural desire for someone else's possession; intense desire; lust of the eye; the window to the heart; depth and maturity of spiritual things; ability to see beyond the norm; knowledge and understanding revealed; evil desires; spiritual dullness; being of the world; illumination and future glory; unworthiness for service; the state of one's moral behavior; spiritual incapability and dullness; contact with eyes reveal unspoken agreement; grief; resentful or painfully bitter desire to have what someone else has (envy); one's moral state revealed; revealed desire for retribution; revealed evil desires of the heart; not fit for service; promise of tears being wiped away and seeing Jesus;

inability and dullness of seeing clearly in the Spirit; God leading us and His protection; omnipotent power; holiness. *(Num. 24: 3; Rev. 1: 7; Judges 17: 6; 7: 17; Is. 29: 18; 33: 17; 42: 6-7; 52: 8; 2 Chron. 16: 9; Ps. 19: 8; 32: 8; 33: 18; Hab. 1: 13; 1 Sam. 18: 9; 2 Peter 2: 14; 1 John 2: 16; Eph. 1: 18; 6: 6; 1 Cor. 2: 9; Is. 52: 8; Jer. 9: 1; Matt. 5: 38; 6: 22, 23; 7: 3-5; 13: 15; Mark 8: 17-18)*

Winking: Flirting with sin; concealing something; trying desperately to draw attention away from true desire.

Closed: Slumbering; refusing to see; lack of faith; purposefully remaining ignorant.

F

Face: Expression shows feelings; something portrayed; the spirit of man; revealed true through a face; face reveals the nature of someone; notice expression and mood; nature; to hide: disapproval: to fall on: worship; to cover: mourning; to turn from: rejection; setting toward something:

In A Dream, In A Vision of the Night
Job 33:15-18

determination. *(Gen. 1: 26-29; 3: 19; 17: 3; Prov. 21: 29; Rev. 4: 7; 10: 1; 22: 4; 2 Chron. 30: 9; 2 Kings 12: 17; 2 Sam. 19: 4; Du. 31: 17-18)*

Factory: **See Places**.

Falling: Watch for a fall into sin; not fully being supported; complete loss of support; immense and intense trial; surrender; separation from God; falling back into sin; born in sin; power of God to change; to be depraved; evil heart; corrupted, perverse; bondage to satan or/and sin; dead in sin; spiritually blind; Falling and getting up: A righteous man seven times. *(John 3: 6; 3: 16; Titus 1: 15; Eph. 4: 18; Heb. 2: 14, 15; Matt. 15: 19; Rom. 3: 12-16; 6: 19; Col. 2: 13; James 1: 2; Prov. 16: 18; 22: 14; 11: 28; 24: 16; Micah 7: 8)*

Family: **See People: also for Father, Mother, Daughter and Son**.

Fan: Work of the flesh to imitate a cool breeze of the Spirit; division of the impure and pure; Christ's fan in one's hand: purging His threshing floor. *(Matt. 3: 12; Luke 3: 17; Is. 441: 16; Jer. 15: 5)*

Farmer: **See Places: also for Barn and Field**.

Father: **See People:** **also for Family, Mother, Daughter and Son.**

Father-in-law: **See People:** **also for Mother-in-Law.**

Feathers: Protective spiritual covering; weightless; God's protection. *(Ez. 17: 3, 7; Ps. 91: 4; Matt. 23: 37; Dan. 4: 33)*

Feeding: **Also being Fed:** To be supplied in a spiritual or supernatural way; narcissism; works that are righteous; basic teaching; change in basic traits of one's nature; to become impure in character. *(Rev. 12: 6; 1 Cor. 3: 2; Hos. 12: 1; Matt. 25: 37; Is. 11: 7; Ps. 49: 14)*

Feet: **See also Shoes or Sandals:** To walk in Spirit; ways; the way you walk before God, is the way you think; behavior; formal possession; offense; one's heart attitude; conduct before God and man; obstinate and strong willed if not moving; messenger of God; humble walk; lowly stance. *(Ex. 3: 5; 24: 10; Gal. 2: 14; Rev. 1: 15; Ps. 35: 15; 40: 2; 1 Sam. 2: 9 Eph. 6: 15; Rom. 10: 15; 16: 20; Heb. 12: 13, 15; Prov. 25: 19; Acts 9: 5; 2 Chron. 16: 10, 12; 1 Tim. 5: 10; Luke 7: 44)*

In A Dream, In A Vision of the Night
Job 33:15-18

Barefoot: No preparation; without salvation and protection; easily offended; tender; good if one is standing in His presence (Moses and the Priest took their shoes off in His presence).

Diseased: Resentment and ill will toward someone.

Kicking: Rebellion against authority.

Lame: Skepticism and unbelief.

Washing: A saint's duty to brothers and sisters.

Fence: Freedom of the Spirit endangered by being encircled and surrounded; self-control; security; tradition that hinders; lines or areas separating us from doing God's will or from sin (a wall or fence keeps things out, both righteous things and evil things); partition; obstruction; safety area; belief systems; to be held back or restrained. *(Is. 5: 2; Ps. 62: 3; Num. 32: 17; Gen. 11: 6; Jer. 15: 20)*

Field: Harvest or reaping of what has been sown; occasion that is presented to accomplish great things; the great deeds of God; the earth or world in the sense of all that it

Susan Noone Riddle

>offers to meet natural needs, but it cannot do so without man's help; droves of people or great numbers of people. *(Matt. 13: 24, 38, 44; Luke 15: 15; John 4: 35; 2 Tim. 4: 10)*

Fifteen: **See Numbers**.
Fifty: **See Numbers**.
Finger: Pointed finger: could be finger of God to accuse or direct; perverse heart; teach or give instruction; clear-sightedness in seeing evil or good; specific convicted heart; deeds, encouragement; God's mighty work; authority of God. *(Luke 11: 20; Dan. 5: 5; Ex. 8: 19; 29: 12; 31: 18; Prov. 6: 13; Is. 2: 8; 58: 9; Du. 9: 10)*
Fire: Heat; burden; trial; persecution; words or the tongue; burning fervency; emotion, longing, aching and craving; power; Holy Spirit; angels; Christ Jesus; evil speaking; renewal in the hearts of men; anger to violence; envy; discord; affliction; removal of impurities; God's: protection, word and vengeance; love; fiery trial; lake of fire; eternal judgment for: devil, false prophets, sinners; consuming and driving lust. *(1 Sam. 17: 40; Matt. 3: 11; 14: 17-21; 25: 2,*

In A Dream, In A Vision of the Night
Job 33:15-18

15-20; Luke 12: 49-53; 19: 18-19; Jer. 5: 14; 23: 29; Ex. 22: 6; Prov. 6: 27, 28; 26: 20; James 3: 5-6; 1 Cor. 7: 9; Ps. 79: 5; 89: 46; Zech. 2: 5; Is. 43: 2; 6: 5-7; Heb. 1: 7; 12: 39; Mal. 3: 2; Acts 2: 3; Song 8: 6; Rev. 19: 20; 20: 10, 14; 21: 8)

Five: **See Numbers.**

Flea: **See Animals, Reptiles, Insects and Birds.**

Flood: Judgment on those who use whatever power they have to inflict violence on others; sin judged; overcome; to be overcome and unable to recover; enticed to sin and fall; overcoming sadness and grief; great destruction and trouble; worldly powers that are hostile; invading army; trial; persecution. *(Ps. 29: 10; 32: 6; 93: 3; Jer. 46: 7, 8; Dan. 9: 26; Matt. 7: 25-27; Rev. 12: 15-16; Is. 28: 15-17; 43: 2; 59: 19; Gen. 6: 17)*

Flowers: Man's glory of the flesh that is passing away; an offering; glory of God; the Holy people and land of God, Israel. *(1 Peter 1: 24; Song 2: 1; James 1: 10, 11; Is. 28: 1; 40: 1-3; Job 14: 2; Esther; Hos. 14: 5; Song 2: 1-2; 5: 13; 7: 2)*

Lily: Death; funeral; mourning; beauty; splendor; Esther: city of Shushan.

Rose: Christ and His Church; love; courtship, romance.

Fly: **See Animals, Reptiles, Insects and Birds**.

Fog: **See also Cloud**: Concerns or mindsets that are darkened by fog or clouds; something concealed; vagueness. *(James 4: 14; Hos. 6: 4; Job 10: 15)*

Food: **See also Eating**: Strong meat: For the mature; deep and satisfying teaching of the Word of God; work of God. Milk: For the immature or babies. *(Matt 25: 35; 32: 4; Psalm 19: 9-10; 22: 26; John 6: 27, 48-63; 4: 32, 34; Is. 55: 1-3; 1 Cor. 3: 1-2; Heb. 5: 14)*

Forehead: Perception and thought processes; inspiration; shamelessness; stronger power; devotion to the Lord; true servants of the Lord; reason; the memory that lingers; revelation in dreams and vision; the human mind; the ability to retain and recall events of the past. *(Rev. 7: 3; 13: 16; 14: 9; 17: 5; 22: 4; Ex. 28: 38; Ez. 3: 8-9; 9: 4; 28: 48; 1 Sam. 17: 49; 2 Chron. 26: 19)*

In A Dream, In A Vision of the Night
Job 33:15-18

Foreigner:**See People**: **also for Sojourner, Stranger, Unknown Man and Alien**.

Forest: Nations; forewarning of trial; showing a place of danger and darkness where one can be easily lost and harmed; person lost; confusion and lack of direction; nations of the world or church; a grove. *(Hos. 2: 12; Jer. 12: 8; 21: 4, 14; 26: 18; Is. 10: 18-19; 44: 23; Ez. 15: 1-6; 20: 46-49; Ps. 104: 20; 107: 4-5)*

Forty: **See Numbers**.

Four: **See Numbers**.

Fourteen: **See Numbers**.

Fox: **See Animals, Reptiles, Insects and Birds**.

Friend: **See People**: **also for Brother and Sister**.

Frog: **See Animals, Reptiles, Insects and Birds**.

Front: Future; now; in the presence of; a prophecy of future events; impending; visible; out front. *(Gen. 6: 11; Rev. 1: 19)*

Furnace: The origin of heat; the heart; rage; zeal; anger; trouble through great, heated and painful experiences; retaliation; the final wrath of God. *(Gen. 19: 28; Du. 4: 20; Prov. 17: 3; 1 Kings 8: 51; Isa. 31: 9; 48: 10; Ps. 12: 6; 39: 3)*

G

Garbage: The pit of hell; abandoned things; pure corruption; reprobate or unclean; unclean spirit; departure from all that is Godly. *(1 Cor. 9: 27; Mark 9: 47)*

Garden: Increase; work; ministry of the body of Christ collectively; euphoric paradise; fruitfulness; prospering ministry; field of labor; fertile ground. *(Gen. 2: 8-10; 4: 2-3; Is. 51: 3; 58: 11; Jer. 2: 21; 1 Tim. 4:14-15)*

Gasoline: Energy; strife that is kindled by words; faith filled; prayer; contention; danger; if fumes: doctrine that is toxic; deceiving spirits; sinful motives; accusation that are not true. *(Jude 1: 9; Prov. 26: 20-21; 24: 28; James 3: 14-15; Matt. 24: 4)*

Gate: **See also Door**: Entering into; domination; dominion; power of authority; satanic power; righteousness; death; heaven; salvation; thanksgiving; entering the presence of God; gates open up to: cities; prisons; sanctuaries; graves. *(Gen. 19: 1; 22: 17; 24: 60; Hos. 2: 15; Ex. 32: 26-27; Heb. 13: 12; 1 Cor. 16: 9; 2 Cor. 2: 12;*

In A Dream, In A Vision of the Night
Job 33:15-18

Col. 4: 3; Matt. 16: 18; 27: 60; John 10: 7, 9; Rev. 4: 1; 3: 8, 20; Ps. 24: 7; 100: 4; 107: 16; 122: 2; 141: 3; Judges 16: 3; Ez. 44: 1-2; Acts 12: 5)

Giant: **See People**.

Girdle: **Also to Gird up**: Vigor, might and potency for battle; a belt. *(Ps. 18: 39; 30: 11; 65: 6; Is. 22: 21; 45: 5; Ex. 28: 4, 39; 1 Sam. 18: 4; John 13: 3-4; Luke 12: 35; Job 12: 18; 30: 11; Eph. 6: 14; 1 Peter 1: 13)*

Gloves: **Also see Hands**: Protective covering for service; safety in the work of the ministry. *(Ps. 24: 3-4)*

Goat: **See Animals, Reptiles, Insects and Birds**.

Gold: **See Metals**.

Governor: **Also Kings, Judges, Caesars, Emperors, Princes, Pharaohs and Rulers**.

Grandchild: **See People**.

Grandmother: **Also Grandfather**.

Grapes: **See also Vine and Vineyard**: Fruit of the Spirit; His Word in seed form; The Lord's vow to us; coming wrath of God; Word of God; abiding in the vine who is Jesus. *(Song 7: 7; Matt. 7: 16; Rev. 14: 18; Num. 6: 3; 13: 20-34; Gen. 40: 10-11; 49: 11; Ez. 18: 2; Gal. 5: 22-23; Matt. 20: 1-6;*

Susan Noone Riddle

Hos. 14: 7; John 15: 1-2, 6; Is. 5: 1-7; Ps. 128: 3; 1 Kings 4: 25)

Grass: Life of fleshly desires; weakness of the desires or lust of the flesh; fragile failing flesh; revelation knowledge; shortness of life; the wicked prospering; God's grace. *(Ps. 9: 5; 23: 2; 72: 6; 90: 6; 92: 7; 102: 4; Is. 15: 6; 40: 6-8; 51: 12; Prov. 27: 25; Jer. 14: 5-6; 1 Peter 1: 24; Gen. 1: 30; 9: 3; Job 5: 25; Amos 7: 1-2)*

Dried: Death of the flesh through repentance.

Mowed: Turning from sin; circumcision of the flesh; crucified flesh.

Grasshopper: **See Animals, Reptiles, Insects and Birds**.

Graveyard (and Grave): Curse of the law; behaving sanctimonious; death; demonic influence; resurrection life of God, resurrected from grave. *(Matt. 23: 27; Luke 11: 24)*

Gray: **See Colors**: **also Silver in Metals**.

Green: **See Colors**.

Groom: **See also Marriage and Bride**.

Guard: **See also Police**.

Guest: **See People**.

In A Dream, In A Vision of the Night
Job 33:15-18

Guns: **See also Arrows**: Spoken words that wound; to bring a charge against the elect; malicious and venomous speaking; power of words in prayer; dominion through speaking the Word of God. *(Ps. 64: 4; Luke 11: 21-22; Acts 19: 13, 15-16)*

H

Hail: Soldiers of Christ; wonders; power; judgment that can only come from God; wrath; glory; chastening; to have a barrage of something hit one as an onslaught of something that can be distressing. *(Is. 28: 17; Hag. 2: 17; Rev. 8: 7; Ps. 18: 12; 147: 17; Job 38: 22)*

Hair: To be covered or protected; man's glory; absolute safety; respect; grief; attractiveness; affliction; destruction; relationship that is binding as in a covenant; a belief system that is taught and practiced; fall; great numbers; humanity; numbered on our head showing His love for us; the old sin nature; religious ritual; on body standing up means fear. *(Pro. 16: 31; 31: 30; Hos. 7: 9; Ps. 40: 12; 1 Cor. 11:14-15;*

Susan Noone Riddle

Lev. 19: 27; 1 Sam. 14: 45; 2 Sam. 14; 25, 26; Judges 16: 17, 22; 20: 16; Is. 3: 17, 24; Song 5: 2, 11; Job 4: 14-15; Ezra 9: 3; Jer. 7: 29; John 11: 2; Luke 7: 38)

Haircut: Breaking a good or bad habit or tradition.

Long: Man: Provocative and defiant behavior; strong will and opposition to God's will and purpose.

On a Woman: Glorified person in the Lord; or church in the Lord; submissive wife or church.

Short on a Woman: short like a man: manliness; rebellion; unsubmissive, desire to be in control.

Shaving: Removal of the things of the flesh.

Hammer: Living Word; preaching the Word hard and fast; to hit repeatedly at something; used to drive pegs in to put up a tent; never used in Temple; used to straighten metal; God's Word; Babylon; speaking words that pound and hurt. *(Jer. 23: 29; 50: 23; Prov. 25: 18; Is. 41: 7; 1 Kings 6: 7; Judges 4: 21)*

Hands: Activity of serving; something done as in an act that changes something; might; work

In A Dream, In A Vision of the Night
Job 33:15-18

both natural or spiritual; ownership; labor; service; idolatry; spiritual warfare; God's hand: Pleading; defense; judgment; chastening; miracles; vigor; punishment; provision; destiny. *(1 Tim. 2: 8; Ps. 16: 8; 17: 7; 28: 4; 31: 15; 45: 9; 75: 8; 90: 17; 109: 31; 110: 1, 5; 139: 10; 145: 16; Job 9: 30; 19: 21; Is. 1: 15; 62: 8; 65: 2; Zech. 3: 1; Ex. 3: 20; 9: 3; 15: 26; 115: 4; Prov. 14: 1; 17: 16-18; 22: 26; Jer. 2: 37; Mark 14: 62; Song 2: 6; Matt. 5: 30; Gal. 2: 9; John 10: 29; 2 Kings 10: 15; 11: 12; Num. 24: 10; Gen. 47: 29, 31)*

Clapping: Joy and worship.

Fist: To be enraged; mad enough to physically or verbally hit someone.

  Hands covering the face: Despair; showing great grief; joy; show of a merry heart.

  Holding hands: Agreement.

  Raised: Surrender to God; praise and worship.

  Right hand: Oath of allegiance, power, devotion and love, honor; self denial; fellowship; opposition.

Susan Noone Riddle

Shaking hands: Relationship that is binding between two people or churches or ministries; similar to kiss.

Stretched out hands: Desire to totally surrender; a cry for help

Striking: In security or anger.

Trembling: To fear terribly; a weakness of the flesh that is very powerful; awe at God's presence.

Under Thighs: In oaths.

Washing: Innocence.

Harlot: Idol worship; one who has been unfaithful or has committed adultery; prostitute; the church committing spiritual adultery; no shame; painted up to look different; enticing; no home; expensive; cause of divorce; causes one to error spirituality; idolatry; profaning God's name; forbidden; priest should not marry; should be shamed; should be punished; Israel; Tyre. *(Is. 1: 21; 23: 15, 17; 57: 7-9; Rev. 1-18; Jer. 3: 3, 8, 14; Prov. 5: 3-20; 7: 12; 9: 14-18; 29: 3; Ez. 23: 30, 40; Amos 2: 7; Ex. 34: 15-16; Hos. 4: 10-19; Lev. 19: 29; 21: 1, 7, 9, 14)*

In A Dream, In A Vision of the Night
Job 33:15-18

Harp: If used for God, praise and worship in heaven and in the earth; if used for the world or devil; symbol of lust; self satisfaction; not playing: in captivity; the wicked; prophets. *(Ps. 33: 2; 43: 4; 71: 22; 137: 2; 147: 7; 150: 3; 1 Chron. 16: 5; 1 Sam. 10: 5; 16: 16, 23; Is. 5: 11-12; 2 Chron. 20: 27-28; Rev. 5: 8; 14: 2-3; 15: 2)*

Harvest: Glean; assemble; seasons of grace; judgment; God's wrath; to reap what has been sown; opportunities to share the Gospel; fruitfulness; end of the world; patience; rain promised; failure to caused by: drought; locusts; sin. *(Matt. 9: 37-38; 13: 30, 39; Rev. 14: 14-20; Lev. 23; 2 Cor. 9: 6; Jer. 8: 20; 51: 33; Rev. 14: 15; Jer. 5: 24; 8: 20; 51: 33; James 5: 7; Joel 1: 4; Is. 17: 4-12)*

Hat: **See also Head and Helmet**: Covered with certain type of thoughts; protection for the head. *(Eph. 6: 17; Is. 59: 17; 1 Thess... 5: 8; Is. 59: 17)*

Head: Belief systems; center of the intellect; the Lord Jesus; master or boss; pastor; thought processes; leadership in position to rule and protect; director; power; husband;

protection; exaltation; self appointed manager or leader; someone who can be depend on. *(Matt. 6: 17; 22: 37; 27: 39; Is. 15: 2; Ex. 29: 10; Lev. 1: 4; 3: 2; 13: 45; 1 Cor. 11: 3-7; Eph. 1: 22; 5: 23-24; 2 Sam. 13: 19; 15: 30; Jos. 7: 6; Ps. 23: 5; 27: 6; 83:2; 140: 7; Luke 21: 28)*

Anointed: Being set apart; well-being and joy.

Covered: A grieving person; to be in submission.

Covered with dust: To be appalled or dismayed.

Covered with the hand: Deep regret and sorrow.

Uncovered: Sin nature revealed.

Swaying: To suffer disdain.

Hedge: **See also Fence and Wall**: God's safeguard or removal of safety if missing; unconcerned; blight; tradition restricts. *(Job 1: 10; 3: 23; 19: 8; Is. 5: 5; Ez. 13: 5; Mark 12: 1; Ps. 80: 12; Matt. 21: 33; Prov. 15: 19)*

Heel: Power to step on and apply pressure that destroys; crucified with Christ; the

In A Dream, In A Vision of the Night
Job 33:15-18

woman's seed; the wicked. *(Gen. 3: 15; 49: 17; Ro. 16: 20; Ps. 41: 9; Job 18: 5-9)*

Helmet: **See also Hat and Head**: Salvation; preparation; promise from God; covering to protect the head of a person. *(Eph. 6: 17; Is. 59: 17; 1 Thess. 5: 8)*

Herb: Poison; a root of bitterness. *(Eph. 6: 17; Is. 59: 17; Heb. 6: 7; Num. 9: 11; Job 10: 1; Prov. 14: 10; Ex. 12: 8; 2 Kings 4: 39-40)*

Highway: **Also Road**: Holy way; the path of salvation and life; truth; Christ; a person; title or name of the way of the Christian; the wrong way; two destinies; the Gospel's call; restoration of Israel; refuge to cities used by robbers; beggars seat; animal's plague. *(Du. 19: 2-3; Luke 10: 30-33; Is. 11: 16; 35: 8-10; 40: 3; Matt. 7: 13-14; 20: 30; John 14: 6; Judges 5: 6; Prov. 16: 17; Nah. 2: 4)*

> **Dead end**: Stop; repent; certain failure; stop and review everything and seek direction for necessary changes in direction.
>
> **Gravel**: Way; God's Word and way; stony ground.

Muddy: Dirt or dust mixed with water or spirit; led by flesh.

Construction: In preparation; change; hindrance.

Hills: **Also see Tower, Mountain, Stairs, Up and Elevator**: Exaltation; uplift high above the natural; arrogance through self exaltation; Throne of God; Mt Zion. *(Ps. 68: 16; 95: 4; 98: 8; Gen. 7: 19)*

Hips: **Also Loins**: The thought process; joining; vigorous wholeness in power and strength; reproduction. *(1 Peter 1: 13; Prov. 31: 17; Ps. 66: 11; Eph. 6: 14; Ez. 47: 4; Heb. 7: 10)*

Honey: To be naturally sugary; not to be offered at the alter; strength; jurisdiction with change; wisdom; Spirit of God; the abiding anointing; the sweet Word of our Lord. *(Ps. 19: 10; 81: 16; 119: 103; Prov. 24: 5-14; 27: 7; Ez. 3: 13; Rom. 5: 6; Judges 14: 14; Rev. 10: 9; 1 Sam. 14: 29; Ex. 3: 8-17)*

Horns: **See also Trumpet**: The power and testimony of Jesus; the power of the reprobate life; kings; anointing; conquest tremendous strength of the Spirit of God (breath). *(Ps. 18: 2; 22: 21; 75: 10; 89: 17;*

In A Dream, In A Vision of the Night
Job 33:15-18

118: 27; 132: 17; Hab. 3: 4; Luke 1: 69; La. 2: 3; Rev. 5: 6; 13: 1; 17: 12; Ez. 29: 21; 1; 34: 21; 1 Cor. 1: 24;)

Horse: **See Animals, Reptiles, Insects and Birds**.

Hospital: **See Places**: **also for Healing**.

Hotel: **See Places**.

House: **See Places**: **also for different locations of the House**: **Attic, porch, den, etc. as well as Sanctuary, Temple, Tent or Tabernacle**: **Also Home**.

Husband: **See People**: **also for Marriage and Groom**.

I

Incense: Prayer; worship; praise; service unto God that is acceptable; If offered improperly: chastised; forbidden to be used for idol worship. *(Ps. 141: 2; Rev. 5: 8; 8: 3-4; Is. 60: 6; Luke 1: 10-11; Jer. 1: 16; 11: 12-13; Lev. 5: 11; Ex. 30: 34-38)*

Iron: **See Metals**: **also for Steel**.

Ironing: Difference in "wrinkled" matters; to consecrate; the correction of God through a pressing and heated trial; working out problem relationships; turning from sin and

Island: being reconciled to ones brother/sister in Christ; applied heat and force due to trials. *(Eph. 5: 2)*

Island: Nations of the world; heaven; a place of total tranquility and rest. *(Gen. 10: 5; Zep. 2: 11; Is. 41: 1; 42: 12, 15; Acts 28: 1, 7)*

Israel: The nation of Israel; the Christian community; the redeemed ones; authority that only can come from God over men and everything in the earth. *(Gal. 6: 16; Rom. 9: 6-13; Is. 49: 3; Gen. 32)*

J-K

Jerusalem: The establishment of peace; called "The City of Our God;" the remnant of God. *(Heb. 12: 22-28; Gal. 4: 6; Rev. 3: 12; 21: 2, 10)*

Jewelry: Prized possessions that are preferential to someone; precious person; God's people; gifted person who has received abilities from the Lord; truth; desire; to exalt oneself; worship of idols; arrogance. *(Mal. 3: 17; 1 Cor. 3: 12; Ex. 19: 5; 2 Tim. 4: 3; Prov. 11: 22; 17: 8; James 2: 2)*

In A Dream, In A Vision of the Night
Job 33:15-18

Judge: **See People: also for Kings, Governors, Caesar's, Emperors, Princes, Pharaohs and Rulers**.

Key: Kingdom access; knowledge; authority that is prophetic; capability to overcome and understanding of the Word; ruler over evil through the power of the cross; the Lord Jesus; the dominion and standing given to the children of God to defeat sin and the devil; possessor of supreme power both good or evil. *(Is. 22: 22; Rev. 3: 7; 9: 1; 20: 1; Matt. 16: 19; 18: 18; Luke 11: 52; John 1: 3; Ex. 31: 3)*

Kiss: Similar to a hand shake showing an agreement; allurement toward evil; betrayal; betrayal from a trusted friend or brother/sister in Christ. *(Ps. 2: 12; Prov. 7: 10, 22-23, 27; 27: 6; Hos. 13: 2; Luke 22: 48; Gen. 23: 4; 50: 1; 2 Sam. 20: 9-10)*

Knees: Worship by total surrender; to minister to God or man in the power of the Spirit; If unwilling to bend the knees: hardheaded and strong will; unbelief; If bruised: a wounded will from a forced authority figure who forced one to bend and submit. *(Gen. 41: 3; Ro. 11: 4; 14: 11; Is. 45: 23; 35: 3;*

Susan Noone Riddle

>Matt. 27: 29; Phil. 2: 19; Eph. 3: 14; Ez. 47: 4)

Knives: **Also see Sword**; Speaking the Word of God; gluttony; to be accused of something falsely; correction that cuts away the flesh; correction that wounds; revelation knowledge; cruelty; cutting by speaking against someone. *(Ps. 52: 2; Titus 1: 13; Josh. 5: 2-3; Prov. 23: 2; 30: 14)*

L

Ladder: To rise or to decline; to become empowered to touch the heavens; provision to break away from captivity; provision to enter something where there was no way; promotion the Spirit if going up. *(Gen. 28: 12-13; John 3: 13; 1: 51)*

Lamb: **See Animals, Reptiles, Insects and Birds: also for Sheep**.

Lame: Shortcomings; a flaw in one's walk with God; a lack in agreement or activity; not fit for priesthood. *(Prov. 26: 7; 2 Sam. 5: 8; Lev. 21: 17-23; Job 29: 15; Is. 35: 6)*

Lamp: **See also Candle and Electricity**: Inward part of man or spirit; Holy Spirit; Word of

In A Dream, In A Vision of the Night
Job 33:15-18

God; similar to candle; fellowship gatherings of believers; Jesus; to prosper; justice. *(Ex. 25: 31-35;Job 29: 3; Prov. 20: 27; Rev. 1: 12, 20; Zech. 1: 12; 4: 1, 2, 11)*

Land: The dwelling place of man; separated from because of sin; given by God to the obedient. *(Du. 5: 16; 28: 49-68; Gen. 1: 9, 10; 2: 11-13)*

New cleared land: New place of ministry.

Land covered in root crops: Fruitful work of the ministry.

Bare earth: dust: Curse; stated of being humbled.

Neglected, unwanted land:
Unresponsiveness to the calling and conviction of the Holy Spirit.

Laugh: Rejoicing; joy of worship and walk with God; sarcasm. *(Ps. 59: 8; Job 5: 20; Gen. 18: 11-15; 2 Chron. 30: 10; Prov. 1: 26; 2: 4; 22: 7; 37: 13; 80: 6; 126: 2, 3)*

Lawyer: **See People**: **also for Attorney**.

Lead: **See Metals**.

Leaven: Disposition towards things; sin that spreads to others; false belief system; saying one thing yet living another way; righteousness that comes from self; habitual activity that is evil and has been taught that way to others; action arrested by fire. *(1 Cor. 5: 5-8; Luke 12: 1; Matt. 2: 13; 14: 6-9; 16: 6, 12; Mark 8: 15; Gal. 5: 1-9)*

Leaves: Cover up or hide; trees with healthy leaves are planted by the rivers of life; ability to survive under whether under pressure of abundance. *(Ps. 1: 3; Is. 1: 30; 34: 4; 64: 6; Jer. 17: 8; Matt. 24: 32; Rev. 22: 2)*

Left: That which is of the Spirit; God manifested through the flesh of man; rejection; unity to meet a goal; the honor and riches of wisdom. *(2 Cor. 6: 7; 12: 9-10; Judges 3: 20-21; 20: 16; Matt. 6: 3; 25: 33; Song 2: 6; Ecc. 10: 2; Prov. 3: 16)*

Legs: **See also Lame, Limping and Thigh**: The walk of man before God; lack of strength in the things of the flesh; frailty of the fleshly man; that which supports the body of Christ; spiritual strength. *(Song 5: 15; Ps. 147: 10; Prov. 18: 14; 26: 7; Dan. 2: 33, 40)*

Lemon: Something gone sour; acidity; bitter doctrine. *(Matt. 27: 34; Acts 8: 23)*

Leviathan: **See Animals, Reptiles, Insects and Birds**: **also see Crocodile and Dinosaur**.

In A Dream, In A Vision of the Night
Job 33:15-18

Leopards: **See Animals, Reptiles, Insects and Birds: also for Tigers, Cheetahs, Cats**.

Library: **See Places**.

Lice: **See Animals, Reptiles, Insects and Birds**.

Light: **See also Daytime**: Unveiled or uncovered; no longer hidden; to show forth; the appearing of the Lord; the church of the Lord; messengers on the front line; those who will inherit the glory; those changed and transformed; models of life in Christ; to have God's grace; leading of the Word. *(Eph. 5: 8-14; John 1: 5-14; 3: 21; 5: 35; 8: 12; 12: 35-36; 2 Cor. 4: 6; 1 Peter 2: 9; Acts 20: 8; Ps. 18: 11; 27: 1; 89: 15; 104: 2; 1 Tim. 6: 14-16; Matt. 4: 16; 5: 14-16; 119: 105; 1 John 1: 5; James 1: 17; Rev. 21: 23)*

Dim light: Need of fullness of the knowledge of the Word.

Light Absent: In need of Jesus, of understanding.

Small Lamp or Flashlight: Just enough light to guide the pathway.

Lightning: God's grandness and glory; voices or God's voice, and earthquakes; the Lord interrupting an activity to get attention of

Susan Noone Riddle

someone; satan's fall; powers that are demonic; intense, sudden power; miracle that interrupt's time; the judgment of God; devastation; rapid ruin. *(Luke 10: 17-18; Dan. 10: 6; Ex. 19: 16; Ez. 1: 14; Matt. 24: 27; 28: 3; Rev. 8: 5; 11: 19; 16: 18)*

Lion: **See Animals, Reptiles, Insects and Birds**.

Lips: **See also Mouth**: Producing spiritual fruit; offer prayer, praise and worship; can be used to: tempt; adulate; bring a charge against; speak falsehood. *(Prov. 7: 21; 10: 19-21; 18: 6; Heb. 13: 15; Ps. 12: 2-3; 34: 13; 51: 15; 63: 5; 66: 14; 71: 23; 119: 13; 140: 3-9; Josh. 2: 10)*

Lost: Inability to find the way to Jesus; in need of guidance; confused over a certain situation. *(Col. 2: 8; John 6: 12; Jer. 15: 16)*

M

Machines: Productive Kingdom work of the Spirit; unproductive of the flesh. *(Ecc. 7: 29; Matt. 12: 36; Rom. 7: 5)*

Man: **See People**: **also for (unknown person)**: Old Man and Foreigner:

Moving Van: **See Vehicles**.

In A Dream, In A Vision of the Night
Job 33:15-18

Manna: Jesus as the bread of life that came down from heaven; provision; bread; Spirit lead preaching; the glory of God. *(Ex. 16: 14-15; Du. 8: 3; John 6: 30-57; Rev. 2: 17)*

Map: Directive commandment; path of important; instructions; recommendation. *(Prov. 6: 23)*

Marble: The majesty of the Kingdom of God. *(1 Chron. 29: 2; Esther 1: 6; Songs 5: 15; Rev. 18: 12)*

Mark: Something being set apart; a symbol of preservation; identification; mark of God on the forehead; mark of the beast. *(Ge. 4: 15; Ez. 9: 4-6; Rom. 16: 17; Rev. 13: 16-17; 14: 9-11; 15: 2; 16: 2; 22: 4)*

Marriage: **See also Bride and Groom**: A covenant being entered into; the joining of Jesus and the Bride of Christ; the church; agreement; joined; one in agreement; union of the Lord and Israel; could be natural marriage; not entering into marriage: interference in intimacy with the Lord. *(Gen. 1: 26-28; 2: 21-25; Matt. 19: 4-6; Eph. 5: 31-32; Nem. 13: 27; Rev. 2: 12)*

Susan Noone Riddle

Meat: Strong doctrine both good or evil. *(Ps. 42: 3; John 6: 27; 1 Cor. 3: 2; 10: 3; Heb. 5: 12-14; Job 6: 7; 20: 14)*

Mercy Seat: Rest; position; concentration; receiving; place of authority; inner court of the temple; throne of God; satanic powers; chair; atonement; place where God and man meet; Kingship of the Lord. *(Rev. 13: 2; Ps. 1: 1; 7: 7; Job 23: 3; 2 Chron. 9: 18; 19: 8; Matt. 17: 19; Heb. 9: 5-12; Ex. 25: 22; 29: 42-43; 1 John 2: 2; Num. 7: 89; Rom. 3: 24-25; 2 Cor. 5: 20; 1 Tim. 2: 5)*

Microphone: Voice of God; prophetic ministry; tremendous ability to impact a situation in the Spirit; power to bring about change. *(Matt. 10: 27)*

Microscope: Careful inspection of one's self, someone or something else; clear-sightedness; magnifying a problem. *(1 Cor. 11: 28)*

Microwave Oven: Left over preaching instead of fresh Spirit-filled Word; not willing to wait for the real thing; looking for the easy way out. *(Rom. 9: 28)*

Milk: Foundational teachings; baby's nourishment; ample supply; doctrine that is

In A Dream, In A Vision of the Night
Job 33:15-18

uncorrupted. *(1 Peter 2: 2; Heb. 5: 12-13; 1 Cor. 3: 2)*

Mirror: The Word of God; looking into self; looking back; reflecting on something; egotism, seeing through a glass darkly; knowing in part. *(1 Cor. 13: 12; Prov. 27: 19)*

Miscarriage: Judgment that was sent forth wrongfully; death or loss of the seed of ministry through trauma; a plan aborted. *(Hos. 9: 14; James 1: 15; Hab. 1: 4)*

Money: Talents that are natural; spiritual or natural wealth; powerful authority; man's strength; greed. *(Du. 8: 18; Gen. 31: 15; Luke 19: 23; 1 Tim. 6: 10; Jer. 7: 8-11; Ho. 19: 5; Ecc. 7: 12; Luke 16: 11)*

Moon: The body of Christ, things that are eternal; God's faithfulness; reign over; used as an object of worship in the occult and underworld stories; that which the works of darkness demonstrated through; indication of end times. *(Gen. 1: 16; 37: 9; Eph. 1: 3; Jer. 31: 35-37; Du. 33: 14; Is. 30: 26; Mark 13: 24; Acts 2: 20; 2 Kings 23: 5; Phil. 2: 15; Rev. 12: 1; Ps. 129: 6)*

Moon to Blood, The church being prosecuted; light in darkness; sign of the Son of Man; church shining in the darkness.

Morning: A new age; the rising sun; the return of the Lord; light of the Lord; exposing the sins of man; a time of mercy and kindness; rejoice. *(Ps. 30: 5; 92: 2; 130: 6; Mark 16: 2; Hos. 6: 4; Zeph. 3: 5; Lam. 3: 22-23; Rev. 2: 27-28)*

Mother: **See People**: **also for**

Mother-in-law: **See People**: **also for Father-in-law**.

Motor: **See Vehicles**: **also for Engine and Battery**.

Motorcycle: **See Vehicles**.

Mountain: **Also see Tower, Skyscraper, Hill, Up and Elevator**: Great power and strength; place of protection; grandeur and glory; wholeness and solidity; kingdom built by man or built by God; elevate; obstacle; difficulty; face bravely; transfiguration; place of prophecy; place of agony; nation. *(Josh. 14: 12; Acts 1: 13-14; 20: 7-8; Ps. 103: 11; 1 Sam. 9: 12-14; Matt 5; 1 Kings 18; 12: 31; John 3: 7; James 3: 15, 17; Heb. 1: 3; 1 Thess. 4: 13-18; 1 Cor. 13: 2; Luke 21: 21; Is. 8: 18; 27: 13; 31: 4; 40: 9; 44: 23; Rev. 6: 14)*

In A Dream, In A Vision of the Night
Job 33:15-18

Mouth: **See also Lips**: Words; speaking evil; speaking the Word. *(Prov. 2: 6; 8: 7; Col. 3: 8, 28; Ps. 62: 4; 63: 5-11; Eph. 6: 9; Rev. 19: 15-21)*

Moving: Transformation in ministry; or job; dissatisfaction with where you are. *(Ez. 12: 3; Gen. 11: 31; 12: 1-3; Acts 7: 2-4)*

Music: Worship of oneself, God, or an object; idol worship; the abundance of the heart overflowing; cheerfulness and joy; praise; prophesying; Spiritual gifts flowing; temptation to sin; mesmerized; seduced; words are important to know what the message is; entertainment; teaching; admonishing; edifying. *(Ez. 33: 32; Dan. 3: 5; Is. 5: 1; Jer. 7: 34; Gen. 31: 27; Matt. 9: 18, 23; Ex. 15: 20-21; 2 Chron. 5: 11-13; Eph. 5: 19; Col. 3: 16)*

Mustard Seed: **See also Seed**: The Word of God; Sowing it: faith. *(Matt. 13: 31; 17: 20; Mark 4: 31; Luke 13: 19; 17: 6)*

N

Nails: Words that are fastened in the memory; constant; permanent; incapable of being moved; unyielding; something that is affixed. *(Ez. 12: 11; Is. 22: 20-25; 41: 1-7; Col. 2: 14; Jer. 10: 4; 1 Chron. 22: 3; Ecc. 12: 11)*

Name: Notability; designate; rank or status; individualism; jurisdiction; notoriety; personage; look up what the name means; could be about the person in the dream; a person with a similar name or same initial or similar personality. *(Hos. 1: 9; Gen. 11: 4; Matt. 1: 21; Mark 14: 61; Rev. 2: 17; 3: 12)*

Nation: **See Places: also for Country**.

Neck: **See also Yoke**: Obstinate; reluctance to believe truth; control; to reign; servitude. *(Jer. 17: 23; Gen. 27: 40; 41: 42; Prov. 29: 1; Hos. 10: 11; Gen. 27: 40; Ex. 13: 13; Du. 28: 48; 31: 27; Is. 8: 9; Song 7: 4)*

Nest: Tabernacle made by oneself; security that is not real; not in the correct location; to be in need of help; God's place of rest. *(Ps. 84: 3; Prov. 27: 8; Is. 10: 14; 16: 2; 34: 15; Jer. 22: 23; Num. 24: 21-22; Matt 8: 20; Job 29: 18)*

Net: To ensnare; plans of an enemy; entrap; winning souls; the superior plan of God;

In A Dream, In A Vision of the Night
Job 33:15-18

flattery serves as a net; the plans of evil men to destroy. *(Ps. 9: 15; 10: 9; 57: 6; 31: 4; Job 19: 6; Prov. 1: 17; 29: 5; Ez. 12: 13; 17: 20; Matt. 13: 47; John 21: 6-11)*

Newspaper: Proclamation of peace or turmoil; events that are vital; something being laid open that one desire to be hidden; prophetic utterance; evil carrying of news in the form of slander. *(Luke 2: 8-18; 8: 17; Is. 52: 7; 61: 1-3)*

Night: Absence of the Spirit; trial; real lack of understanding; hidden thought or event; sin; show of the glory of God; judgment; seeing truth through a glass darkly; time for singing; time of partying; drunkenness; and doing evil deeds; time when evil spirits may gain entrance. *(John 3: 2; 9: 4; 11: 10; 12: 35; Luke 5: 5; 22: 53; 1 Thess. 5: 5-7; Rev. 8: 12; 21: 25; 22: 5; Rom. 13: 11; Micah 3: 6; Is. 5: 11; Ps. 19: 10; 42: 8; 104: 20-22; Matt. 2: 12-19)*

Nine: **See Numbers**.

Nineteen: **See Numbers**.

Noise: Something that is intrusive; loud noise, alarm; irritation; sound of loud, powerful music; battle sounds; feelings of having little value; resistance that is dynamic; sudden fright. *(Ex. 32: 17; Is. 31: 4; Jer. 46: 17; Amos 5: 3; Jer. 47: 3; Prov. 21: 19)*

North: Great power; exalted and majestic; Spiritual judgment by God; where heaven is; warring in the Spirit; taking an inheritance and possessing it; the throne of God. *(Job 26: 7; 37: 9; Prov. 25: 23; Is. 14: 13; 41: 25; Ps. 48: 2; 89: 12; 107: 3; Jer. 1: 13-14; 4: 6; Dan. 11: 6-44)*

Nose: The Spirit or breathe of Life; the power of God; His ultimate control; to seek to gratify abundantly; a pleasant or unpleasant odor; a gossiper. *(1 Peter 4: 15; Prov. 30: 30-33; Ps. 11: 6; 18: 8; 133: 2; Job 4: 9; 27: 3;39: 20; 2 Kings 19: 28; Ex. 15: 8; 2 Sam. 22: 9, 16; Is. 31: 4; Jer. 46: 1)*

O-P

Oil: Extravagance in use; the anointing; prosperity; complete joy; love one to another; grace; Holy Spirit. *(James 5: 14; Ps. 23: 5; Is. 61: 1; 55: 21; 1 John 2: 20, 27; Luke 4: 17; Lev. 2: 1-2; Du. 32: 13; 33:*

In A Dream, In A Vision of the Night
Job 33:15-18

24; 2 Cor. 1: 21; Acts 19: 38; Prov. 5: 3; 21: 17; Matt. 25: 4; 1 Sam. 10: 1)

Old Man: **See People**.

One: **See Numbers**: **also for First**.

One hundred: **See Numbers**.

One hundred and Fifty: **See Numbers**.

One hundred and Fifty-three: **See Numbers**.

One hundred and forty-four: **See Numbers**.

One hundred and forty-four thousand: **See Numbers**.

One hundred and Twenty: **See Numbers**.

Orange: **See Colors**: **also for Peach and Tan**.

Oven: Matters of the heart; fervency of heat; fantasy of the heart; thinking on something. *(Hos. 7:4-6; Luke 12: 28; Mal. 4: 1; Matt. 6: 30; Ex. 8: 3; Ps. 21: 9; 1 Cor. 7: 9)*

Painting: To revamp or renew something; to create something out of nothing. *(1 Peter 4: 8; Matt. 23: 27; Titus 3: 5; Acts 18: 24)*

Park: **See Places**: **also for Garden and Yard**.

Path: **See also Highway**: Way; direction of life; For evil doers: is dark and crooked; ends in death; is caused to be hard by the Lord; plagued with evil; For the lover of God and His ways: private walk with God; smooth; in peace; righteous; filled with contentment; to be safe; falsehood; discernment that is spiritually off. *(Jer. 6: 16; Heb. 3: 10; 12: 13; Ps. 17: 5; 23: 3; 25: 10; 27: 11; 65: 11; Prov. 1: 15-16; 2: 13, 18-20; 3: 17; 4: 18; 12: 28; Job 6: 18; 24: 13; 13: 27; 30: 13)*

Pearl: Truth in the things of the Spirit; glory of heaven; the purified people of God; the embellishment of the things of the world; developed because of trials. *(Matt. 7: 6; 13: 45-46; Rev. 17: 4; 21: 21)*

Pen/pencil: Words that are permanently resistant to fading; contract; accordance; enter into a formal agreement; to pledge one's complete bond; to bring to public notice; record; a fixed documented record of something. *(Ps. 45: 1; Job 13: 26; Jer. 8: 8)*

Perfume: The glory of God; fragrance of death that deceives; fragrance of the redeemed; spiritual allurement. *(Prov. 7: 17-18; Song 3: 6; Ecc. 10: 1; Ps. 45: 8;)*

Picture: To bring to mind; former time of undergoing something in particular; a significant occurrence; imagination; to bring to remembrance; something hidden brought to light. *(Num. 33: 52; Heb. 9: 14; Ez. 23: 40)*

Frames: Mind set.

In A Dream, In A Vision of the Night
Job 33:15-18

Old frame: Dated.

Pig: **See Animals, Reptiles, Insects and Birds: also for Sow and Swine**.

Pillar: Physical or spiritual might; soundness in leadership, support of the earth; someone who is important; people of foundational truths; the presence of God; believer in God; the feet of angels. *(Gal. 2: 9; Rev. 3: 12; 10: 1; Jer. 1: 18; 1 Tim. 3: 15; Song 5: 15; Job 9: 6)*

Pink: **See Red, Tan and Orange (Peach)**.

Pit: **See Places**.

Play: Worship; idolatry; covetousness; true worship; deeds that are evil; spiritual warfare; striving; competition. *(1 Cor. 9: 24; 10: 7; Is. 11: 8; Ps. 104: 26; 2 Sam. 6: 45, 21; Col. 3: 5)*

Platter: Delivering something evil as a victory (John the Baptist head on a platter); hypocrisy; externalize. *(Matt. 14: 8, 11; 23: 25-26; Num. 7: 13)*

Plow: Cultivate by means of separation; cracked; unremitting sin; to be afflicted; getting ready for implanting; turning away: activity that is corrupt; to resolve steadily; not fit for kingdom when turning back; the work of the ministry; total destruction; to do wrong. *(Hos. 10: 11-13; Jer. 4: 3; 26: 18; Judges 14: 18; Luke 9: 62; Ps. 129: 3; Is. 28: 24-25; Prov. 20: 5; 21: 4; Job 4: 8; 1 Cor. 9: 10; Amos 6: 12; 9: 13)*

Poison: Deadly, evil teachings. *(Ps. 58: 4; 140: 3; Du. 32: 33; Rom. 3: 13; James 3: 8)*

Police: **See People**: **also for Guard, Lawyer and Judge**.

Postage Stamp: Seal; authority; authorization; small or seemingly insignificant; but powerful. *(Esther 8: 8; John 6: 27)*

Pot: (Bowl and Pan): Vessel; doctrine; tradition; a determination or resolve; quick devastation; totally transformed; the destruction of a nation; to be punished without mercy; form of truth; a person. *(Rom. 2: 20; Ex. 25: 29; Jer. 1: 13; Zech. 14: 20-21; Mic 3: 2-3; Ps. 58: 9; 2 Kings 21: 13; 1 Thess. 4: 3-5)*

Preacher and/or Pastor: **See People**: **also for Priest and Prophet**.

Pregnancy: **See also Baby**: Seed of the Word conceived; His prophetic Word to the church and to us personally planted, growing, ready to be birthed; something in progress of happening or being birthed; sin

In A Dream, In A Vision of the Night
Job 33:15-18

or righteousness; anticipation; expectancy. *(Jer. 1: 4-5; Gal. 1: 15; Is. 66: 9; James 1: 15; Mark 13: 8)*

Labor pains: Trials.

Prison: **See Places**.

Pumpkin: Witchcraft; deception; snare; witch; trick. *(Psalm 21: 11)*

Purple: **See Colors**.

Purse or Wallet: Treasure; heart; personal identity; precious; valuable; *(Matt. 6: 21; 12: 35; John 12: 6)*

When empty; spiritually bankrupt.

Q-R

Rabbit: **See Animals, Reptiles, Insects and Birds: also for Hare**.

Radio: Continuous; unrelenting; unceasing; unbelieving; tradition; important news; broadcasting the gospel; hearing God. *(Prov. 9: 13; 27: 15)*

Tower: Broadcast; truth or error; gospel.

Raft: **See Vehicles**.

Rags: **Also Sackcloth**: Poverty, humility. *(Is. 64: 6; Jer. 38: 11-13; Prov. 23: 21)*

Railroad track: Tradition; unchanging; habit; stubborn; gospel; caution; danger. *(Mark 7: 9, 13; Col. 2: 8; 2 Thess. 2: 15; 3: 6)*

Rain: God's blessings; God's Word and Spirit outpoured; life; revival; Holy Spirit; trial; disappointment; the outpouring of blessings; the judgment of the last days. *(Ps. 11: 6; James 5: 7; 72: 6; Hos. 10: 12; Zech. 10: 1; Is. 55: 10-11; Matt. 7: 24-27; Jer. 3: 3)*

    Drought: Blessings withheld because of sin; without God's presence.

Rainbow: God's covenant with man; beast and the earth; promise that the storm is over; His throne and glory. *(Gen. 9: 12-17; Rev. 4: 3; 10: 1)*

Reap: Fruitfulness because of acts; harvest; judgment of the last days; reaping what one has sowed; perverse or uprightness deeds being rewarded. *(1 Cor. 9: 6, 11; Prov. 22: 8; Hos. 8: 7;10: 13; Rev. 14: 14-16; Gal. 6: 8-9; Lev. 26: 5; John 4: 35-38; Matt. 6: 26; 13 30-43; :25: 26)*

Red: **See Colors**: **also Scarlet and Crimson**.

Reed: Spiritually weak person; fallen flesh; affliction through trial. *(Is. 42:3; 2 Kings*

In A Dream, In A Vision of the Night
Job 33:15-18

18: 21; Matt. 11: 7; 26: 41; Ez. 42: 15-20; Luke 7: 24)

Refrigerator: Heart; motive; attitude; thoughts. *(Matt. 12: 35; Mark 7: 21-22)*

    Stored food: Memories stored in the heart.

    Spoiled food: Harboring a grudge; unclean thoughts and desires.

Refuge: Protection; shelter from death and affliction. *(Heb. 6: 18-19; Ps. 46: 1; 9: 9; 142: 5; Du. 33: 27; Is. 4: 5-6)*

Reins: Symbols of motives of the heart; pull to a halt; stop what you're doing. *(Ps. 7: 9; 26: 2; 73: 21; Is. 11: 5; J ob 19: 27; Rev. 2: 23)*

Rend: Anger; deep grief; repenting of sin discord and disunity. *(Matt. 7: 6; 9: 16; 26: 65; Luke 5: 36; 1 Sam. 28: 17; Joel 2: 13)*

Rest: Refreshing; ceasing from activity; relaxation; too relaxed; not paying attention; insolent behavior; being slothful; complete salvation. *(Ps. 132: 8, 14; Is. 11: 10; 14: 63: 14; Gen. 18: 4; Matt. 11: 28-30; Matt. 26: 45; Heb. 4: 3-11)*

Restaurant: **See Places**: **also for Cafeteria and Kitchen**.

Right: Natural (instead of spiritual) authority; power; man's strength in the flesh; or the power of God revealed through flesh (as in the body of Christ); accepted. *(Gen. 48: 18; Ex. 15: 6; Matt. 5: 29-30; 25: 33; 1 Peter 3: 22)*

Right turn: A natural change.

Ring: **See also Circle and Ring**: Covenant relationship; good community standing; Kingdom authority; never ending; prestige; unchanging; uninterrupted. *(James 2: 2; Esther 1: 6; 3: 12; 8: 8; Gen. 41: 42; James 2: 2; Luke 15: 22; Ex. 25: 12-27; Is. 40: 22)*

> **Wedding Ring**: Covenant in marriage with man and woman, or God and man.
>
> **Engagement ring**: Promise of commitment.
>
> **Rings worn as jewelry**: Self glorification.

River: **See also Brook, Sea and Waters**: Flow of life; Spirit or life; sin; wickedness; prosperity of God's people; judgment; righteousness; trial. *(John 7: 38-39; Ez. 47: 5; Amos 5: 24; Prov. 18: 4; 21: 1; Job 6: 15; 20: 17; Jer. 50: 38; Ps. 36: 8; 46: 4; 110: 7; Is. 19: 6; 32: 2; 41: 18; 43: 2)*

In A Dream, In A Vision of the Night
Job 33:15-18

> **Deep**: Depths of the Spirit; deep calls unto deep.
>
> **Muddy**: Flesh (dust) mixed with water (spirit).
>
> **Dangerous currents**: Not good for swimming in the Spirit; difficult; impassable; stay away because of danger.

River that is dry: Void of Spirit and life; legalism; traditional worship empty of power; in need of repentance.

Robe: Righteousness. *(Ex. 28: 31-34; Rev. 7: 9-14; Is. 61: 10)*

Rock: **See also Stone**: Safe refuge; the base of the assembling of the believers; to be buried or covered in Christ; the stone that causes stumbling. *(Ex. 17: 5-6; 33: 18-23; Job 24: 8; Matt. 7: 24-25; 16: 18; John 4: 14; 7: 37-39; 1 Cor. 10: 4-5; Ps. 31: 3; 95: 1; Is. 2: 10; 8: 14; 32: 2; Rev. 22: 17)*

Rocket: **See Vehicles**.

Rocking Chair: Intercession; recollection; prayer; relaxation. *(Jer. 6: 16)*

Rod: **Also Staff and Scepter**: Governing anointing; mercy seat; to gauge; fruit bearing; authority; discipline. *(Is. 9: 4; 14:*

Susan Noone Riddle

> 5, 29; 11: 1; Mic. 5: 1; 1 Cor. 4: 21; Ps. 2: 9; 110: 2; Rev. 19: 15; Ez. 42: 15-20; Prov. 13: 24; 26: 3)

Roller Coaster: **See Vehicles**.

Roller Skates: **See also Shoes**: Gliding; speed; fast; swift advancement or progress; skillful walk with God. *(Rom. 9: 28)*

Roof: **See also Upstairs and Attic**: The mind; meditation; logic or natural; shield or covering of protection; heavenly revelation; prayer; declaration; complete overview; ability to see all, both good and evil. *(Acts 10: 9; Matt. 10: 27; Luke 12: 3; 2 Sam. 11: 2; Is. 30: 1)*

Root: The origin of something; originating from King David; disposition; ungodly attitudes and moral values that ROOT into man's heart: evil at it's origin; bitterness; love of money; low self-esteem; fearfulness; rebelliousness; Godly values in the heart, such as: steadfastness; pure motive; reason; conviction; fixed. *(Matt. 3: 10; 1 Tim. 6: 10; Ps. 80: 9; 1 Tim. 6: 10; Heb. 12: 15; Is. 11: 1, 10; 14: 29; 53: 2; Jer. 12: 2; Judges 5: 14; Is. 14: 3; 1 Kings 14: 15; 2*

In A Dream, In A Vision of the Night
Job 33:15-18

Kings 19: 30; Hos. 14: 5; Eph. 3: 17; Rom. 11: 16; Rev. 5: 5; 22: 16)

Rope or (Cord): Bond in covenant; to pledge; deliverance; to tie yourself to something healthy or unhealthy. *(Prov. 5: 22; Ps. 118: 27; Is. 5: 18; Acts 27: 32; Judges 16: 11-12; 1 Kings 20: 31)*

Round (shape): **See also Circle and Ring**: Favor with God; love and mercy. *(Lev. 19: 9-10, 27; Is. 40: 22; Esther 1: 6; 8: 8; James 2: 2; Luke 15: 22; Ex. 25: 12-27)*

    IF Moving: Following the Spirit (like wheels).

Rowboat: **See Vehicles**.

Rowing: Striving to get somewhere; hard work; intercessory prayer; to travail in the Spirit. *(Mark 6: 48; Phil. 2: 30)*

Rug: Protection from cold; protection for foundation or floor; cover up. *(Mark 4: 22; 2 Cor. 4: 2)*

Running: Quick reaction; toiling; to labor over one's salvation; flee from truth; the race of serving the Lord and believing. *(1 Cor. 9: 24; Jer. 12: 5; Prov. 1: 6; Rev. 9: 9; 1 Cor. 9: 24; Is. 40: 31)*

S

Sacrifice: Bloodshed; one laying down their life in death for another; paying a high price; Old Testament: animal sacrifice covered sin; New Testament: Jesus Christ shed His blood once in for all; praise. *(Lev. Chapters 1 through 7; Is. 53: 7; Titus 2: 14; Heb. 10: 1-10; John 10: 18; Eph. 5: 2; Col. 4: 6; 1 Tim. 2: 5)*

Sailboat: **See Vehicles**.

Salt: Purity; protection from sin and evil; covenant that never ends; unfruitfulness which leaves a void; that which remains and is lasting; seasoning; acceptable; leaving a good and lasting impression; immorality; careful speaking; well being within; God's final judgment; monument as a memorial; rejected; Godliness; divine nature. *(Du. 29: 23; Matt. 5: 13; Mark 9: 49-50; 2 Chron. 13: 5; Lev. 2: 13; Num. 18: 19; Du. 29: 23; Col. 4: 6; Ezra 6: 9; 2 Chron. 13: 5; Gen. 19: 26; Ez. 47: 11)*

Salt Water: Spirit of the world; unclean; source of evil.

In A Dream, In A Vision of the Night
Job 33:15-18

Sand: **See also Seed**: Flesh; poor foundation; the descendants of someone; the Lord's thoughts about us; weak and faulty foundation; hard work; obstacle; multitudes of people; seed; spiritual and earthly seed of Abraham; multitudes that are unsaved. *(Matt. 7: 26-27; Prov. 27: 3; Heb. 12: 1; Rom. 9: 27; Rev. 13: 1; 20: 8; Ps. 78: 27; 139: 18; Gen. 13: 16; 22: 17; 32: 12)*

Sanctuary: Tent, Tabernacle, House and Temple: God's abode in men of clay; tabernacle; the dwelling place of God; where the Lord dwells in heaven; His habitation in the body of Christ; God's household; heaven; the believer. *(Heb. 8: 2; 9: 23-24; 13: 11; Ex. 25: 8-9; Amos 7: 9; Ps. 20: 2; 102: 19; 150: 1; Lev. 21: 23; 26: 31; Jer. 51: 51; Eph. 2: 19-22; 1 Cor. 6: 19; John 1: 14)*

Scepter: **Also see Rod and Staff**: Authority of the believer. *(Is. 9: 4; 14: 5; Mic. 5: 1; 1 Cor. 4: 21; Ps. 2: 9; Rev. 11: 1-2; 19: 15; Ez. 42: 15-20; Prov. 13: 24; 26: 3; Gen. 49: 10; Heb. 1: 8)*

School: **See Places**: **also for Classroom**: **also for different types of schools and areas of instruction**.

Scorpion: **See Animals, Reptiles, Insects and Birds**.

Sea: **See also Brook, Waters and River**: People; false-hearted teachers of the Word of God; nations of the world; gentiles; obstacle; unsettled multitude of humanity; the through faith; fast progress; right standing with God; the Gospel being increased and sent forth. *(Is. 11: 9; 48: 18; 60: 5; Ps. 68: 22; Jude 13; James 3: 11-12; Rev. 4: 6; 15: 2)*

Sea of glass: Peace; stillness before the throne of God; transparency.

Seacoast: Borderland; confinements of the emotions and will. *(Jer. 5: 22; 47: 6-7)*

Seal: Covenant that is binding and can be either evil or good; mark of God (seal on forehead) or satan (666). *(Rev. 7: 2; 20: 3; Dan. 12: 4; Songs 8: 6; Rom. 4: 11; 2 Tim. 2: 19)*

Seat: **See also Chair and Throne**: Power; position of authority; rulership; rest; concentration; receiving; place of authority; inner court of the temple; throne of God; satanic powers; mercy seat; Kingship of the Lord. *(Rev. 13: 2; Ps. 1: 1; 7: 7; Job 23: 3; 2 Chron. 9: 18; 19: 8; Matt. 17: 19; Heb. 9:*

5-12; Ex. 25: 22; 29: 42-43; 1 John 2: 2; Num. 7: 89; Rom. 3: 24-25; 2 Cor. 5: 20; 1 Tim. 2: 5)

Seed: The Word of God; Christ; sin that has been conceived; fruit of the Spirit; man's word; descendants; to be reborn in Jesus; blessings that are spiritual in nature. *(1 Cor. 9: 11; 15: 36-38; Gen. 1: 11-12; 3: 15; 13: 15; Matt. 13: 38; Luke 6: 45; 17: 6)*

Serpent: **See Animals, Reptiles, Insects and Birds: also for Snake**.

Seven: **See Numbers**.

Seventeen: **See Numbers**.

Seventy: **See Numbers**.

Seventy-five: **See Numbers**.

Sewage: Dishonesty; defiled flesh; perverse authority that is exploited. *(Is. 4: 4; Du. 23: 13-14; Gal. 6: 8)*

Sewing: Joining; union; reunion; counseling; revalidation of a relationship. *(1 Sam. 18: 1)*

Shadow: Covered by the Lord for safety; to be protected; the time of the Old Covenant; an example of something else; transitional events bringing change; brevity. *(Ecc. 8: 13; Heb. 10: 1; Luke 1: 79; Matt. 4: 16; Job 3: 5; 8: 9; 10: 21-22; James 1: 17; Col.*

2: 17; Ps. 17: 8; 23: 4; 36: 7; 57: 1; 63: 7; 91: 1; 102: 11-14)

Dark shadows: demons.

Sheep: **See Animals, Reptiles, Insects and Birds: also for Lamb**.

Shepherd: Christ, God; Eldership; separation of goats and sheep; position for the prophetic to occur; A just one: full of faith; not self centered; believes the Word; considers others; no fear; An unjust one: self-centered, not faithful; unprincipled; faint-hearted; disbelieving. *(Ez. 34: 1-31; Heb. 13: 20; John 10: 1-18; 1 Peter 5: 4; Jer. 23: 1-5; Is. 40: 10-11; 56: 11-12; Ex. 2: 17-19; Jer. 50: 6; Gen. 31: 38-40; 33: 13-14; 1 Sam. 17: 34; Luke 2: 8-20; John 10: 12-13)*

Shield: Saving grace; God's truth; protection; faith. *(Gen. 15: 1; Ps. 3: 3; 5: 12; 18: 35; 28: 7; 33: 20; 59: 11; 84: 9-11; 91: 4; 115: 9-10; 119: 114; Eph. 6: 16; Du. 33: 29; 2 Sam. 22: 3)*

Ship: **See Vehicles: also including different types and speeds**.

Shoes/Boots/Sandals: To be alert; a person's words; prepared to share the gospel (see more below). *(Eph. 6: 15; Ruth 4: 7; Josh. 5: 15;*

In A Dream, In A Vision of the Night
Job 33:15-18

Gal. 5: 16; Luke 3: 16; Ex. 3: 5; 12: 11; Ruth 4: 7-8; Is. 5: 27; Du. 33: 25; Song 7: 1; 1 Kings 2: 5)

Boots: Warring in the Spirit.

Giving them away: A way to validate something.

High Heels: Seduction; discomfort; walking tall in a manner.

Need of Shoes: Mourning.

New Shoes: Changing direction. Calling may be redirected to a "new and fresh" thing.

Putting them on: Preparation for a journey.

Slippers: Too comfortable.

Snowshoes: Faith; walking in the Spirit; supported by faith in the Word of God.

Taking them off: Honoring God; ministering to the Lord.

Taking someone else's off: To show respect.

Tennis Shoes: Running the race; comfort; Spiritually sports minded, like "playing games"; or "staying fit."

Shopping Center: **See Places**: **also for Marketplace**.

Shoulder: Strength; government; to be a servant; assist; carrier of burdens; Kingdom authority; safety; also road shoulder can represent the same things. *(Ps. 81: 6; Is. 9: 6; Zech. 7: 11; Is. 9: 4; 10: 27; 22: 22;46: 7; Luke 15: 5; Ez. 2: 4; 24: 4-5; 29: 7; 2 Chron. 36: 13; Du. 31: 27; Ex. 12: 34; 28: 10-12)*

Broad Shoulders: Strong authority and ability to carry large burdens.

Drooped shoulders: Defeated attitude; overworked, over tired,;burned out.

Shovel: acknowledgment of wrong; ashes that are being removed; speaking ill of a brother or sister; digging up something. *(2 Kings 3: 16-17; Du. 23: 13; Prov. 16: 27; 26: 27; Ex. 27: 3; Is. 30: 24)*

Sickle: Reaping what has been sowed; God's Word; the harvest. *(Mark 4: 26-29; Du. 16: 9; Joel 3: 13; Rev. 14: 14-19)*

Sieve: To set apart one from another; the chaff and wheat being separated; tried and instituted. *(Am. 9: 9; Is. 30: 28; Luke 22: 31)*

Sign: Something that is of spiritual importance that indicates something requested; witness of something; miraculous marker; the wonderment of God; validation of the prophetic; a memorial to the blessings of

In A Dream, In A Vision of the Night
Job 33:15-18

God; confirmation of the Word of God; a sure promise fulfilled. *(1 Kings 13: 3-5; 2 Kings 19: 28-29; 20: 5-11; Heb. 2: 4; Hos. 12: 10; Du. 13: 1; 26: 8; Josh. 24: 15-17; Is. 7: 11; Judges 6: 17; 1 Sam. 2: 31-34; Ps. 65: 8; 1 Cor. 10: 32)*

Crossroad or Intersection: Time to make a decision about a change.

Stop Sign: Stop and pray for guidance.

Yield: A sign of submission!

Silver: **See Metals**: **also gray in Colors**.

Singing: **See also Song**: Rejoicing; thanksgiving; warfare intercession; overflow of the redeemed; one may sing in: victory; when imprisoned; in revelry; praise; worship of God or of idols. *(Ps. 7: 17; 9: 2; 13: 6; 18: 49; 21: 13; 27: 6; James 5: 13; Ex. 15: 1; Is. 12: 5; 23: 16-19)*

Sister: **See People**: **also for Brother**.

Sister-in-law: **See People**: **also for Brother-in-Law**.

Six: **See Numbers**.

Six-Six-Six: **See Numbers**.

Sixteen: **See Numbers**.

Skiing: Assistance provided by the power of through faith. *(John 6: 19-21; Matt. 14: 29-31)*

Skins: Death's seal; deceptive attitude; covering. *(Num. 4: 1-25; Ex. 26: 14; Josh. 9: 4; Job 19: 26; Jer. 13: 23; Lev. 13: 1-46; Gen. 3: 21; 27: 16)*

Sky: God's presence; judgment; righteousness. *(Jer. 51: 9; Ps. 18: 11; Is. 45: 8)*

Skyscraper: **See Places**: **also for Tower, Ascend, Up, Mountain, Hills and Elevator**.

Sleep: Death; state of rest; not conscience or aware of things needed to be tended to; lack of knowledge; danger; refreshing; spiritual lethargy; indifference; when unable to sleep: working too hard; worry; working in the flesh; in a state of watchfulness. *(Is. 29: 10; Rom. 13: 11; Ps. 127: 2; Prov. 20: 13)*

    Overslept: Missed a divine meeting with God.

Smile: To show kindness; to be charitable; to go about doing good; to try and fool someone with an outward appearance. *(Prov. 18: 24)*

Smoke: Manifested presence of God; to manifest something; God's glory; praise and prayer; the life of man; lying or boasting; to be offended; uneasiness of spiritual things; to be blinded by smoke; attempt to hide. *(Is. 6: 4; 34: 8-10; 65: 5; Ps. 102: 3; 119: 83;*

Prov. 21: 24; 1 Cor. 8: 1; Du. 29: 19-20; Gen. 15: 17; 19: 28;31: 40; Dan. 2: 1; Rev. 8: 4; 15: 8)

Snake: **See Animals, Reptiles, Insects and Birds: also for Serpent**

Snare: Idol worship; trap of the devil; man's fear of other men; immorality; swift devastation; overcome by evil; to bring into bondage. *(2 Tim. 2: 26; Prov. 6: 2; 29: 25; Luke 21: 34-35; Ps. 9: 16; 18: 5; 91: 3; Hos. 9: 8; Judges 2: 3; 1 Tim. 6: 9; Ex. 10: 7; Ecc. 7: 26; 2 Sam. 22: 6; Is. 8: 14-15; 1 Kings 11: 4)*

Snow and Ice: **See also White**: Wicked nations; risen Lord; angel of the Lord; redeemed believer; totally pure; covered with forgiveness and the purity of the Word. *(Is. 1: 18; 55: 10-11; Job 16: 3-4; Rev. 1: 14; John; 6: 60; Ps. 51: 7; 147: 16; 73: 2; Dan. 7: 9)*

  Dirty Snow: No longer pure.

  Ice: Cold attitudes.

Soap: Forgiveness; act of total cleansing; intercession. *(Jer. 2: 22; Mal. 3: 2; Is. 1: 16)*

Socks: Protection for feet; not fully ready to share the Gospel in ministry. *(Eph. 6: 15; Gal. 5: 16; Ps. 24: 4)*

Susan Noone Riddle

White socks: Heart and walk before God that is unblemished.

Dirty socks: Heart and walk before God that is blemished.

Soldier: **See People**: **also for Guard and Police**.

Son: **See People**: **also for Daughter**.

Songs: **See also Singing**: Worship and praise; new song; to be filled with joy. *(Ps. 7: 17; 9: 2; 13: 6; 18: 49; 21: 13; 27: 6; 96: 1; 98: 1; James 5: 13; Ex. 15: 1; Is. 12: 5; 23: 16-19; Rev. 5: 9; 14: 3)*

Sour: Teaching that is false; carnality. *(Ez. 18: 2; Jer. 31: 29-30; Hos. 4: 18; Is. 18: 5)*

South: Tranquility; south wind opposes the North wind; place of refreshment; enemy's camp; temptation; natural as opposed to spiritual. *(Josh. 10: 40; Job 37: 9, 17; Acts 27: 13; 28: 13; Ps. 126: 4; Luke 12: 55)*

Sowing: Dispersing seed of the Word; seed can be righteous or evil; life everlasting. *(Gal. 6: 7-8; 2 Cor. 9: 6; Job 4: 8; Ps. 126: 5; Matt. 13: 3-9; 11-33; 37-53; Is. 55: 10; Mark 4: 1-20; Luke 13: 18-19)*

Spear: **See also Knife and Sword**: Sharp and penetrating; words formed against someone. *(Ps. 57: 4; John 19: 34)*

In A Dream, In A Vision of the Night
Job 33:15-18

Spider: **See Animals, Reptiles, Insects and Birds**.

Spot: Flawed; Jesus' death; instructors that are false; without spot: the church in true glory; made right in God's eyes; to obey. *(1 Peter 1: 19; Lev. 13: 1-3; Heb. 9: 14; 2 Peter 2: 13; 3: 14; Jude 12; Eph. 5: 27; 1 Tim. 6: 14)*

Sprinkle: Washing for cleansing; consecrating; to be made pure. *(1 Peter 1: 2; Lev. 1: 5-11; 14: 7; Heb. 9: 13; 10: 22)*

Square: Not open to truth; religious as in a form of Godliness but powerless; worldly; mercy seat; the altar of God; breastplate; the city of God; mercy seat. *(Lev. 16: 14-15; 19: 9; 2 Tim. 3: 5; Rev. 21: 16; Ex. 27: 1; 39: 8-9; Matt. 15: 9)*

Staff: **See Also Rod and Scepter**: Potency; direction. *(Is. 9: 4; Mic. 5: 1; 1 Cor. 4: 21; Ps. 2: 9; Rev. 19: 15; Ez. 42: 15-20; Prov. 13: 24; 26: 3)*

Stairs: **See also Elevator**: Steps; process of time; advancement; strong desire to reach a goal; procedure; position change; Jesus returning from the heavens to earth; symbolic of victory; Jesus being lifted up on the cross; wisdom that comes from above; Beatitudes in the Sermon on the Mount. If going up: moving up into the Spirit realm; elevated; Prophetic church of great revelation moving upward; high places of the Lord or of the flesh; moving above earthly experience; higher spiritual things; Mt. Zion; sacrifice of worship; Mt. Sinai and the Ark of the Covenant in the Temple; Songs of ascent unto Him; If going down: spiritual demotion; trial; backsliding. Tower of Babel; Mt. Carmel; dominance; control; obstacle; Spiritual decline; backslide; falling away; humility; prostration. *(Du. 22: 8; 2 Cor. 12: 18; Ps. 37: 31; Acts 1: 13-14; 20: 7-8; Ps. 103: 11; 1 Sam. 9: 12-14; Matt 5; 1 Kings 12: 31; 18; John 3: 7; James 3: 15, 17; Heb. 1: 3; 1 Thess. 4: 13-18)*

Down: Demotion; backslide; failure.

Guardrail: Safety; precaution; warning to be careful.

Standing: Incomplete task; virtue; standing on or committed to a point of view or belief. *(Acts 7: 55-56; Heb. 10: 11; Eph. 6: 13)*

Stars: The coming of the Lord; a false sense of well being; generations multiplied; Israel;

In A Dream, In A Vision of the Night
Job 33:15-18

saints of God; ministers of the gospel; people; the rising Lord Jesus; an apostle of God; dignitary or mentor. *(Gen. 1: 17; 15: 5; 22: 17; 37: 9-10; Dan. 12: 3; Ez. 32: 7; Obad. 4; Numbers 24: 7; Rev. 1: 16-20; 2: 28; 12: 4; 22: 16; Jude 13; 2 Peter 1: 19)*

Falling: Apostate church.

Stiff-necked: Obstinate; rebellion against authority; unyielding; domineering; desire to control situations or others. *(Ps. 75: 5; Ez. 2: 4; 2 Chron. 36: 13; Du. 31: 27)*

Stone: Sturdy; believer; witness of the Holy Spirit; the Word of God; good works; a believer; Jesus the chief cornerstone; unruliness; strength; allegation; a strong sense of rightness; persecution; disinterest; bearing false witness; defiance; a reprobate mind; foundation laid in Christ; a void or emptiness. *(Rev. 2: 17; Zech. 7: 12; Hab. 2: 11; Ez. 11: 19; Jer. 51: 26; Is. 28: 16; Dan. 2: 34-35; 1 Sam. 25: 37; 2 Sam. 16: 6-13; Josh. 24: 27; Lev. 20: 2-5; 27; 24: 15-23; Acts 1: 8; 1 Cor. 3: 12; Matt. 3: 12; 21: 42-44; 1 Peter 2: 5; Num. 15: 32-36; Du. 17: 2-7; 21: 18-21; 22: 22)*

Stoning someone: Adultery; idol worship; blasphemy; practicing forms of sorcery or witchcraft; giving children over to idols as a sacrifice; not honoring the sabbath; rebellion of the youth; apostasy.

Storm: **See also Clouds, Thunder, Tornado, Whirlwind and Wind**: Emotional turmoil; great mourning; commotion; transformation; warfare in the Spirit; judgment; sudden disaster or devastation; testing; trial at the hand of others; satanic activity. *(Is. 25: 4; 1 Thess. 5: 3; Nam. 1: 3; Eph. 4: 14; John 3: 8; Acts 2: 2-4; Job 1: 12, 19; 8: 2; Matt. 7: 27; Ex. 9: 23-25; Josh. 10: 11)*

Black Storm: Enemy power; attack coming.
White Storm: God's power; revival.

Straight: Going in the right direction; spiritually on the right track; unyielding. *(Heb. 12: 13; Matt. 3: 3; Ps. 5: 8; Luke 3: 4-5)*

Stumbling: Barrier in the way preventing the truth; sin; backslide; mistake; become deceived; to be overcome; lack of knowledge; alcohol usage; the Christian's freedom is a stumbling block to others. *(Jer. 50: 32;*

In A Dream, In A Vision of the Night
Job 33:15-18

Rom. 11: 9; Is. 5: 24; Ex. 15: 7; 1 Cor. 1: 23; 8: 9; 1 Peter 2: 8; Prov. 3: 23)

Suicide: Self ruin; pride and fatigue of life; self hatred; mournful feelings; to be without hope; result of betraying the anointed one; dishearten and cast down; a sinful act. *(Ecc. 7: 16; Matt. 27: 5; Is. 28: 7; 1 Peter 2: 8; Prov. 3: 21-23; 1 Cor. 1: 23; 8: 9; Judges 16: 29-30; 1 Kin. 16: 18-19; 2 Sam. 17: 23; Luke 4: 9)*

Suitcase: Private things; hidden things of the heart; time for moving on; move; transition. *(Ez. 12: 3; Gal. 6: 5)*

Summer: Time for collecting the ripe crops; significant of a covenant with God; harvest of fruit of the Spirit; opportunity; time of testing; heat of mental and physical torment; opening or chance for something to happen. *(Prov. 6: 8; 10: 5; Gen. 8: 22; 2 Sam. 16: 1-2; Ps. 74: 17; Matt. 24: 32; Jer. 8: 20)*

Sun: The glory of Jesus; connected to moon and stars; fiery; God; Light and truth; virtue; physical and mental suffering; torment at the hand of others; testing of faith; the Old Testament law; the coming glory; the god

Susan Noone Riddle

of this world; rising of the people of God. *(Ps. 19: 4- 7; 84: 11; Ecc. 1: 3-14; Mal. 4: 2; Matt. 13: 43; 17: 2; Mark 4: 6, 17; 1 Cor. 15: 41)*

Supper: Jesus' broken body; Jesus' blood that was shed; marriage supper of the Lamb. *(Mark 14: 22-26; 1 Cor. 11: 23-33; Rev. 19: 7-9)*

Sweating: Man's efforts; fleshly works; price paid because of sin; striving in the flesh; agony as Jesus in garden -(great drops of blood). *(Gen. 3: 19; Luke 22: 44)*

Sweeping: Cleaning house (own tent, tabernacle that the Holy Spirit lives in); repenting of sins; transformation; actively taking barriers down; admonishment of sinners. *(Is. 28: 17; Eph. 4: 31; 2 Cor. 7: 1; 2 Cor. 7: 11; 1 Tim. 5: 20)*

Sweet: Reflection and meditation in the Word of God; rest for the physical body; Christians in service unto God; the Old Testament Law; the Word of God; words that are gratifying; fellowship in the spirit. *(Prov. 3: 24; 16: 24;Ps. 19: 10; 55: 14; 104: 34; 119: 103; Eph. 5: 2; 2 Cor. 2: 15)*

Swimming: Activity of the Spirit; worship; gifts of the Spirit being applied; service to God;

prophecy in operation. *(Ez. 47: 5; Eph. 3: 8)*

Swimming Pool: Condition in the Spirit; a ministry; God's favor.

    Dirty or Dry: Corrupt or destitute spiritual condition; backslide.

Swing: Rhythm of a life at rest or peace. *(Is. 30: 15)*

Swinging High: Thrill seeking and not counting the cost.

Sword: **Also see Knife**: Word of God; utensil for warfare; ruling over the wicked; judgment of the flesh; words that are faultfinding; prophetic words that cut away flesh; vengeance of God; one who is in mental agony; victory through the Word of God; enforcing compliance by threatening; conflict; oppressive conduct in order to persecute. *(Eph. 6: 17; Ps. 64: 3; Du. 32: 41; Josh. 5: 13; 6: 21; Prov. 5: 3-4; 12: 18; Rom. 13: 4; Luke 2: 35; Rev. 6: 4)*

T

Tabernacle: **See also House, Sanctuary, Tent, Temple**: God's place of meeting with man;

Susan Noone Riddle

          refuge; God's household; heaven; the believer. *(Heb. 8: 2; 9: 23-24; 13: 11; Ex. 25: 8-9, 23; 29:42-44; Amos 7: 9; Ps. 20: 2; 102: 19; 150: 1; Lev. 21: 23; 26: 31; Jer. 51: 51; Eph. 2: 19-22; Num. 1: 50-53; 1 Cor. 6: 19; John 1: 14)*

Table: Altar; spiritual food that is consecrated; priestly communion with God and one another; covenant; needs being met; place of surrender and agreement. *(1 Cor. 10: 20-21; Dan. 11: 27; Ps. 78: 19)*

Tail: The end of something; poisonous and deadly; last in time or in line for something; he who is last shall be first; the least of. *(Rev. 9: 10, 19; 12: 4; Job 40: 17; Is. 9: 15; Du. 28: 13, 44)*

Tares: People whose father is the devil; those who depart from the faith; false teaching; degenerates; grain that is deceptive and dangerous. *(Matt. 13: 25-40)*

Tasting: Testing; using perception; to judge righteously. *(Ps. 34: 8; 119: 103; Heb. 2: 9; 6: 4; Ex. 16: 31; John 2: 9; Matt. 27: 34)*

Tea: Iced: God's grace; refreshing in His presence. *(Prov. 25: 25; Is. 28: 12; Acts 3: 19)*

Teacher: **See People**: **also for Classroom and School**.

In A Dream, In A Vision of the Night
Job 33:15-18

Tears: To be grieving; distress of the soul; mourning; to come to repentance; intercession; judgment; to feel and show humility and/or sadness; sometimes tears of joy. *(Is. 25: 8; Mark 9: 24; Ps. 34: 6; 42:3; Rev. 7: 17)*

Teeth: **See also Arrows, Spears, Mouth**: Experience that brings wisdom. *(Zech. 9: 7-8; Is. 7: 16; Rev. 9: 8; Rom. 5: 3-4; Col. 2: 8; 1 Tim. 6: 20; Prov. 25: 18-19; Heb. 5: 8, 12-14; Ez. 18: 2; Ps. 1: 2; 3: 6; 35: 16; 45: 5; 57: 4; 64: 3; 76: 3; 91: 5; 119: 9; 127: 4; Jer. 9: 8; Job 4: 10; 6: 4; Du. 32: 23, 42)*

Animal teeth: Sharpness; devouring; serious endangerment.

Baby teeth: Childish; without wisdom or knowledge; inexperienced; unblemished.

Broken teeth: A difficult issue; broken relationships; learning obedience through suffering; approaching agony.

Brushing teeth: Making words or thoughts pure.

False teeth: To replace spiritual understanding with reasoning; substitute for truth; wisdom of the world; teaching error.

Toothache: Tribulation coming; heartache.

Telephone: Intercession; Godly counsel; ungodly speaking; bearing false witness against someone; enemy's voice; dead line: miscommunication or not hearing and in need of being able to hear God. *(Acts 2: 21; Rom. 10: 12; Is. 59: 1-2; Lev. 19: 31)*

Telescope: Seeing into the future; making a small problem bigger. *(Rev. 4: 1)*

Television: A prophetic vision; taking into the "eye gate" information that is both evil and good as in eating from the tree of the knowledge of good and evil (as opposed to the tree of life). *(Num. 24: 16; Dan. 2: 19; 1 Chron. 13: 7, 9-10; Rom. 1: 32)*

Temple: **See also House, Sanctuary, Tent or Tabernacle**: God's habitation or dwelling; man's human body; of the Lord Jesus Christ. *(Heb. 8: 2; 13: 11; Ex. 25: 8-9; Amos 7: 9; Ps. 20: 2; 102: 19; 150: 1; Lev. 21: 23; 26: 31; Jer. 51: 51; Eph. 2: 19-22)*

Ten: **See Numbers**.

Ten Thousand: **See Numbers**.

In A Dream, In A Vision of the Night
Job 33:15-18

Tent: **See also House, Sanctuary, Temple or Tabernacle**: Covering that is impermanent for flexibility; man's dwelling; foreigner traveling with no permanent dwelling. *(Gen. 12: 8; 13: 3-18; Heb. 8: 2; 13: 11; Ex. 26: 36; 25: 8-9; Amos 7: 9; Ps. 20: 2; 102: 19; 150: 1; Lev. 21: 23; 26: 31; Is. 38: 12; 2 Cor. 5: 1; Jer. 51: 51; Eph. 2: 19-22)*

Thief: **See People**.

Thigh: **See also Leg**: Strength; flesh; the walk of a man's life; natural man; works of the flesh; to attempt to entice one to sin. *(Gen. 32: 25-32; Num. 5: 21; Ps. 45: 3; Is. 47: 2)*

Thorns: A curse; something that hinders through trial; gossip; perverse occurrences; persecution; life's cares and concerns; place of defense. *(Gen. 3: 18; Heb. 6: 8; Ex. 22: 6; Matt. 13: 22; Mark 4: 7; Luke 8: 7)*

Throne: **See also Chair and Seat**: Rulership; place of authority; inner court of the temple; God's seat of authority; satanic powers; mercy seat; Kingship of the Lord. *(Rev. 13: 2; 20: 11; Ps. 1: 1; 7: 7; 9: 7; Job 23: 3; 1 Kings 16: 11; 2 Chron. 9: 18; 19: 8; Matt. 17: 19; Heb. 9: 5-12; Ex. 25: 22; 29: 42-*

Susan Noone Riddle

>*43; 1 John 2: 2; Col. 1: 16; Num. 7: 89; Rom. 3: 24-25; 2 Cor. 5: 20; 1 Tim. 2: 5)*

Thunder: **See also Clouds, Storm, Tornado, Wind and Whirlwind:** The Lord speaking; in judgment or blessing; change; without understanding of what the Spirit is saying; not seeing the signs of the times; warning of judgment coming. *(John 12: 28-29; Ps. 18: 13; Ps. 18: 13; 77: 18; Rev. 11: 19; 19: 6; 1 Sam. 2: 10)*

Thirteen: **See Numbers**.

Thirty: **See Numbers**.

Thousands: **See Numbers**.

Three and Third: **See Numbers**.

Three hundred: **See Numbers**.

Three hundred ninety: **See Numbers**.

Tin: **See Metals**.

Tractor: **See Vehicles**.

Trailer: See Places.

Train: **See Vehicles**.

Tiger: **See Animals, Reptiles, Insects and Birds: also for Cheetah, Leopards and Cats**.

Title/Deed: Indication of possession; having the authority to own or be in possession of something. *(Gen. 23: 20)*

In A Dream, In A Vision of the Night
Job 33:15-18

Tongue: **See also Teeth and Arrows**: Language of a certain nationality or country; manner of speaking; fountain for blessing or curing God's own; cannot be tamed by man; life and death in it's power; can start a fire for good or evil. *(Zech. 9:7-8; Is. 7: 16; Rom. 5: 3-4; Col. 2: 8; 1 Tim. 6: 20; Prov. 25: 18-19; Heb. 5: 8; Ez. 18: 2; Ps. 11: 2; 45: 5; 64: 3; 76: 3; 91: 5; 119: 9; 127: 4; Jer. 9: 8; Job 6: 4; Du. 32: 23, 42)*

Tornado: **See also Clouds, Storm, Thunder, Whirlwind and Wind**: Distress; overcoming irresistible power; great trouble; sudden disturbance from the norm; swift change; spiritual warfare; judgment; sudden disaster or destruction; trial; persecution; opposition; witchcraft. *(Is. 25: 4; 1 Thess. 5: 3; Nam. 1: 3; Eph. 4: 14; John 3: 8; Acts 2: 2-4; Job 1: 12, 19; 8: 2)*

Tower: **Also see Tower, Mountain, Hill, Skyscraper, Up and Elevator**: Prophetic church of great revelation; high places; above earthly experience; higher spiritual things; strength that protects; Tower of Babel; dominance; control; obstacle; Jesus returning from the heavens to earth;

Susan Noone Riddle

symbolic of victory; Jesus being lifted up on the cross; wisdom that comes from above. *(Acts 1: 13-14; 20: 7-8; Ps. 61: 3; 103: 11; 144: 2; 1 Sam. 9: 12-14; Matt 5; 1 Kings 18; John 3: 7; James 3: 15, 17; Heb. 1: 3; 1 Thess. 4: 13-18; 1 Kings 12: 31; Prov. 18: 19; Is. 30: 25)*

Tree: Individual person or church; Jesus; covering; leaders; sanctuary; power of evil people; note the health of the tree and where it is planted; a nation or denomination. *(Is. 7: 2; 44: 14-17; 55: 12; 1 Kings 4: 25; Jer. 24: 1-10; Hos. 9: 10; 14: 6-8; Matt. 12: 33; 21: 19; 24: 32-33; Rev. 6: 13; Luke 13: 6-9; Ps. 37: 35; 52: 8; 92: 12; 137: 1-2; Ez. 17: 24; Job 14: 7-9)*

Cedar Tree: Power; majestic power; King and Priest.

Christmas Tree: Celebration; false-worship; self-glory.

Cypress Tree: Fairness; used to make idols.

Evergreen: Life everlasting.

Fig: Prosperity; peace; final judgment; the return of the Lord; the Jewish

In A Dream, In A Vision of the Night
Job 33:15-18

nation; barren religion; fathers of Israel; the righteous and the wicked.

Myrtle Tree: God's blessings; great beauty.

Oak Tree: Great strength to weather storms; solid place of refuge.

Olive Tree: Israel; anointing oil; the true, anointed church. the two olive trees as the two witnesses of Revelations.

Palm Tree: A highly righteous fruit producing person of the church.

Tree Stump: Lack of faith; tenacious; to take a hard stand and not move; cut off from the life of Jesus; possibilities of hope or promise of restitution and resurrection.

Willow Tree: Sadness; tears and sorrow.

Trophy: Victory; to contend for a prize; winning in warfare of the Spirit. *(1 Kings 20: 11; 1 Sam. 17: 57)*

Truck: **See Vehicles**.

Trumpet: **See also Trumpet**: Christ's second coming; final judgment; announcing blessing; voice of the Prophet; important proclamation; preaching the Gospel; the prophetic; warning; worship and praise; the gathering and being caught up with the Lord when He returns; a call to rise from slumber or to gather. *(Josh 6: 5; 2 Sam. 2: 28; Heb. 12: 19; 1 Cor. 14: 8; 15: 52; Joel 2: 15; Eph. 5: 14; Is. 58: 1)*

Tunnel: A passageway; time of transition; a dark and troubling event. *(1 Cor. 10: 13)*

Twelve: **See Numbers**.

Twelve Thousand: **See Numbers**.

Twenty: **See Numbers**.

Twenty-four: **See Numbers**.

Two: **See Numbers**.

Two Hundred: **See Numbers**.

Two Thousand: **See Numbers**.

U-V

Up: **Also see Tower, Mountain, Hill, Skyscraper, and Elevator**: Prophetic church of great revelation; high places; above earthly experience; higher spiritual things; spiritual ascension; pride; self exaltation; strength; protection; safety; Tower of Babel; dominance; control; obstacle; Jesus returning from the heavens to earth; symbolic of victory; Jesus being

In A Dream, In A Vision of the Night
Job 33:15-18

lifted up on the cross; wisdom that comes from above; Mt. Zion; sacrifice of worship; Mt. Sinai and the Ark of the Covenant in the Temple; songs of ascent unto Him; Mt. Carmel; Beatitudes in the Sermon on the Mount. *(Acts 1: 13-14; 20: 7-8; Ps. 61: 3; 103: 11; 144: 2; 1 Sam. 9: 12-14; Matt 5; 1 Kings 18; John 3: 7; James 3: 15, 17; Heb. 1: 3; 1 Thess. 4: 13-18; 1 Kings 12: 31; Prov. 18: 19; Is. 30: 25)*

Unclean: Defiled; abomination; demonic; unclean demonic spirits; unclean animals may represent. *(Acts 5: 16; 10: 14; 2 Cor. 6: 17; Eph. 5: 5; Rev. 16: 13; Matt. 10: 1; 12: 43; Mark 1: 23-27)*

Urinating: Pressure relieved by repenting of sin for self or others; strong desire; tempted to sin. *(Prov. 17: 14; 1 Sam. 25: 22)*

Van: **See Vehicles**.

Vapor: **See also Cloud**: Temporary nature of natural life; ominous or occultic; manifestation of the presence of God; cloud of His presence; filling of the temple of God (born again, Spirit-filled men and women). *(Is. 19: 1; 44: 22; Ex. 13: 21-22; 14: 19-20; 16: 10; 19: 16; 40: 35; Rev. 14:*

Susan Noone Riddle

> 14; Ps. 18: 9; 104: 3; 97: 2; Num. 9: 15-22; Heb. 12: 1-2; Jude 12; 2 Chron. 5: 13; Luke 9: 34-35; Matt. 24: 30; Prov. 25: 14; 2 Peter 2: 17; 1 Cor. 10: 1-2; Lam. 2: 2; Dan. 7: 13)

Veil: Camouflaged; covered glory or sin; deceitfulness; spiritual understanding blocked; the Old Testament law; the flesh; to be segregated from God; that which divide; love that covers a multitude of sin; making a transition from flesh to spirit. *(Luke 24: 45; 2 Cor. 3: 13-16; Mark 15: 37-38; Ex. 26: 31-35; Heb. 6: 19; 9: 3; 10: 20; Matt. 27: 51; 2 Chron. 3: 14)*

Vessel: Body of the Christian believer; tool for the glory of God; vessels of the body of Christ (as He is the head). *(Matt. 25: 4; 1 Cor. 4: 7; Rev. 2: 27; 1 Thess. 4: 4; 2 Tim. 2: 21; 1 Peter 3: 7; Rom. 9: 22-23)*

Vine: **See Grapes and Vineyard**: Christ and His church; Christ is the true Vine; Church and the believers are the branches; Israel; family; any established institution like a city or a nation. *(Song 7: 7; Matt. 7: 16; Rev. 14: 18; Num. 6: 3; 13: 20-34; Gen. 40: 10-11; 49: 11; Ez. 18: 2; Gal. 5: 22-23;*

In A Dream, In A Vision of the Night
Job 33:15-18

Matt. 20: 1-6; Hos. 14: 7; James 4: 14; John 15: 1-6; Jer. 2: 21; 10: 13; Judges 9: 13; Is. 5: 1-7; Ps. 128: 3; 1 Kings 4: 25)

Vineyard: **See Places**.

Voice: Thunder; compelling; words of Christ; indication to open the door of our hearts to receive Jesus; sound of many waters; but sheep know HIS voice; sign of a covenant; requires obedience; important to test the spirit by the Word. *(John 10: 4; Heb. 12: 26; Rev. 1: 15; 3: 20; Is. 66: 6; Matt. 3: 3; Josh 24: 24-25; Gen. 3: 1-19; 22: 6-18; 1 John 4: 1)*

Volcano: Something very explosive blowing up and bringing change; unexpected pressure that brings an out of control reaction; emotional instability that is unpredictable; the judgment of God. *(Du. 32: 22; Ps. 11: 6)*

W

Walking: Living a life in the Spirit; living a life in sin; the lifestyle of the dreamer. *(Gal. 5: 16-25; Eph. 4: 17; 1 John 1: 6-7; 2 Cor. 5: 7)*

Wall: Can be a hindrance or obstruction; enormous power; leaders; Kingdom or City of God; peace; can be protection and defense. *(Is. 2: 15; 5: 5; 26: 1; 56: 5; 62: 6; 2 Chron. 8: 5; Ps. 18: 29; 51: 18; 122: 7; 2 Sam. 22: 30; Nam. 2: 5; Prov. 18: 11; Neh. 6: 6-15; 12: 27-47)*

War: Total devastation; death; great ruin; prayer and worship; final war in heaven and in earth. *(Rev. 12: 7-17; 17: 14; 19: 11-19; 1 Peter 2: 11; 1 Tim. 1: 18; James 4: 1-2; 2 Cor. 10: 3; Eph. 6: 10-18; 2 Chron. 20)*

Washing: Cleansing from sin and the filth of this world. *(John 9: 7; 13: 5-14; Lev. 1: 13-19; Is. 1: 16; Gen. 18: 4; Ps. 26: 6; Acts 22: 16)*

Washbasin: **Also Sink and Bathroom**: Prayer if repentance; intercession; cleansing. *(Is. 1: 16; Jer. 4: 14)*

In A Dream, In A Vision of the Night
Job 33:15-18

Washcloth:Means of cleanings and applying the Word and Spirit to one's life. *(Ps. 51: 7; John 15: 3; Job 14: 4)*

    Dirty Cloth: False teaching and doctrine.

    Very dry cloth: Word without Spirit; dry and abrasive.

Watch: **See also Clock**: Vigilant; a Prophet; being alert; on guard. *(1 Cor. 16: 13; 1 Peter 5: 8; Jer. 31: 28; Jer. 31: 28; 51: 12)*

Watermelon: Restoring of the soul; refreshened; fruitfulness. *(Num. 11: 5; Prov. 1: 31; Is. 3: 10; Prov. 18: 21)*

Waters: **See also River, Brook, Ocean and Sea**: Flowing in the Holy Spirit; nations of the earth; restlessness; note if there is an undercurrent or cross current; eternal life in Jesus; Word; spirit of man or enemy; instability; tremendous suffering or bitterness. *(Prov. 18: 4; Eph. 5: 26; Amos 8: 11; Gen. 49: 4; Job 34: 7; James 3: 11-12; Rev. 17: 15; 21: 6; Jer. 2: 13; 47: 1-3; Ex. 15: 23-27;17:1-6; Matt. 3: 11-16)*

    Stagnant or muddy or polluted: Sin; flesh; the doctrine of men.

    Troubled Water: Place of healing; deep grief.

Water fountain: Man's spirit; God's Spirit; salvation.

Water Well: Revive and refreshes the soul; springs up as water of life to make us whole; man's spirit; God's Spirit. *(Prov. 4: 23; 5: 15; 10: 11; 16: 22; 2 Peter 2: 17; John 1: 10; 4: 10, 13-14; Is. 12: 3)*

Weeds: Fleshly deeds; failure to attend to something; slothfulness; overwhelmed with concern; iniquity made full. *(Gen. 2: 15; Prov. 24: 30-31; Jonah 2: 5; Gen. 15: 16)*

Weight: Heavy responsibility; load or burden to carry; to be encumbered; heaviness. *(Ez. 4: 10-16; Heb. 12: 1; 2 Cor. 4: 17; 10: 10; Matt. 23: 23)*

West: Coming of night or evening; where the sun goes down; God's favor; sunset; day closing; behind or finished; frontier; pioneering spirit; spiritual warfare; completed. *(Du. 20: 10; Josh. 3: 4; Ps. 75: 6; 103: 112; Matt. 24: 27)*

Wheel: **See also Ring, Round and Circle**: For transporting; life's cycle; eternal things; swiftness. *(Ez. 1: 15-23; 10: 1-22; James 3: 8)*

In A Dream, In A Vision of the Night
Job 33:15-18

Whirlwind: **See also Clouds, Thunder, Tornado, Storm and Wind**: Power on a large scale; inability to overcome; judgment; if white, could be revival. *(Prov. 1: 27; 10: 25; 2 King 2: 1-11; Ps. 58: 9; Eph. 4: 14; John 3: 8; Acts 2: 2-4; Job 1: 12, 19; 8: 2)*

White: **See Colors**.

Wife: **See People**: **also for Bride and Marriage**.

Wilderness: Separation from the Lord; desolation; place of provision; guidance; God's mighty deeds; where the heart is tested; wandering and temptation. *(Ex. 7: 16; Matt. 3: 1-12; 4: 1; 15: 33-38; Du. 2: 7; 8: 2; Ps. 78: 17-19, 40, 52; Job 12: 24; Heb. 3: 7-19; Gen. 16: 6-8; 37: 22; John 3: 14)*

Wind: **See also Clouds, Thunder, Tornado, Storm and Whirlwind**: Powers of God or satan; breathe of life; Spirit; doctrine of devils; Holy Spirit; to challenge; empty words such as boasting; vanity; calamity; God's adjudication and correction and quota or portion; demise and failure of man; false teaching. *(Eph. 4: 14; John 3: 8; Acts 2: 2-4; Job 1: 12, 19; 8: 2; Prov. 25: 14; Ez. : 10; Eph. 4: 14; Is. 32: 2; Hos. 8: 7; 13: 15)*

Susan Noone Riddle

Window: Revelation knowledge; unobstructed view; heavenly favor; revealed or laid open; seeing truth; prophecy; understanding; exposed; if unguarded or unlocked: could mean danger of enemy attack; if veiled: could me truth or revelation hidden. *(Gen. 6: 16; 8: 6; 26: 8; 2 Kings 7: 19; Joel 2: 9; Mal. 3: 10; Song 2: 9; Dan. 6: 10; Josh. 2: 15-18; Song 2: 9)*

Wine: Teaching blessing; blessing of wisdom; feelings that are potent; the anger of God; Spirit of God or spirit of man; revelation; sorcery. Drinking with someone: fellowship; communion; the blood of Christ; committing spiritual fornication. *(Eph. 5: 18; Luke 5: 37-38; Prov. 4: 17; 9: 2-5; 20: 1; 31: 6; Acts 2: 1`3-17; Du. 32: 32; 1 Cor. 10: 16; Mat. 26: 27-29; John 2: 1-10; Ps. 75: 8; Is. 55: 1; Rev. 17: 2)*

Wine Skins: The church; the body of Christ; the harlot church.

Wine Press: Production of true doctrine in Spirit and Truth.

Wings: Prophet or preacher; Spirit of God; safeguard and shelter. *(Mal. 4: 2; Is. 40:*

In A Dream, In A Vision of the Night
Job 33:15-18

31; Ex. 19: 4; Ps. 17: 8; 36: 7; 61: 4; 91: 4; Luke 13: 34; Rev. 12: 6-14)

Winter: Unfruitfulness; death of a vision; abide during latent times; cold emotions or situation. *(Jer. 8: 20; Is. 1: 30)*

Witch: **See People**.

Wolf: **See Animals, Reptiles, Insects and Birds**.

Wood: Life; temporary; flesh; the human part of the Lord; dependence on the flesh; fleshly appetite; eternal with respect to a living tree. *(Jer. 5: 14; Prov. 26: 20-21; 2 Tim. 2: 20; Rev. 9: 20; Is. 53: 1-3; 1 Cor. 3: 12-15; Ex. 7: 19; Lev. 14: 4-6)*

Woman (Unknown): **See People**: **also for Man and Harlot**.

Worm: **See Animals, Reptiles, Insects and Birds**: **also for Maggots**.

Wrestling: Perseverance; travail; to be salvaged; opposition to something; tribulation; struggle over who is going to be in control. *(Gen., 32: 24-28; Eph. 6: 12; 2 Tim. 2: 24)*

X-Y-Z

Year: Time in circulation; specified period of blessing or judgment; time as it is in

Susan Noone Riddle

              circulation. *(Job 36: 11; Ps. 65: 11; 90: 4, 15; Luke 4: 19; Is. 23: 15; 61: 2; Ez. 4: 5)*

Yellow: **See Colors: also see Gold in Medals**.

Yoke: **See also Neck**: Servitude or bondage to sin; to be enslaved; fellowship with believers, not allowed with unbelievers; complete union; discipleship; legalism; marriage. *(Ez. 4: 5; Gen. 27: 40; Gal. 5: 1; 2 Cor. 6: 14; 1 Tim. 6: 1; Lev. 26: 13; Jer. 27: 8-12; Du. 28: 48; Matt. 29: 3; Lam. 1: 14; 1 Kings 12: 4-14)*

Zion: **See Mountain; Hills; Up and Elevator**: Strength; place of protection; majesty; stability; kingdom of God or of Man; exalted; obstacle; difficulty; challenge; transfiguration; place of prophecy; place of agony; kingdom; nation. *(Josh. 14: 12; Acts 1: 13-14; 20: 7-8; Ps. 103: 11; 1 Sam. 9: 12-14; Matt 5; 1 Kings 18; 12: 31; John 3: 7; James 3: 15, 17; Heb. 1: 3; 1 Thess. 4: 13-18; 1 Cor. 13: 2; Luke 21: 21; Is. 8: 18; 27: 13; 31: 4; 40: 9; 44: 23; Rev. 6: 14)*

In A Dream, In A Vision of the Night
Job 33:15-18

Dealing with Symbols, Types and Shadows

In using symbols, types and shadows from the Bible to understand dreams and visions from the Lord, there are symbols which come directly out of the Bible. There are also symbols which come from our own personal life and walk with the Lord. We must remember that all symbolism does originate with the Lord and His Word. Some of these may be intimate between ourselves and the Lord. Many of them will be in modern terms with Biblical basis. An example of this is the word chariot that is used in the Bible to express an angel or a man's fighting vessel. This is relatively unlikely that in our world today, we would dream of a war fought with chariots. Of course some of us do still dream about chariots. However, most of us living in the 21st century would dream of high tech war vessels instead. Some have even seen what they believe to be future vessels of war, like John may have seen in Revelations. The Lord will take that symbol into modern terms and language so that the dreamer can relate to the message through the surroundings he or she live in. He may use a fighter plane, or army tank! When we are walking in intimacy with the Lord,

Susan Noone Riddle

we begin to find His language and manner of speaking to us very understandable and intimate. Please use the symbols as a guide only. All symbolism is meant to lead us to the Author and Finisher of our Faith. We should never let ourselves get locked into a "code" or into "bondage" to symbols. We are creatures of habit. When change comes "into the picture" we get uncomfortable. The Lord loves to push us out of our comfort zone to keep our lives fresh and teach us that He is sovereign. Always remember that the Lord may use a symbol one time to mean something and then use it to mean something else another time. The Word of God is multilevel as well. Everything should stay fresh and new in the Lord. Sometimes He will change gears just to keep us from getting stale or stuck in a rut!

There are books that I personally recommend. These teachers of Bible symbolism and types and shadows have taught me so very much. I would highly recommend that these books are obtained for anyone's personal library. These books are: (see Bibliography for information on obtaining these books): "<u>Dreams and Visions With a Difference For All Believers</u>." by Paula M. Cavu, "<u>Interpreting the Symbols and Types</u>." by Kevin Conner, "<u>Understanding the Dreams You Dream</u>." by Ira Milligan, "<u>Dictionary of Biblical</u>

In A Dream, In A Vision of the Night
Job 33:15-18

Imagery." by InterVarsity Press, and "Biblical Mathematics, Key to Scriptural Numerics" by Ed F. Vallowe.

Remember that simply having symbols without spiritual insight does little good and can even be harmful. It is much like having the Word of God without the Holy Spirit. *2 Corinthians 3* teaches us that the letter of the law without the Spirit kills. We can view this as the "letter of the symbol" kills without the Holy Spirit! We run into difficulty, deception, and frustration when dealing with symbols and their meanings if we try to force the interpretation into a box with a bunch of symbols. Religious cults have been built around one man's vision or dream that was so real to him that he mistook it as reality. There have been those who believed in their visionary experience so strongly the he or she was able to convince many others that the vision was a "new revelation" that no one else has received. This is how many groups of people become seduced and deceived. The Bible says that the Lord is doing a new thing. The new thing that He is doing is not new to Him! The Word of God is balanced. God cannot be forced into a box, but neither can He lie against His Word. If we continue to seek wise counsel in the Word and through others we will not be deceived by the dreams we dream or by the

Susan Noone Riddle

symbolism in them. We should also remember that seeking counsel does not mean surrounding ourselves with only those that we know will agree with us. Let's not ever be afraid of some healthy loving, Spirit filled criticism. A good indication of a true leader and counselor is that they will lead you toward the Word and Jesus, not toward themselves. They will not tell you only what feels good to hear. They also will not set themselves up as always being the one who knows it all. A true elder will guide and lead not tell and demand!

I will give some examples of dreams and symbolism in the next chapters.

In A Dream, In A Vision of the Night
Job 33:15-18

Chapter Six
Dreams That Do Not Necessarily Use Symbolism

Some dreams are easy to understand right up front. With these kinds of dreams, the dreamer may awaken and just know what it means. This is, however, not the most common way that parables and dreams come from the Lord. Receiving supernatural communication from the Lord is no different from studying the Word of God. There are some passages that we read over and over and just don't understand the full meaning. The longer we know Jesus and walk side by side with Him, the more we begin to understand what He is saying. We may even understand the scriptures on a simple level when we first begin studying the Word. Then, as time passes and we grow in grace, the passage develops a deeper meaning to us. A dream from the Lord is the same. We may not understand what any of it means at first. We must always remember to ask the Lord first what He is saying.

Even though the most common way of understanding dreams for the believers is that they are symbolic in nature, there are some dreams and visions that we receive from God that are exactly what they say and involve little or no symbolic interpretation. Here are some examples of dreams that have been light on symbolism, and heavy on literal understanding!

My husband was running for public office in our Parish. In Louisiana we have Parishes that are comparable to the counties in other states. We knew in our hearts that God had called him. Yet, we suddenly had opposition that stunned us. We felt vexed in our spirits. We were confused. Things looked disheartening on the outside. We knew that the Bible says, "Faith is the substance of the things hoped for, and the evidence of things not seen," but we were concerned about whether or not we had missed God. *(Hebrews 11:1)*

I began to pray and really seek God. "Lord, have we missed it? Are we doing the wrong thing? What is going to happen?" Then I had this dream.

Dream - Signs of Victory

The wife of the opponent and I were sitting on our front steps. People kept coming up to me, asking for a campaign sign to put in their yard. I would say, "Yes," and give them one. Suddenly a woman came up to the

In A Dream, In A Vision of the Night
Job 33:15-18

wife of my husband's opponent and shoved her over the guardrail of our front steps. I ran to her aide. She was lying on her back and was completely paralyzed. I looked up into the kitchen and called out to my husband, asking him to call 911. When I woke up at about 3:00 in the morning, I heard the Lord say, "This is a sign; they will be knocked flat on their back."

When I meditated on the dream, I really began to feel compassion for these people. I lost all fear and became concerned for our opponents. I began to pray for them. As the Election Day approached there were many things that happened that could have caused us to lose heart. My husband and I would be tempted to get discouraged, until we would remember the dream as well as other things that confirmed the promise we received from the Lord.

On the night of the election returns, it became evident that Charles had won a landslide victory. We felt such compassion for our opponents knowing that they too had worked hard. The dream had shown us that our opponents had been deeply hurt and wounded, feeling betrayed. The dream was indeed a "sign" from the Lord that we needed to concentrate our energies on praying for them and trusting Him. My husband served in this position for several years and is now

Susan Noone Riddle

serving in another capacity. We are dear friends with our past opponents.

It was not that the Lord wanted to exalt us and hurt someone else. The Bible tells us that the Lord appoints our leaders both in the secular realm and in the natural realm. Pharaoh was even raised up by the Lord for one purpose, to show forth His power and so that the name of the Lord would be known in all the earth *(Romans 9: 17, Exodus 9: 16)*. We may go to the polls here in America and vote, but God still appoints! In every experience, we have the opportunity to grow and learn. God designs all of our experiences for the best interest of all, even when it does not look that way at the time.

The symbolism in this dream was minimal. The opponents were "knocked flat on their back." The people asking for signs showed me that the dream was a "sign" from God about the election. The numbers "911" were used as a warning that the injury to their spirits would be severe. We did our part and prayed, and loved them.

Another dream I had concerning the realm of government was about an election for a high office here in Louisiana. The person who had held that office had announced that he would not run for another term. He had been a very popular politician that most knew not to even try to run against and win. There were so

In A Dream, In A Vision of the Night
Job 33:15-18

many people that wanted to hold that office. It was wide open to all. There was a lot of speculation about who would win.

Dream: And the Governor Will Be...

I was at was a beautiful mansion in the Southern part of our state. I sensed that something divine was happening. There were wonderful relics all around that were family collections. I sensed that these relics were inherited things. When I awoke, I knew in my heart that the owner of this home would be the man to win this election. I knew some other things, which the Lord has put in my heart for a later time.

When I shared this news with my husband, he just sort of chuckled. After all, at that time, the man was considered a "Dark Horse" in this race. No one really thought he would come up in the race from the percentages he was showing in the polls. The next week, as I sat and visited with friends, I was informed that we were going on a tour of an antebellum mansion in South Louisiana, owned by one of the candidates in the race. While I stood in his home I marveled at the awesome power of God.

Susan Noone Riddle

I considered that to be a confirmation. Isn't the Lord just so amazing!!! The man in the dream did win the election and once again, the Lord showed us that He has the answers before we even ask the questions.

Night Communication

At another time, I was seeking the Lord on a very important matter. In the middle of the night, my son was used of the Lord to answer the question! I had retired from teaching in the public school system. Being involved in ministry and raising three boys was keeping me extremely busy! I was soon asked to take the place of someone while they took a maternity leave. This would mean going back to work for 6 to 8 weeks. The pay sounded wonderful!! However, I was unsure about what was truly God's will. I went to bed one night asking the Lord what to do. About 2:00 in the morning my middle son John came in and snuggled in between my husband and I. He quickly fell asleep. I was thinking over and over in my head, "Lord, do I speed up or slow down? You told me to stop teaching so I could slow down. If I take this job, I'll be speeding up again?" My middle son, John, sat up in bed and yelled at the top of his lungs, "SLOW

In A Dream, In A Vision of the Night
Job 33:15-18

DOWN!" Then he lay back down and continued sleeping. The next day he had no memory of this at all, except that he had dreamed something about baseball! Needless to say I did not take the job. I knew beyond a shadow of a doubt that I had heard the Lord loud and clear through my son. This was not a dream that I had, but a supernatural happening nonetheless. Why the Lord chose to speak in this manner really does not matter to me. I am grateful nonetheless that He did. There was no symbolism in this event.

Another amazing prophetic dream was concerning my Father. My Father and I were always extremely close. I began to have a series of dreams about 4 years before he died. These dreams would leave me very troubled, crying almost uncontrollably.

Dreams: My Father's Death
The First Dream
(Repeated several times in a 4 year period)

I dreamed Daddy was dead. He was lying in a coffin. The people around were saying he died of lung cancer.

One of the Other Dreams (In this Series of Dreams)

Susan Noone Riddle

I dreamed that Daddy was very, very sick. We were all so concerned. We knew that he had a serious lung cancer that could not be cured.

There were at least 6 or 7 of these type dreams over a 4-year period. Each dream deeply affected me. I would sob and cry in prayer for him. I asked the Lord to let me warn my Dad if this was truly to come to pass. My main concern was his salvation, but I also asked for healing in his body. He had smoked for 58 years and worked around dangerous chemicals all his working years.

I never told he or my mother about the dreams until after he got sick.

One of the Last Dreams

One night I dreamed that my youngest son, Michael, was hurt badly. He appeared much younger in the dream than he really was. We needed to take him to the hospital for x-rays. His foot was sliced open, Inside of his foot; it looked like a fishes gill.

When I woke up I noticed it was exactly 2:00 a.m. In his younger years, Michael stayed with my mom and dad during the day while I worked. Daddy was close to all three of my sons, but was retired and had

In A Dream, In A Vision of the Night
Job 33:15-18

more time to spend with Michael. They had a special relationship. My Dad, Michael and myself are all the baby of our families with similar personalities. I knew a fish's gill meant "lungs" to us because my dad also went fishing two times a week. Two is also the number of separation. I told my husband, "Something is about to happen with Daddy." It was October the 7th, 1997. Exactly one week later on October 14th, at 2:00 in the morning, my Dad woke up with severe pain in his chest. He could not move. That morning my mother called me obviously upset. She expressed to me what had happened to my Father in the night. He had asked her to call me, because he wanted my help. He died three months later on January the 14, 1998, of lung cancer.

I miss him dearly. Not long before he died he surrendered his heart to the Lord. It was very plain to see that he was going on to glory to live with Jesus. I realize now that the dreams were given to my husband and me to be prepared for my Father's passing, as well as for us to pray for his salvation. The preparation was much appreciated and needed by us. It is one of those miracles that cannot be explained in words.

I spoke to Daddy concerning the dreams in the months before he died. He told me he was glad that I had not told him about them before. He said he would not have listened. But, at the end of his life, he did listen. That is what really matters. He left this realm and entered into life in Christ Jesus! Praise His name!

One night I woke up from a very short dream.

Warnings in the Night

I saw a woman that was working for my husband at the time. She was holding three papers in her hand. One was yellow and the other two were white.

There was a time period that we were greatly persecuted because we were dreaming dreams. Joseph was hated by his brothers because his father favored him. His brothers were very mad because Joseph enthusiastically shared the dreams the Lord gave him with them. He ended up in "DEEP" trouble because of it! I didn't know at the time I had this dream, but my husband had left three typed dreams on his desk that I had dreamed and given him to read. We had at one time attended church with the woman who was working for him. There had been serious conflicts over the issue of dreams and visions within the church that she still attended. There was a group of people that really wanted to prove that we were from the enemy's camp. A few days after the dream we learned

In A Dream, In A Vision of the Night
Job 33:15-18

that she had found the papers on his desk and taken them to show her Pastor and others in the church!

This dream was not very symbolic, but an outright warning from the Lord of what had happened. Because of the dream we were prepared in prayer and in the Spirit for the confrontation that followed. We were also able to pray death to the charismatic witchcraft type words that were being spoken against us. *(Romans 8: 33, Psalms 64: 3)*

One night I woke up to another very short dream.

Psalms 46: 4

I was holding a Bible in my hands. Someone was pointing to *Psalm 46: 4* which reads, "There is a river whose streams thereof; shall make glad the city of our God, The holy place of the tabernacle of the most high God."

I decided to pull out a song that I had written from *Psalm 46* and sing it the next Sunday morning. I was much amazed when I discovered that our Pastor began a series of teachings from *Psalm 46* for the next few Sundays! This was simply the Lord giving me direction for the praise and worship on that Sunday!

Another example of a dream that did not require much interpretation was one that some very good friends of ours were in. They lived in another town. We did not see them often, but always stayed in touch. We were in college together many years ago. We hadn't heard anything from them in a long time when I had this dream.

Dream of Suffering Marriage

I was talking to the couple. They tell me that things are not going well in their marriage. They say they may be getting a divorce. I feel deeply grieved.

I decided to pray for them and wait for direction from the Lord. I was not sure at all if the dream was about them or someone else. About two weeks later, I felt directed of the Lord to call them. The wife was home alone. I felt led of the Lord to just make small talk at first. She began to open up to me. She shared with me that she and her husband were having serious troubles. I told her about the dream. She began to weep. I told her that the Lord loved them so much that He shared this with me so that I could help and pray. She was deeply touched. As a result, she drew closer to the Lord. Unfortunately, their marriage did not

In A Dream, In A Vision of the Night
Job 33:15-18

make it. However, my friend is clinging to Jesus though it all. She was deeply hurt, yet I know that the Lord is even now strengthening her. After all, He alerted us ahead of time because of His heart of love for her. What an awesome God!

Sometimes the Lord will speak to us about something that is coming to let us know that even though it is hard to let go of people we love, it is still his will for the change to take place. Because of this, we can rest in Him. A Pastor and his wife that were once in our community were very close friends of ours. He and his wife had helped us through great difficulties. I could say there was and is a very special love between us. One night I had this dream.

The Dream of a Move

I was on a journey with my Pastor and his wife. We were WALKING (no short distance, 3 driving hours) to New Orleans. There were many people walking with us that were members of a church where another Pastor (a man that is no longer in ministry) had fallen in sin. When we got there we attended a service. The service was on television. The T. V. lights shown on my Pastor and his wife as they announced that they were moving.

I was so upset! I wanted so much to ignore this dream. However, soon afterwards, our Pastor resigned. He ended up transferring to a church in New Orleans where there was a large television ministry. The church was at one time the church of the same well-known minister that had fallen and left the ministry, just like in the dream! Once again, this dream prepared me for their leaving. It was very hard to say good-bye, but the dream helped us accept the Lord's will for our church as well as for our Pastor and His family.

At one time our church had been without a Pastor for about nine months. We were looking for a Pastor.

This is NOT My Will

I dreamed that a gray-headed man was coming to preach and consider our church. The Lord said in the dream that the people would be deceived into thinking that he was the one, but he was not. He also said to me in the dream that this man was full of deception.

In A Dream, In A Vision of the Night
Job 33:15-18

Sure enough, the next morning the man that came to preach was a very nice, good preacher who was gray headed! He seemed very nice and sounded very good as he preached, ON THE OUTSIDE! The denomination I was attending at that time voted as a means of choosing a Pastor. We actually conducted an election for this man that same morning. He only lost by six votes! Men and women may vote, but GOD APPOINTS! When the man of God that God sent arrived we knew he was the one!

The Gospel is Preached on an Exploding 747

June 27, 2002

These two dreams and then excerpts from the actual account of the news story of the China Airlines 747 that broke apart in midair on May 25th 2002 will stretch your spiritual mind of Christ as well as open your hearts to a new understanding of what may be part of the end time move of God in this earth.

In a time that technology is increasing at a rapid pace, the things of the Spirit of our God are also escalating expeditiously. In *Daniel 12: 4*, we are told that at the end of the age people will run to and fro and knowledge will increase. At this time as no other time, knowledge is expanding at such a rate that we are barely able to keep up with it all. We know that at the end of the age the activity of the Holy Spirit will also become more profound and to those who will listen and follow Him, more spectacular events will occur. He is Light, and Light is expanding and expelling the darkness!

I find it interesting that it was a Philip who was the one who asked the question that got the "greater works" answer from our Lord *(John 14: 12)*, and it was also a Philip that was translated from one location to another! Philip was translated or taken away supernaturally by the Spirit after preaching the Gospel and baptizing the Ethiopian Eunuch in *Acts 8*. Paul spoke of a man he knew that was caught up in the third heaven, whether in the body or out of the body, he did not know, but he was satisfied to say that God knew as though that was all that really mattered *(2 Cor. 12:1-6)*. Most agree that the man Paul was speaking of was himself. He just didn't know how to relate or explain it. In the time we live in, we are experiencing things that are difficult to relate but must be related nonetheless. The natural mind wants to reject the signs and wonders and miracles and supernatural

In A Dream, In A Vision of the Night
Job 33:15-18

occurrences because spiritual things cannot fit into the boundaries of the wisdom of the world *(1 Cor. 2: 14)*. *In Revelations 12*, a Male Child is born that is to rule all nations with a rod of iron, and is caught up with God and His throne. I believe that this Child is the greater works ministry that is coming forth in these last days at a rate just as fast as the increase in technology in the natural.

The day of the honor of man and the one-man show in the church is over. We have come to a place that our Lord is drawing us away from mindsets that no longer produce life and toward the mind of Christ to produce changed lives.

I woke up at exactly 3:30 a.m. on May the 18th, 2002, which is my youngest sons birthday. Whether in the body or out of the body, I do not know, God knows, in a dream or a vision, I was sitting near the back, left of the 747 jet airplane. Looking over the airplane interior, I could see the back of the seats. Every passenger appeared to have dark, Asian type hair. I knew the plane was about to crash as I began to shout, "Jesus Christ is the Lord of all! Turn to Him now and repent of your sins, He loves you and He will receive you now! King of Kings and Lord of Lords Jesus is!" I continued to say these things until the plane seem to crash and I instantly woke up.

Most dreams come through the soul and are symbolic; therefore I began to seek the Lord for answers. Daniel, Ezekiel, John and many others in the Bible did not fully know the meaning of their visions even at the time of their death, as far as we know. When Peter saw the sheet in the book of Acts, he was perplexed over the vision that he had seen. But Peter did not have to wait long before the Lord revealed to him what his vision meant. Daniel was sick and greatly despaired over the visions of his head, but he probably went to be with the Lord not understanding completely with what they meant. Joseph was a very young man when he first saw the dreams that he saw. But it was many miles and years before he saw the answer comes to pass.

On May 22, four days later I awoke after seeing a different perspective of the same airplane. This time I was standing on the ground and looking up into the sky as I saw very large 747 dangerously low to the ground. It was white with some kind of stripe along the side. I turn to people standing around me and said, "That plane is about to explode." I turned back around to look at the plane just as it exploded in mid air. As we ran for cover, I heard a small still voice inside of me say, "That plane is 40 minutes away from here."

In A Dream, In A Vision of the Night
Job 33:15-18

On May 25th at 3: 30 p.m. a China Airlines 747 exploded and broke apart in midair not very long after takeoff from an airport in Taiwan. To the best of my knowledge I have never seen a China Airlines plane with my natural eye, but when I saw an aircraft in a news picture, it was the same one I saw explode.

Another unusual coincidence was the fact that my son, whose birthday was the day of the first dream, was flying to Mexico the very same day that the plane crashed. Michael's jet flew near the spot that the airliner crashed, only on the other side of the world.

I began to do some research wanting to understand why the small still voice said, "40 minutes away from here." I suddenly remembered that when we were children, we used to say that if we drove a stake through the earth, straight from where we were to the other side, it would come out in China! I did not major in geography, I began to dig to find information about latitude and longitude. There was a picture on the Internet of the exact location where the airplane exploded off the coast of Taiwan. I began to do the math, and discovered that this 747 exploded in the air exactly on the other side of the earth from where I am. I still wanted to understand what the 40 minutes was all about. The only minutes that were familiar to me were the hours and minutes of the day. But as I looked into longitude and latitude, I discovered that the earth is mapped out in degrees and minutes. From where I live in the United States, this plane and these people lost their lives exactly 42 minutes within a 10 degree space of longitude, south from where I am. This plane crashed at 3:30 p.m. in Taiwan, and I awoke a week before having had the first dream at 3:30 a.m. our time. The other side of the world is daylight while we're experiencing nighttime. In real time, excluding daylight savings time, when it is 3:30 a.m. here where I live, it was 3:30 p.m. at the plane crash site.

The place where we are the most influential at sharing the Gospel of the Lord Jesus Christ is our own homes and communities. There is nothing more spiritual than looking at those we live with and see on a daily basis in the eye and sharing His grace, love and Word. When the fruit and gifts of the Holy Spirit flow from our lives like a river onto those who know us personally, lives are changed and saved.

But, think for a moment of a situation where many people may need to know of His saving grace, and no one in their community or families have either known the Lord or spoken to them. Then, suppose someone on the other side of the world prayed mysteries *(1 Cor. 14: 2)* and the Lord moved, giving 200+ people an opportunity to repent and live eternally with Him?

I don't know, but God knows…

In A Dream, In A Vision of the Night
Job 33:15-18

Chapter Seven
Dreams that Use Symbolic Language Based on Bible Truths

Fed By an Angel

I was walking away from a city, trying to persuade the women walking with me not to leave, but they continued onto a dark path. We entered a cold dim National Guard Armory Building. I was still pleading with them to turn around, when armed men entered the building. They began to shoot the women in the forehead in a cold calculated manner. I got on my knees and lifted my face toward God as man pointed a gun right at my forehead. He fired, but the gun kicked up and the bullet barely grazed the top of my head.

I fell and played as though I were also dead. I then rolled under a bed to hide. As I hid there, the men loaded all of the women that were dead into trunks of cars, and left. I stayed under the bed for what seemed like a long time. After I was sure they were not coming back, I ran out and across a field into an ark like structure where an angel and a small child were feeding me.

Susan Noone Riddle

Soon afterwards, many very disturbing things took place. The fellowship in the dream did leave the city of our God and conformed to the will of man. Many people were spiritually wounded and killed. They were warned and even told exactly what was going to happen by many different sources and ways, but pride held them back from seeing. The Lord never tears down without building up. He has restored what was taken that was of Him. The enemy was allowed to attempt to destroy the ministry and the prophetic anointing that He has placed within me, but failed as the angel of the Lord fed me. It was an opportunity for my husband and me to grow in grace. We have asked and continue to ask the Lord to burn away the wood, hay and stubble, and refine us as gold. Sometimes that means suffering for His Kingdom to grow!

Many times a dream will not be about the people in the dream. Most of the time the people in a dream represent something within us, or a group of people, or someone similar to the person in the dream. However, these dreams were actually about the people in the dreams. The people were not symbolic of someone else. What about dreams that are symbolic? How can we be sure that we understand the mind and heart of God in order to discern the difference?

In A Dream, In A Vision of the Night
Job 33:15-18

My husband had a dream about a man and a mosquito.

The Mosquito Dream

He saw in the dream, Sam Walton sitting in a chair. There were mosquitoes around. He was getting great pleasure in pulling the legs off of them as well as tying their legs together.

Suddenly he grabbed his heart and fell over dead.

There was a man who soon thereafter decided to try to destroy my husband. He was a very powerful man with the means to do just that. This man called my husband into his office and told him he was going to do everything in his power to bring him down. He spent the next few years trying to do all that could to bring Charles into a ruined state. Sam Walton was a symbol of someone who was comparable in power and influence in our community. We were brand new Christians. This dream told us that this man was in danger for "torturing" innocent people without feeling or care. We began to pray for him, asking for mercy for him. He did finally back off the overt attacks, but never really gave up the quest. However, one night he suddenly died in the night of a massive heart attack.

Susan Noone Riddle

We hope and pray that he was able to find forgiveness and peace with God.

My husband and I really take elections seriously. We seek the Lord about who to vote for in all elections. There was one election that was really difficult. One of the candidates was proclaiming to be a Christian, while the other was not. Something just did not seem right. One of our sons told us of a dream that he and about one of the candidates. We have learned in this family when someone dreams, it is time to listen!

The Fly Dream

The candidate that was proclaiming to be a Christian was a fly!

It was really strange because many Christian people were planning to vote for the fly guy! We were feeling that though he was, on the surface, the most appealing candidate, he was more dangerous than the other. The dream just confirmed our feelings on the matter. To the best of our knowledge, our son had never heard us discuss the issue. We actually did not realize that he knew who the candidates were.

In A Dream, In A Vision of the Night
Job 33:15-18

The candidate we voted for won the election. As a result of this election a position opened up that first enabled Charles to run for and win public office in government.

There was a time when we were involved in a fellowship that believed in "dealing" harshly with people and their problems. Confrontation was the main method used to "expose" people and their sin. Many people were wounded and some gave up trying. My husband had this dream during this time when we were seeking the Lord about this method of ministry.

Just Chop It Off!!!

The Elders of the church were at a hospital. They were cutting people's arms and legs off. People were bleeding to death. The Elders were very proud of their "cutting" limbs off of the bodies of people.

This dream was a wonderful eye opener. My husband was able to see that what was going on was not helping but hurting people.

Another time the Lord decided to let me experience just a taste of being crucified with Him at the hand of those who were my brothers and sisters. This was a *1 Peter 4: 12-19* experience, and surely not the last.

Suffering according to His will is about being a reproach for the name of Christ. It usually comes at the hand of our brothers and sisters in Christ. We can nail our feet down, and even one hand. But it takes someone else to nail that last hand down on that cross. That is usually the one that hurts the most. Jesus was crucified, buried risen and then fully glorified. We desire to see His glory, but we must first die to our own desires and will. This dream was a preparation for me to accept the suffering I was about to experience at the hand of the brethren.

Snakes in the Living Room

I dreamed I was asleep on the couch in our living room. This is the room where our music equipment is kept. Two small black snakes came and bit me on the inside of my left thigh. I woke up in the dream knowing that the bite had put deadly poison in my system.

My first reaction was that God was judging me for something. I cried and condemned myself. I was sure the Lord was telling me I had done something wrong. Once I stopped feeling sorry for myself, I began to dig in the Word of God for help; I realized what the Lord

In A Dream, In A Vision of the Night
Job 33:15-18

was saying. He led me to *Psalms 140: 1-3* which says, "Deliver me, o Lord, from evil men; Preserve me from violent men, Who plan evil things in their hearts, They sharpen their tongues like a serpent; The poison of asps is under their lips. Selah." Another scripture I found was *Psalm 58: 3-5* which says, "The wicked are estranged from the womb; They go astray as soon as they are born speaking lies, There poison is like the poison of a serpent; They are like the deaf cobra that stops its ear, Which will not heed the voice of charmers. Charming ever so skillfully." After seeing these scriptures, I realized that the Lord was warning me that there would soon be an attack of accusations against my husband, my Pastor and myself at the time.

I arrived at church one morning ready for service, and felt a cold chill in the Spirit. As I approached the prayer room I knew something was wrong. As we began to pray together, I was alerted to the fact that someone was praying in a manner that was not of the Lord. I went to our Pastor and told him that there was something wrong. He took action right away. We soon learned that there had been an effort made to discredit us all. Someone had been visiting each member of the worship team as well as others we fellowshipped with speaking the "poison of asps (snakes)" and trying to sway their opinions of us.

Within a weeks time they announced to our Pastor that they were leaving and there were eighty people coming with them. After a month of great personal distress and turmoil within the body, they left alone. Through prayer and good leadership, very few remained deceived. Thank God for warnings and prayer!

I also had a dream about this same situation around the same time.

Drug Addicts or Sorcerers?

A man and his wife were doing drugs. They were very intoxicated. There was a great amount of darkness surrounding them.

The dream seemed at first that it was to be interpreted out right in the natural. Maybe they were doing drugs. I began to pray for them thinking that possibly they had a drug abuse problem. As I prayed I began to feel that I was missing it somewhere. Then the Lord began to reveal to me that the drug abuse was an example of charismatic witchcraft! As time progressed, the fact that this was true became very apparent. They were spreading contention and strife by using words to manipulate people.

In A Dream, In A Vision of the Night
Job 33:15-18

Something very interesting is that one of the words for sorcery, in the Greek language is "pharmakos." This is where we get our English word for pharmacy. I have seen many dreams that I have had as well as others where drugs represented sorcery and witchcraft. A person does not have to be a devil worshipper chanting prayers to satan in order to be doing witchcraft. A Christian can let their mouth be used to form weapons against another Christian and cause much harm. *(Psalm 64)* A word spoken against the brethren, true or false, can change someone's opinion of someone else. There are times this damage is never repaired. In God's eyes, this is a serious offense in the church. *James 3: 16* says, "Where there is ENVY and SELF SEEKING (STRIFE) there is confusion and every kind of evil work." Envy and strife are manifested with words. First come envy and strife, next confusion, and then all of the hordes of hell. James was talking about the church, not the world!

Many times the Lord will use weather systems to get a message across. Time after time the Lord has gotten my attention through dreams of tornadoes or hurricanes. I have found this to be true in increasing numbers within the body of Christ in the last few years. In the months before the world trade center disaster in New York City, there was a multitude of dreams that I received through my web site, message board, and e groups about tornadoes. Many people were discerning trouble for themselves personally, for the church, and for the United States of America as well as the world. Tornadoes in the Bible are called tempest, great storms, storms, windstorms, whirlwinds, gales, and others. The metaphor and imagery in the symbol and meaning of a storm that whirls round and round at high enough wind speeds to harm everything in its path, is so terrifying and real. In *Psalms 55: 8* the storm is likened to enemies coming against the Psalmist (David). In *Hosea 8:7* it is send by God as judgment against idolatry. In *Jer. 23: 18* it is sent by God against the False prophets. Jesus was resting when His disciples panicked at the sight of a strong deadly storm. They were in a boat and feared for their lives! Jesus was asleep on a pillow in the stern. The men woke Him up asking Him if He even cared! He arose, rebuked the wind, and said to the sea, "Peace be still!" This must not have been a storm of judgment. *(Mark 4: 39)* Every situation must be weighed carefully in the Word and the Spirit. We should never assume that the tornado or storm we are dreaming about is judgment. Though it may be, if it isn't, repenting for the sins of others and ourselves will not stop it until we do as Jesus did; SPEAK PEACE AND

In A Dream, In A Vision of the Night
Job 33:15-18

STILLNESS TO IT! Paul was caught in a tempest when he was in chains on a ship. The Lord gave Paul a warning that he gave to the Captain before they set sail and again after they entered the storm. It is interesting to note that Paul warned, but stayed with the group until the end. He never "jumped ship." He was in chains, but he could have left if it had been God's will for him to leave. It is only the wicked and the foolish that get blown away by the whirlwind. *(Prov. 1: 27, 10: 25).* God's true prophets in the earth will see the destruction coming. We will also see that God has a plan that always results in an opportunity to repent and restore.

Here is an example of just that. Seeing a tornado does not usually say that an actual tornado is going to hit your community. Many times these types of dreams are warnings for intercessors to earnestly pray. The tornado or tornadoes in the dreams are signs or symbols to speak of possible sudden and vast destruction approaching.

Tornadoes Are Coming!

I was standing in the kitchen at my home. I saw three tornadoes headed for our house. One of them

Susan Noone Riddle

was about a mile wide. The other two were smaller. The wide one and one other one was black. One of the smaller ones was white. I began to get everyone into a safe place. We were praying. We all survived. No one was hurt.

There have been times when I have pointed to the storm and said, "Peace be still in the name of Jesus." Other times I have led others to safety. Once I threw myself over someone to cover that person so that they would be safe. Regardless, I have come to know that these dreams must be prayed over. They are either direct warning of possible, coming attacks from the devil, or the possible judgment of a situation or group of people. EVERY TIME I have dreamed of tornadoes there has been a significant event or two that has occurred either personally in our family, within our church or the body of Christ as a whole as well as in our community, state, nation or the world. Sometimes it is clear that the danger was lessened through prayer or intervention on our part because of the directions of the Lord gained through prayer. In this particular dream, the dark tornadoes were demonic attacks. The white one was coming judgment. There is so much misunderstanding in the body about what judgment of God is. The Lord judges in order to offer mercy. He is always looking for opportunities to heal and restore.

In A Dream, In A Vision of the Night
Job 33:15-18

This can also happen with volcano eruptions or earthquakes in dreams.

The Big One

My husband dreamed that there was a large earthquake and many were hurt. This earthquake was in Los Angeles or LA, which is the postal service's code for Louisiana where we live.

This dream was both natural and spiritual. The next week a college friend came to visit Charles from Los Angeles. We ministered to him about overcoming habitual sin. He was deeply hurt by a great deal of rejection from Christian supremacy type attitudes that had been expressed over his lifestyle. We were able to minister to him and see healing in his heart. After he returned home to Los Angeles the terrible earthquake that hit Northridge occurred. This dream was also spiritual. The next weekend our Pastor felt he had to resign because there were some in leadership disagreeing with him. Though he was sure it was time for him to go, it was an event that really shook our church to the very foundation. However, God did a miracle in healing things as a result of much prayer

Susan Noone Riddle

and fore warning to others and as well as ourselves. God is so good.

Many times storms, earthquakes, volcanoes, tidal waves and the like are warnings of judgment. The Lord will judge our churches and our individual lives, not to destroy, but to clean us out so that he can pour out His blessings on us. Judgment, though grievous at the time, brings repentance and great things from God.

Next is a dream from a friend that involved a tidal wave.

The Tsunami Tidal Wave

A Tsunami tidal wave hit the shore of our community. Many were hurt. Two different groups of people got into ships. One group was the lady who had the dream, my husband and his mother, and some others. The other ship full of people were angry and shaving their heads as the floated away in the opposite direction.

The Lord will use the night season to instruct, as well as spark our interest to investigate certain scriptural truths. My friend actually did not know what a Tsunami tidal wave was! After finding out that it was a certain type of destructive wave, she began to

In A Dream, In A Vision of the Night
Job 33:15-18

realize that the enemy was planning an attack. The two ships were two groups of people the Lord labeled for her as "sheep" and "goats." To this very day that separation process is in progress. It began with a slow church split. Some of the sheep have become goats since then and have switched ships! Other goats have repented and become sheep. When the enemy is finished, the Lord will take something meant for destruction and turn it into one of those "all things work together for the good of those who love the Lord, to those who are called according to His purpose," situations! *(Romans 8: 28)*

Some dreams are meant to reveal a specific truth. The danger here is that the devil knows very well how to twist scriptures as he did in the garden with Eve and in the wilderness with Jesus. As I stated earlier, a number one way that cults are able to draw people away from the truth is by placing the major emphasis on one leaders EXPERIENCE and not on the Word of God. We cannot be led by experiences. Experiences vary from person to person. Twice in the book of Romans Paul ask us not to be strong in our own opinions. *(Romans 12: 16, Romans 11: 25)* If someone is following someone that believes they have all the answers, that follower needs to find another leader.

Paul also said that we know in part. He told us that we see through a glass dimly or darkly. As long as we are on this side of heaven, each one of us is going to miss it somewhere. As long as we have a hunger and thirst for the Lord, He will reveal things to us in many ways to help us see through that glass a little less dimly. Here is a dream that helped me begin to understand about Jesus and His three days in the grave.

Sheol and the Pit

A dear friend of mine and I were standing near a great pit. He told me that the Lord wanted to teach us something important about what the Word of God really says about Jesus going down to Sheol.

This simple yet powerful, short dream started me on a long journey in investigating the scriptures about whether or not Jesus died spiritually. As young Christians we were taught one thing, but I began to see a different thing in the scriptures. I began to realize that this was very important to settle in my heart. It is also important when it comes to actually living for the Lord. Each and every one of us was born with a spirit that was not alive. We had to be born again to have the light bulb turned on in our spirit. Jesus wasn't born

In A Dream, In A Vision of the Night
Job 33:15-18

spiritually dead, for the very nature of His father was the BREATH of God! In His flesh, He was fully man. He had every desire and need that every flesh and blood man has. He had a soul as well. He also was a spirit. His spirit was alive and 100% God. It is my belief that He did not have to die spiritually to obtain the keys to the Kingdom. If He had, then there would have been no power for Him to recover from the death that He suffered. *Romans 8: 11* says, "The Spirit of Him that raised Christ Jesus from the dead, dwells in you, He who raised Christ from the dead will also give life to (or quicken) your mortal bodies through His Spirit that dwells in you." It was the life that was IN Him that raised Him. The life of God never left Him. Why is that important to our life in Him? Because when we decide to seek repentance and receive redemption by being "born again" we must know that it is a God thing, not a man thing. That life that causes us to be rejuvenated is actually the same life or Spirit or breath that caused Him to be born the first time. It was the man Jesus that died, not the God, Jesus. GOD CANNOT DIE! The miracle is that much more of a miracle when you realize that He is alive and cannot die. If Jesus had died spiritually, it all would have been over. The Lord God was, and is, and is to come!

In dreams the Lord can reveal truths that open up the spirit realm and make it more real! That is what happened in this dream. What I saw in the Spirit revolutionized my prayer life.

Pray In the Spirit

I was in a place of business. I could barely move. I knew I was being held captive there. I could barely walk, yet I was trying very hard to place one foot in front of the other. I saw a man come out of a door. This man is an unjust judge. I knew he was in charge. I noticed that there were men sitting around in chairs. They were very large, perhaps 9 or 10 feet tall. As I began to pray in the Spirit (in tongues, my personal prayer language), they became energized with strength to get up and fight for me. I could suddenly move faster. As long as I continued praying, I could move, and the ministering spirits were on the move fighting back the evil. If I would slack up, so would they. I would then slow down. I finally caught on. I was able to get to the door and get free as I prayed without ceasing! Suddenly I noticed that many others were getting free as well.

In A Dream, In A Vision of the Night
Job 33:15-18

It was plain to see that the giants were angels. My prayers activated their service. The unjust judge was the devil! He was keeping others and me captive as long as we didn't understand that prayer was the key!

Sometimes dreams and their symbolism don't seem to make much sense at all. These dreams, if from the Lord, can be written down or simply remembered. Then when and if the time is right, God reveals what they mean. There may be times that we have dreams that never make sense to us, but we really believe they are from the Lord. In these cases, we really need to write them down because, like Daniel, Peter and John, if the Lord tarries, these types of dreams may be important to someone someday. It is truly awesome. The Lord will sometimes speak in a dream for no other reason than to let you know that He is a supernatural, awesome God! He wants us to know that He is sovereign and in control. Other times he will reveal something so simple to let you know that He cares about your every concern. He wants to comfort us as we go through a hard time. The Word of God calls the Holy Spirit our comforter. This was evident in the next dream.

Susan Noone Riddle

Dream: Healing an Offense

A sister of mine in the Lord was playing the piano. We had recently had a disagreement between us. I was standing near by. She had on a "grass" green color dress. She got up from the piano. She came to me with a big hug. She said as she hugged me, "I'm sorry. Let's put it all behind us and start over."

This sister and I had a disagreement a few weeks before this dream. After the dream I commented to my husband that I felt she was going to reach out to me to restore the relationship. About four days after the dream, I received a letter in the mail. My friend repented to me in the letter. She asked for restoration, which I was thrilled to do! What was an added excitement to it all was the letter and envelope was the same "grass" green color!

At times my husband and I have dreamed about the same thing on the same night. These next two dreams were given to us the same night at the same time!

Our Dreams About Hitler

MY DREAM: I was in a concentration camp like the ones seen from films and photos of World War II.

In A Dream, In A Vision of the Night
Job 33:15-18

I knew that Hitler was in charge. Several of us were in a fenced in area that was terribly small in the amount of area provided. There were several of these areas. The fences were endlessly high and had a fence over the top of them. The water in the bottom was dreadfully dirty. There was nowhere else to go to the bathroom but on the floor. Everyone was exceedingly thirsty. Many wanted to drink the dirty water. I told them we had to climb up high to get pure, clean water. I did climb up carrying a tin bucket to hold the water in. When I climbed up to the top of our cage I saw small children being put into hot ovens to be incinerated.

At the very same time my husband and I woke up. The first words out of his mouth were, "I had an awful dream about Hitler." It was about 2:00 am. We both knew that this was not a normal time for dreaming or for waking and remembering our dreams. He had just had this dream:

HIS Dream: My wife and I were sitting in our den looking at the television. Hitler was on the TV speaking, and fire was burning all around the screen.

We were both disturbed by the dreams. We prayed and went back to sleep. The next day we discussed the dreams some more. We both bore witness and agreed that the dreams were concerning the Christian church being persecuted in the last days. Hitler represented the spirit of the antichrist. There is no doubt that was possessed with a high-ranking principality from the kingdom of darkness. Hitler professed to be a Christian. He believed he was, as a white Christian, superior to others, especially those of the Jewish race. Even as the Jewish people of race and faith and even some Jewish Christians were tortured and killed, before the coming of the Lord, many children of the royal priesthood, holy nation, the inhabitants of the New Jerusalem, those of us of the chosen generation, kingdom kids, stones in the building fitly joined together, called by His holy name may meet a similar fate. These dreams led us to pray, "Lord, help us prepare for what is to come. Have mercy on us."

I do not know if our tribulation will be physical, though I know some are already suffering in some countries. But as the days of His coming approach, I believe we can expect some type of persecution that will be hard to bear. The Lord told us however in *1 Corinthians 10: 13* that, "No temptation has overtaken you except that which is common to man; but God is faithful, who will not allow you to be tempted beyond that which you are able, but with the temptation will also make a way of escape, that you may be able to bear it." Notice that the Lord did not

In A Dream, In A Vision of the Night
Job 33:15-18

say through Peter that He would REMOVE the temptation. He will however; give us the ability to bear it as well as a way for us to escape.

I believe we are already seeing signs of this high ranking spirit that is closely related to the spirit of the antichrist in the terrorism that we are seeing even in the U. S. A. and other parts of the world at this time in the earth.

Sometimes it is very unclear exactly what the Lord is saying until the event prophesied in the dream comes to pass. This next dream is an example of that.

Dream: Falling Hard

A sister of mine in the Lord and I were walking on a sidewalk. On the left side of the sidewalk was a hill. My friend wanted to climb up the hill on a mightily steep side. I told her we needed to walk down to the more gradual incline were it was much safer to climb up. We could hear noises on the other side of this mount. It sounded like some little boys and girls misbehaving. I knew that we weren't supposed to be able to hear them, but were being aloud to hear the "spiritual noise" on the other side of the hill. I didn't go with her because I could sense the danger. I walked

Susan Noone Riddle

down the sidewalk to where it was safe to climb, as she ran up the steep side. Suddenly she fell down. It was a terrible fall. She was injured badly. Her husband and I were hovering over her, trying to see if she was all right. Her husband realized she was in poor condition. He instructed me to call 911. I had my cell phone and was calling 911 already. Her legs were crushed and she could not get up.

I woke up from the dream feeling so grieved and heavy. I spoke with my husband. We prayed earnestly about what to do. Finally, about a week later we decided that I should tell her the dream, and I did. The dream was not received. She sternly said that the dream was not about her. She said that it was my dream, and therefore; it must be about me. I have learned never to push anything I feel I have received from the Lord on anyone! First of all, it is not my duty to prove that God and His Word is true. The proof of a vision or a dream is time. I love the scriptures in *Acts 5: 38-39* where Luke gives an account of the advice of a man named Gamaliel concerning the Apostles. He says, "And now I tell you, keep away from these men and let them alone; for if this plan or work is of men, it will come to nothing; but if it is of God, you cannot overthrow it lest you even be found to fight against God." So, I responded with telling her that the

In A Dream, In A Vision of the Night
Job 33:15-18

possibility was real that the dream was about me and not her. I knew that time would tell. *Ezekiel chapters 2 and 3* teach that we are responsible to tell and give the warning the Lord has shown us. If the person hears or not, we are no longer responsible. Ezekiel actually says that if we do not tell them, and the Word we held back comes to pass, their blood is on our hands! If we are wrong and we miss it, at least we tried. I have learned that when the Lord speaks to me, I need to speak out the warning, because He is not a man that He should lie. I am not as concerned about making a mistaken in a warning the Lord gives me, as I am in not giving it and it being correct. In this case, it most certainly was correct and had far reaching implications!

I felt that the bad boys and girls were not actual people, but were representing demonic spirits waiting for the chance to attack. They were waiting for an opening. When my sister ran up the hill in her fervor and zeal to know the Lord, she was careless. She ran up the most dangerous place because she was fully exposed to all of the dangers.

Several weeks later a minister came and preached. He laid hands on my sister and she fell to the ground, hitting her head on the floor so hard, she was bruised. I reminded her of the dream. She seemed to take it much more seriously. It is so easy to forget that our battle is not with flesh and blood but with principalities and powers and rulers of the darkness, spiritual wickedness in high places! *(Ephesians 6: 12-17)* Now, years later, the dream has been proven many times over. The troubles did indeed involve me as well. What can we do when warned of trouble? We can hide ourselves in Him. We can keep our eyes open and watch. It is a good idea not to let pride keep us from receiving a warning, real or not.

If we listen we will find that important information can come in the night.

Missing Money

I dreamed that my husband called me from his office. He told me that we were $2000.00 overdrawn in our personal checking account.

I woke up feeling uncomfortable about the dream. We never have that much money in our personal account. We use it for the grocery store, clothes, Wal Mart and other personal things. I asked my husband if everything was all right with all of his accounts at the office. He said he did not know but he guessed they were fine. A couple of weeks later we discovered that

In A Dream, In A Vision of the Night
Job 33:15-18

several thousand dollars had been embezzled from one of his office accounts. Though this event was very distressing, there was such a peace knowing that the Lord knew all along. The person who had stolen the money ended up returning it to us. If we had not paid attention to the information in the dream, this person may have continued to steal money and get away with it. The Lord saved us a great deal of hardship by alerting us to the fact that we were being violated in such a way.

Chapter Eight
So What's All the Fuss About?

1 Corinthians 2 speaks a lot about the conflict between the natural mind and the Spirit. In *verse 14* of this chapter says, "But the natural mind does not receive the things of the Spirit of God, for they are foolishness to him; nor can he know them, because they are spiritually discerned." The natural, carnal part of us will resist and even fight against the things of the Spirit of the Lord. The Lord God does not want us to be MINDLESS. Rather, He has instructed us to renew our minds with the Word of God.

Many people depend too much on "extra revelation" from dreams, visions, voices, and other supernatural manifestations. They actually get their flesh involved with the supernatural and can literally direct it with their flesh. THIS IS VERY DANGEROUS! There are many voices in the Spirit realm. If we are not careful to know the Word of God, we can be deceived by the voices of the Spirit realm. We are in a time of the Lord that we, as Jesus said in *John 4: 21-24*, must take hold of Godly scriptural wisdom and worship in spirit and truth (Spirit and Word). By renewing our minds as Paul said in

In A Dream, In A Vision of the Night
Job 33:15-18

Romans 12: 2, and opening our hearts to the Spirit realm as Paul said in *1 Corinthians 2: 9-16*, we will receive the proper type of messages and not be deceived.

One of the things that people find fault concerning dreams and visions in the body of Christ is that there are many people who are unbalanced. They do not balance the Word of God with the Spirit realm and the supernatural things of God. This sometimes causes many to close the door on the whole message of the supernatural. There are also occasions that people have used dreams that they have had to manipulate the lives of others.

An example of this is a situation I was involved in on one occasion. A woman came to me to tell me a dream she had about another church member. She claimed that she had the dream more than once. The dream supposedly showed that the church member was being called to a far away remote place to minister. She was sure that she must persuade the church member to go away. I counseled her not to tell the person about the dream. I suggested that she pray and really intercede for him. If the church member ever heard for himself the call to go to this place, then the dreamer could share the dream as a confirmation.

Susan Noone Riddle

Sharing the dream outright could really cause confusion and delay in finding God's perfect will.

Another example is something I have seen happen over and over when a church splits. Sometimes people feel a church is not meeting their needs, so they decide to move on to another church nearby or start one of their own. There may be a problem however if they leave a church when the Lord did not tell them to leave. If this is the case, they may soon begin to miss the fellowship with their brothers and sisters from the church they left. They begin to hear about how God is moving in the place that they left. Here is an example of a dream that was used to manipulate a situation such as this:

A Black Wedding Dress

A bride was all decked out in wedding apparel. The only problem was she was dressed in black. She walked down the isle of a church to meet her groom.

A dream like this can be actually a warning from God that a spiritual death is coming to a church or a body. This dream could have been a tool of healing and may have been intended for that when the dreamer received it. If the dream was out of the dreamer's

In A Dream, In A Vision of the Night
Job 33:15-18

heart, it may have been the dreamer who was wearing the black dress and needed to repent of wrongdoing. It could have also been the dreamer's feelings toward a church. It could have also been a dream given to the dreamer meant to stir the dreamer to pray for a church. Unfortunately, this dream was used to persuade people that the particular fellowship was evil and many were hurt.

When anyone uses the precious things of God to promote their own agenda they are using divination. Because the gifts and callings of God are without repentance, sometimes people may actually have some kind of factual information that they may use to promote the strife and division rather than healing and restoration. In speaking of the grandiose vision or revelation they say God has given them, they develop a sense of superiority over groups of people, hearing and seeing things in the Spirit others do not hear and see. The end result is a group of blind followers and an eventual lack of trust in people that claim to have prophetic dreams and visions.

This is one of the things that will cause controversy over spiritual dreams and visions in the body of Christ.

It is very important to keep everything we do under the perfect love and infinite grace of the Lord. *Galatians 5: 22-23* says, "But the fruit of the Spirit is

Susan Noone Riddle

love, joy, peace, patience, kindness, goodness, faithfulness, gentleness, self-control. Against such there is no law." Everything we do in the Lord must line up with these fruit of the Spirit as well as the definition of love the Lord gave us in *1 Corinthians 13*. This word EVERYTHING means EVERYTHING. If we are correcting someone in must be done in love, joy, peace, and on. If we are sharing a dream with someone, the same thing applies.

In A Dream, In A Vision of the Night
Job 33:15-18

Chapter Nine
Tying It All Together

The Lord Jesus Christ will speak to us in a dream in a vision of the night in order to get our attention, reveal Himself and His Word to us, warn us of sin or danger or attack from man or Satan.

As with any and all of the other gifts that come from God, there are abuses. However, we cannot throw out the things that come from God because some people abuse the truth. We must be careful to follow the Word of God, but not without the guidance of the Spirit.

There have been many times that I have heard from the Lord in ways other than a dream. There are some people who don't receive any dreams from God, but they are led by the Spirit in other ways. It doesn't mean that one believer is more spiritual than the other. It simply means that the Lord has developed believers in different ways to hear His voice. The important thing to remember is that dreams and visions are reality in the body of Christ today. There are many other avenues used by the Lord to speak to us. I hope that this information has richly blessed you in your walk with HIM!!!!

Chapter Ten
Frequently Asked Questions

I see a strong pattern in the questions that are asked concerning Biblical dreams. Here are a few of them.

1. If someone dreams about me, does that necessarily mean that the dream is about me?

No, it does not. It could possibly be about you, but most of the time it is about the person who is dreaming or someone similar to you in character. It is understandable why the dreamer would automatically assume that the dream is about you. The important thing is that you and the dreamer pray and ask the Lord who or what the dream is about.

2. Are our dreams always literal or always symbolic?

Most of the time dreams are symbolic. See the section of this book (Dreams and Parables as Dark Sayings, Chapter One) that explains why dreams are symbolic most of the time.

In A Dream, In A Vision of the Night
Job 33:15-18

3. If I dream that I am going to marry someone or have a baby, should I expect to marry this person or have a baby?

This is a question that many single people ask as well as married people who are hoping to have children. It is a natural desire to want to find a mate for companionship and to have children. It is really not a good idea in the first place to be led by one dream alone, or even several dreams whether from others or ourselves. Remember, the Lord is not in a hurry. He does not miss it. Yes, He is coming soon and it is important to follow Him everywhere He goes. However, the Lord is not worried or forceful or pushy. If He has a plan for someone to marry, He is able to bring it about. He doesn't want us to force what we believe His will is. I can give you testimony after testimony of the big problems that can develop by seeking to fulfill God's will when it is not His will, or not in His timing. WE DO NOT EVER WANT TO RUSH INTO SOMETHING THAT IS NOT OF THE LORD!

Most of the time the dream of a baby represents the birth of a ministry or something new, and even the birth of sin. See the symbols in the dictionary part of this book under, baby, marriage, bride, groom and other related topics.

4. I sometimes do not remember my dreams. Should I be concerned?

No, there is no need to be concerned. *Job 33: 15-16* tells us that the Lord speaks to us and then seals the instruction of the dream. If there is something we need to know, He will be sure that we know. He is so wonderful. If you sense that the Lord really does want you to remember, simply begin to pray and ask Him to help you remember your dreams. Ask Him to reveal the interpretation to you. He gave it, He can explain it, in His time.

5. Do all dreams come from God?

No, they do not although ultimately the Lord is the creator of all things. Dreams can come from the enemy, from the Lord and from out of our own hearts. Read more in Chapter Three.

6. Are only certain people anointed to interpret dreams?

Just like some people are gifted at playing on an instrument or healing the sick, some people are especially gifted to understand the language of dreams

In A Dream, In A Vision of the Night
Job 33:15-18

and visions. They are just that though, people anointed of God. It is my belief that the Bible teaches that the same Spirit that raised Christ from the dead dwells in each of us *(Romans 8:11)*. In *1 Corinthians 13: 9, 12* the Bible says that we prophesy and know in part. Anyone who understands dreams and visions only knows in part. I also believe that it is the responsibility of those who do understand to guide and teach others to understand so that no one becomes dependent on anyone else to "interpret" their dreams. Our responsibility is to build up and edify the body of Christ and not draw God's people unto us. There are some great web sites that teach and release people. I have the web sites I have found listed on the links page on my web site: http://www.tehillah.org/links.shtml

7. If someone interprets a dream I have, do I have to accept their interpretation?

No, you do not. However, if you went to them and asked for help, then you should pray and seek God about what they have shared with you. If what they said does not agree with you, pray. By going to them, you opened the door to receive what they say and pray about it. Don't get mad at them if they don't tell you what you wanted to hear! It may not sit right with you because it upsets your flesh. It may not agree with you because it came out of their flesh! It is important to remember that dreams and visions don't have to mean only one thing, and may have applications for the present, past and future as well as personal, local and worldwide.

8. If I receive revelation from God in a dream or vision that speaks of warnings that seem to have worldwide implications, what am I supposed to do with it?

Don't call the FBI and the television news stations and the radio stations and expect everyone to jump on it, that is a certainty! Do speak to someone you trust and pray, pray, pray. There is such a thing as casting your pearls before the swine. Joseph was so eager and innocent when he shared his dreams with his brothers. They were filled with envy and strife. Joseph may have felt an urgency, but his dreams did not come to pass until many, many years later. Remember that anything spiritual from the Lord is a seed. It will go into the ground and die before it grows up and bears fruit. If you know this from the onset, you will go through it with patience and endurance.

If we push doors open and force our way into places that we feel we need to be in order for God's message to come across, then we will get nailed to the

In A Dream, In A Vision of the Night
Job 33:15-18

cross faster and for longer than was really necessary. That is what is called building kingdoms according to self will. Those kingdoms have to be torn down. It is a very painful process. How do I know? I've done it! Let God make a way. His way is everlasting.

9. Why does the Lord speak in dreams and visions, why not just speak plainly?

Very good question! Everything the Lord does is based on the desire to have relationship with us. He desires relationship more than he does anything else. Everything else is an outgrowth of that relationship.

It is my belief that the "riddles" or "parables" or "dark sayings" are given to teach us who He is and how He thinks, as well as to change us in the soul realm and to draw or drive us to the Word and to His feet.

When I was a young, Spirit-filled Christian, I had dreams that must have lasted all night long. I would wake up and start writing them down. There were about four people who would patiently listen to these storybooks and help me sort through it all. I learned so much about deliverance and healing. Some things have been hard to face! I also learned so much about who my Lord is, and what He says about many things. I searched the scriptures wanting to understand what symbols meant and how they related to the Word of God. Through that time period, I fell deeper and deeper in love with Jesus. Our relationship developed and rose to higher levels.

As the years passed, I began to have shorter and shorter, more to the point dreams and more visions. I did not need to go to others as often to understand what the Lord was saying. I still do discuss dreams with others and through them, the Lord draws us to His Word and we fellowship with one another on deeper levels than ever before. I also learned that there are naturally minded people that are like Joseph's brothers who will not accept communication from God on any other level but what they are comfortable with and know. I pray for them, love them and hope that as they walk with the Lord, He will draw them deeper into the things of the Spirit. I can fellowship with them on a level that God provides, but I know that there are some places some people are not ready to go. If I need direction, which I do every day, I simply ask the Lord to teach me and guide me. That guidance may come in plain speech, or it may come in a "riddle." I am a Riddle, so that is all right with me!

In A Dream, In A Vision of the Night
Job 33:15-18

10. How do I judge what I see in a dream or vision?

The same method of judging prophecy or interpretation of tongues or the Word itself apply to judging dreams and visions. The Word is clear about that.

11. If I dream that I stood up and prophesied in the service at the fellowship I attended, and I go to that gathering prepared, but the leaders never give me a chance to speak, yet the whole order of the service lined up with everything I heard and saw in the dream, should I be really upset with the leadership?

NO! There are many reasons you may have seen this in a dream. If the Lord gave you a Word, and it was preached, then why have a problem at all? That is awesome! Your dream came to pass; it just did not come from you. The desire to be recognized by man is probably the reason things happened the way they did. The Lord is working on making us transparent vessels. If we get upset because we did not "get to speak," then we probably need to repent for wanting to control and thank God for letting us have another opportunity to die to self. John the Baptist said that he must decrease and the Lord must increase! Oh how we love to shine! "Lord, let Your glory be all that shines…"

If the message you spoke in the dream was not preached, then there are several things that may have happened. The leadership may have missed it. They may be called and appointed and anointed, but leaders do still live in an earthen vessel and will miss it just like everyone else. The dream my have been for another time. The dream may have been just for the dreamer to prophesy to himself/herself and grow in understanding. The dream may have been out of the dreamer's heart. Time will tell!

There are places or fellowships that may not be walking in the will of the Lord. Jesus told John in the book of Revelation that they were synagogues of Satan. A word of caution on this:

Take very much consideration and prayer and time in determining this. Do not ever make a decision about this quickly, certainly not because of one dream! I cannot stress this enough. The Lord is not a God that chops people up and leaves them bleeding and dying. He does not support the actions of an Absolom, David's son, who spent a great deal of time manipulating people by criticizing King David at the gates of the city, drawing them unto himself. Even in a synagogue of Satan, take great care in handling the situation according to Spirit and truth in love. Self-promotion will leave many wounded and the self

In A Dream, In A Vision of the Night
Job 33:15-18

promoter soon demoted, alone, bitter and angry. David did not touch Saul and even called him God's anointed.

12. Should I be concerned as to whether the parable or dark saying I receive from the Lord is a dream, a vision or from a trance state?

My answer to this question is no. It is interesting to study and learn the differences, but I don't see that it is going to make that much of a difference in the outcome. There are scriptural differences. You can read about it in Chapter One, under the section of this book entitled, "Dreams, Trances and Visions."

13. Are there some common dream topics or subjects that people, both unbelievers and believers dream and why? Does God speak to unbelievers?

Yes, there are common topics or threads in both unbelievers and believers dreams. Some of those topics are:

Tornadoes or storms.

A son or a daughter or a small child being harmed.

Being pregnant or having a baby.

Getting married.

Being pursued by "bad guys."

Trying to talk on the phone and not being able to communicate.

Trying to squeeze through a space that is too small.

Car and plane crashes.

In this day and time we live in many people are dreaming about:

Catastrophic events like massive earthquakes, asteroids, nuclear bombs and/or wars where whole cities are being wiped out.

Tidal waves where many are killed.

Church upheavals where no one will heed the warnings.

Floods.

Hard times and difficulty in surviving.

Coming of the Lord in a cloud.

Other related things.

Yes, God does speak to unbelievers, but in a different manner. Both unbelievers and believers have souls, or minds, wills and emotions, so both types of dreamers can dream out of their own heart about desires and feelings. The Lord will speak to both groups of people in order to wake us out of our slumber and keep us from our own plan, purpose and pride. The gifts and callings of God are without

In A Dream, In A Vision of the Night
Job 33:15-18

repentance, so unbelievers and believers alike may receive visions and dreams that warn of things to come. People who have no relationship with the Lord may dream of the end of the world or warnings about a coming death, etc. That is why we need to not use this type of revelation as a sign of someone's spirituality. It is the fruit of the Spirit that is the indication of a person who has a relationship with Jesus. They can be found in *Galatians Chapter 5*.

A person who is not redeemed and "knows" things is a person that may end up becoming a Psychic and use their gift for dishonest gain. There are many beautiful gifts that worldly Christians and unbelievers use for personal exaltation like playing well on an instrument, singing well, acting well in a drama and even preaching well!

14. What do I do if I can't find the symbols of a dream in the dream symbols?

Seek the Lord, ask for revelation knowledge from Him and be patient. You can also liken the symbol to something similar. If you dream about a bird that you cannot recognize, then liken it to a bird in general then go from there.

Susan Noone Riddle

In A Dream, In A Vision of the Night
Job 33:15-18

BIBLIOGRAPHY

These are great reference books that every dreamer should have!

Cavu, Paula M. <u>Dreams and Visions With a Difference For All Believers</u>. Daystar Ministry Publication, Australia. © - 1996 (Web site also available) e-mail address: daystar@mailbox.uq.edu.au

Cavu, Paula M. <u>Heavenly Communication in the Conscience State</u>. Daystar Ministry Publication, Australia. © - 1996 (Only available from web site) e-mail address: daystar@mailbox.uq.edu.au

Conner, Kevin. <u>Interpreting the Symbols and Types</u>. © 1980. Bible Temple Publishing.

Ellis, Enterprises, Inc. <u>The Bible Reference Library</u>. 1993 IBM 1993 CD - Rom.

Duriez, Colin; Longman, III, Tremper; Penny, Douglas; Reid, Daniel G., Wilhoit, James C. <u>Dictionary of Biblical Imagery</u>. InterVarsity Press

Susan Noone Riddle

© 1998 by InterVarsity Christian Fellowship/USA. www. ivpress.com E-mail: mail@ivpress.com

Milligan, Ira. <u>Understanding the Dreams You Dream</u>. © 1997 - Destiny Image Publishers, Inc. Treasure House

Riffel, Herman. <u>Dream Interpretation A Biblical Understanding</u>. © 1993. Destiny Image Publishers.

Ryle, James. <u>A Dream Come True</u>. © 1995. Creation House.

Strong, James. <u>Strong's Exhaustive Concordance of the Bible</u>. McLean. VA.: MacDonald Publishing Company, n. d.

The New Open Bible. <u>New King James Version</u>. © - 1982 by Thomason Nelson, Inc. [this version used unless otherwise stated] Season. © 1990. Thomas Nelson, Inc., Publishers.

Vallowe, Ed F. <u>Biblical Mathematics, Key to Scriptural Numerics</u>. © 1992. Vallowe Ed F. Evangelistic Association

In A Dream, In A Vision of the Night
Job 33:15-18

Vine, W. E. <u>Vine's Expository Dictionary of Old and New Testament Words</u>. Fleming H. Revell Company. 1981 Webster's New Collegiate Dictionary. G. & C. Merriam Company. 1973

Susan Noone Riddle

HOW CAN I KNOW THE LORD PERSONALLY?

There are no formulas that work to "fix" the condition of our spiritual hearts, but there is a way to know Jesus Christ and begin a relationship with Him. John said in *John 17: 3* that eternal life is to KNOW HIM. Eternal life is not praying one prayer or being baptized nor is it being a member of a church. Many say that man is basically good. The only part of us that is good is the part that is created in the image of God. That part is without life until it is redeemed and made alive or quickened by the life of God.

I believe that the Bible is the Word of God. The Scriptures of the Bible have a wonderful thread that run through them of supernatural imagery that no one or group of men and/or women could have put together. It is a lot like the human body. There are those that believe that the order and the workings of the body have just evolved over billions of years. Can nothing create and design something? It is the same with the Bible. It was written by many and put together by many, but only God could have designed the heart and spirit of it.

In A Dream, In A Vision of the Night
Job 33:15-18

Jesus came from His place of glory and walked among us. He was not religious He was and is real. He spoke the hard truth when necessary. He sat and ate with those that the religious people of His day wouldn't go near. He touched and healed the lepers without fear. He was fully God and fully man. He voluntarily laid down His life and died, shedding His life flow of blood for men and women that laughed and despised Him. They laid Him in a tomb as His followers mourned His death. They had hoped for an earthly, powerful King to deliver them. But, soon, they would learn who that King really was.

Just as He said He would do, on the third day, He rose from that grave. He stayed among them many days until He was taken up into heaven before the eyes of many who followed and believed in Him. On the day of Pentecost, just as He had promised, the Holy Spirit was poured out on those who where waiting in the Upper Room, and many were filled with the Spirit and spoke in tongues. The truth of the Savior of the world is the most widely known truth world wide of any, the Bible the most read book.

Still, many never step passed the "story" or the "religious" experience to really know Him. I invite you today to seek His face. As with anyone that we have a relationship with, we must talk to Him and listen for Him to speak to you. He may speak in a small still voice. He may speak through another. He may speak in a dream, or a vision of the night.

Here is the way that we can begin our life anew and be born again. He can and will take our hearts of stone and turn them into a heart of flesh. We can each become and be a new creation in Christ Jesus. None of us can be good enough to "earn" eternal life. That is a false belief that man made up. It is not in the Bible. It is not our good or bad deeds that determine whether or not we will spend eternity with Him, it is our relationships with Him and with one another. If it were our deeds, then how good would we have to be and where would we draw the line? Jesus said that many would stand before Him on that day and speak of all the great deeds that they did, and He will say, "Depart from me you workers of iniquity, I never KNEW you."

Would you like to KNOW Him? Many know about Him, but knowing Him personally can be compared to nothing. Pray this prayer now, and begin the journey of your life!

"Father, I thank you for sending Your Son, Jesus Christ, conceived of the Holy Spirit, to be born of a virgin, walked among man, died on the cross bleeding His life blood for me, was buried and on the third day

In A Dream, In A Vision of the Night
Job 33:15-18

rose from the grave, walked among men and ascended into heaven. Jesus, my Savior, You are now seated at the right hand of the Father, and I love You. I want to know You. Come and live on the inside of me. Take my life. I confess that You are Lord of me and of all. I believe in my heart and confess that You are my God with my mouth. Lord Jesus, lead me now, by Your Holy Spirit, and take control of the direction of my life. Reveal Yourself to me! AMEN!"

The Lord said that it was not good for Adam to be alone, and He took a rib from Adam and made Eve. This is not only talking about marriage, but of fellowship with others who believe in Him. Not every building that has the word "church" on the top of it is going to necessarily be where the Lord would have you fellowship. Some people have home meetings, others attend services in a building. Ask the Lord where He would desire to direct you. Is there someone in your community that you know and admire who seems to have something REAL in God that you have noticed? Call them and ask them to pray with you about fellowship. If you don't have a Bible, find one. Begin to read the book of John in the New Testament, and ask the Lord to reveal Himself to you through the scriptures.

Susan Noone Riddle

If you are interested in the Baptism of the Holy Spirit, I have a teaching tape available. Just send an offering of $5.00 to:

Susan Riddle - Baptism Tape
419 N. Monroe Street
Marksville, LA 71351`

The $5:00 is just to cover the cost of the production and mailing of the tape. This tape will go through the scriptures and explain the truths of being submerged in the Holy Spirit.

ABOUT THE AUTHOR

Susan was born in Franklin, Louisiana. In 1966 she and her family moved to the Philippine Islands when Susan was ten. They moved back to Franklin, Louisiana in 1972. Susan was born again in Franklin in a Baptist Church under the ministry of James Robinson. Not having the understanding that there was a devil with the intent to steal, kill, and destroy, she fell away from the Lord. All of the time that Susan was not actively serving God, she was longing to return to His side, but stayed away believing that He would never accept her back into His grace.

Susan rededicated her life to Jesus in 1983 and has never left His presence again. She enjoys speaking at meetings, singing, preaching and teaching the Word of God. She has been leading worship since 1985. Mrs. Riddle has written over 90 praise and worship songs. She was a runner up in a song-writing contest in Nashville for the song, "We Ascribe Glory."

Mrs. Riddle has a college degree both in Elementary Education and Theology. She also has a Masters degree in Theology from Christian Life School of Theology. Charles and/or Susan are available to minister the Word of God in your churches by contacting them at:

Mr. and Mrs. Charles A. Riddle III
419 N. Monroe Street
Marksville, LA 71351

Phone #'s: 318-253-6792
or 319-253-4551 (please do not call me with a dream. I prefer email — see last page for these addresses).

FAX: 318-240-9000

e mail: Tehillah77@aol.com (Not for sending dreams).

I do not receive dreams by regular mail or over the telephone. Please read this disclaimer to clarify why:

Tehillah Ministries does receive dreams and visions for prayer and consideration via e mail under these conditions:

I know that your dreams and communication with the Lord are important to you. Please know that if you do not hear back from me, it is because I have not heard anything from the Lord on your dream. It does not mean that your dream is or is not from the Lord. I WILL NOT SEND an interpretation at all unless I am

SURE that the Lord has revealed something to me. No scripture, and therefore no prophecy is of private interpretation. So please feel free to share what the Lord has given to me or anyone else with anyone you feel a need to share it with for confirmation.

Sometimes our dreams are for a later time. In *Job 33: 16* it says that the Lord "opens the ears of men, and then seals the instruction" THAT HE has given in our dreams. This means that even if you don't understand the meaning of the dream right away, or EVER in this life, He has given it and sealed the instruction. When the Apostle John received the vision that he shared with us in the book of Revelation, he did not understand much of its meaning at all. We still do not totally understand its meaning! Other times it is like the Apostle Peter and the vision of the sheets. He wondered over the vision, but soon understood exactly what the Lord was saying to him.

As I am sure you know from reading the purpose of this book and/or web site, I AM NOT A Psychic or Medium. The Bible says that these are demonic and an abomination to Him. This is NOT a "hotline" service (Praise the Lord!!!) It is freely offered in the grace of God. The main purpose of this service unto the Lord is to help His children learn to understand dreams and visions. We can learn so much from one another. It is not my or the Lord's desire that anyone become dependent on me or anyone else to hear the voice of God.

If I receive anything in prayer from the Lord on your dream, I'll write back to you!

God Bless you! In Him, Susan

Susan's web sites are found at:
Play Piano by Ear:
http://www.tehillah.org/playbyear.shtml
Dreams and Visions:
http://www.tehillah.org/dreams.shtml

E groups:
http://www.groups.yahoo.com
dreamsfromHim@yahoogroups.com
Dream-Interpretation@yahoogroups.com
See the tehillah website for details.

Printed in the United States
28953LVS00001B/70

9 781403 393029